JOSEPH ARCH

From a photograph by Dexter   *F. Jenkins, Heliog. Par.*

Joseph Arch

The Story of his Life

Told by Himself

And Edited with a Preface by

The Countess of Warwick

London

Hutchinson & Co.

34, Paternoster Row

1898

PREFACE.

BY THE COUNTESS OF WARWICK.

" To couple my name with that of Joseph Arch gives me no displeasure. I believe him to be an honest and good man. I believe, too, that the cause he has in hand is well founded, and I confide in his using no means to promote it but such as are sanctioned by the law of God and the law of the land." *

These words of the late Cardinal Manning, uttered more than a quarter of a century ago, at a time when Arch and the Union were fiercely assailed, express my own sentiments to-day, when he and the Union have accomplished their work. Joseph Arch is a Warwickshire man, and his people have been connected with Warwick Castle for generations. It seemed to me a pity that the story of his life-work should remain

* " Life of Cardinal Manning."

untold, and I am glad to have been some small help to him in the telling of it. In doing this, I have been careful not to over-edit; I have judged it best that he should speak for himself and express his opinions quite frankly in his own way. The chapters which deal with his early struggles, aspirations, and difficulties—aye, and his early jealousies and prejudices, too—give us an insight to the forces silently working in many an agricultural labourer's breast, and show us with what travail the Union was brought forth. It is good for us to see things sometimes through another's eyes. But it will, of course, be understood that with all the opinions expressed in his pages I do not necessarily agree.

If it were possible to separate the man from the work (which it is not), I should regard the history of the National Agricultural Labourers' Union as far more important than any personal record. I look upon the Union as one of the most remarkable movements of modern times. The phrase is commonplace, but it is true; the Union was remarkable alike in its inception, progress, and achievement; and in the social history of England it must henceforth fill a prominent place. I know of no movement, *working always within the four corners of the law*, which accomplished so much in so short a time. For, what are the facts? A

Warwickshire peasant, at first alone and unaided, started and led an organisation which revolutionised the condition of the agricultural labourer. From small beginnings—a handful of labourers, a hurried meeting under an old chestnut tree in the gloom of a February evening—an agitation was set on foot, which rapidly grew from strength to strength until it permeated the length and breadth of rural England. It was no barren agitation merely; for coincident with its growth was a visible improvement in the moral and material condition of those for whom it was organised. The Union is known by its fruits. We have only to compare the condition of the agricultural labourer before the Union was started, with his condition to-day, to see that these fruits are manifold. The late Dr. J. Fraser, the well-known Bishop of Manchester, then vicar of a country parish, bore eloquent witness before a Royal Commission in the sixties as to the deplorable state of things existing at that time in many rural districts. Bread was dear, and wages down to starvation point; the labourers were uneducated, underfed, underpaid; their cottages were often unfit for human habitation, the sleeping and sanitary arrangements were appalling. Naturally, they took colour from their environment. How could any of the things which make for the beauty and the joy of life, morality, or even common decency, exist in such inhuman homes? In many a country village the condition of the labourer and his family was but little removed from that of the cattle they tended.

If we ask how these things came about and were suffered to continue, we are sorrowfully constrained to admit that the agricultural labourer in those days had few friends, either in his own class or in any other. He had no organisation, the Trades Unions let him alone; he had no money, the professional agitator ignored him; he had no vote, the politician passed him by. His lot was indeed a hard one; and, though of course there were many places where it had ameliorations—villages where the poor were well looked after; estates where the owners made it their duty to see their labourers were well housed and fairly paid—yet the ameliorations were comparatively few; and even they came, not as a right—the right of every honest working-man to a fair wage and decent condition of life—but rather as a charity, and so helped to weaken that spirit of independence which is an Englishman's birthright. Agricultural depression (a very real obstacle now) could hardly then be urged as an excuse; for at the time when wheat was dearest and land most valuable, the lot of the agricultural labourer was at its worst. These are unpleasant facts, but it is idle to blink at them, since they were the things which made the Union possible—and desirable.

The natural result of this state of affairs was a rankling sense of injustice among the agricultural labourers. The discontent was sullen, inchoate, voiceless, hardly apparent on the surface; but it was there all the same. The tide of social betterment was beginning to flow strongly in the towns, and it agitated even the stagnant backwaters of remote agricultural districts. The peasant, ignorant and illiterate though he was, could hardly remain insensible to the fact that, while the condition of workmen in other industries was improving, his remained the same. And this thought added to his dumb discontent. People have said it was the Union which caused discontent; on the contrary, it was discontent which caused the Union. In the Union the legitimate discontent of the agricultural labourer found its legitimate outlet. The labourers were crying for a man to lead them, to organise them, to voice their needs. The time was ripe and the man came; fortunately he was an honest and law-abiding one. One trembles to think what might have happened if the movement had been in less capable hands. The situation had in it all the elements of danger; inflammatory appeals to the prejudices of an ignorant and suffering peasantry would have lighted a fire difficult to quench, and would probably have put back the movement for their betterment at least a generation. Arch was no firebrand, but rather a "village Hampden," who put the welfare of the cause he had espoused before any personal ambition. In my opinion he was the man of the moment, the indispensable man. As Lord Rosebery said recently:

"There are junctures in the affairs of men when what is wanted is a man: not treasures, not fleets, not legends, but a man, the man of the moment, the man of the occasion, the man of destiny, whose spirit attracts, binds and inspires, whose capacity is congenial to the crisis, whose powers are equal to the convulsion. . . . The crisis is the travail, the birth of the man ends or assuages it."*

Such a man was Joseph Arch. The Union was his and he led it; and I think we owe him gratitude—not the labourer only but every one connected with the land—that he led it wisely and well.

It is very difficult for us now, when the turmoil has ended, to realise the state of affairs when Arch came to the front, or the tempest of feeling which his coming raised. Yet we must try to do so, if we

* Lord Rosebery on Sir William Wallace.

are to form a just estimate of his work. In this connexion a friend writes to me:

"I well remember the immense surprise which the revolt of Hodge occasioned in the North. It was as if the dead had come to life. We regarded the movement with intense expectation and hope. It had seemed to us impossible that there should be any stirring of the dry bones. The agricultural labourer had seemed hopeless. The serfs of the plough had lost even the aspiration to be free men. Such at least was the prevailing opinion when Joseph Arch arose.

"We hailed him as another Moses, and rejoiced exceedingly in the belief that his advent heralded the dawn of a happier social system, more compatible with the natural dignity of man.

"Several things combined to interest the public in the movement. It was a time of unrest. The town workmen had only a few years before received the franchise. The French Empire had just gone down under the blows of the German Army. The Education Act was just getting into working order. Everywhere there was a ferment in the minds of men. That it had at last affected even the Midland peasants proved how deep and wide the leaven of change was working.

"The old order was indeed changing and giving place to the new, and those who believed in progress, and were perhaps more alive to the evils and abuses of the old, than to the danger of the new, were loud in rejoicings over the revolt of Hodge.

"One thing that much helped the movement was the

direct and unmistakeable religious sentiment which found expression at the early meetings of the labourers. The revolt was thereby linked on to the old Civil Wars, when the Puritan preacher was the soul of the army of the Commonwealth. Most of the leaders of the strike were Methodist local preachers. In no instance, I am told by one who was in the midst of the movement, was one of the agitators trained for the work in the Established Church. This linked the movement on to Nonconformists everywhere, and when Bishop Ellicott uttered his famous remark about the horsepond the Midland Dissenters felt that the hour of victory was nigh.

"Another thing that appealed to the imagination was the extent to which the meetings of the strikers were inspired by song. The hymn tunes were easily linked to the verses in which the labourers expressed their hopes, and embodied their demands. The industrial revolt had in it some of the elements of a religious revival, and one of the most conspicuous of these was the resort to singing as a relief of emotions otherwise difficult to articulate.

"The industrial significance of the Union and its religious suggestiveness were, however, less important than the effect which it had on politics. The revolt of Hodge was the finishing blow to the old régime. It heralded the advent of rural democracy. The politician had never hoped much from the rural labourer. Logically he was of course entitled to a vote. But it was feared he would be as clay in the hands of the potter, in the hands of the squire and the parson. Joseph Arch dispelled that dread. He revealed the labourer as a factor, a real, living, potent factor, in the land. From that conviction sprang the Reform Bill which in 1884 enfranchised the country householders, and placed the constitution of the House of Commons on a frankly democratic basis.

"Great things, therefore, have sprung from that revolt of the serfs, and although many hopes were disappointed, and the millennium is still to seek, who can say that Joseph Arch has not been justified by the results of the great impetus which he gave to the cause of progress at a critical moment?"

The Union was necessary. What power has the poor man if he have not combination? The right to combine belongs to us all. The agricultural labourer has used his right with excellent results. First the grain, then the ear, then the full corn in the ear. First organisation, then higher wages and all which that means, and then the protection and power of the Parliamentary vote. With the franchise the agricultural labourer became politically a free man. And recent legislation, in the direction of allotments, free education, parish councils and so forth, has recognised that henceforth his interests are to be considered. The vote procured him this recognition and legislation; the Union procured him the vote. More than that, the vote is exercising an educational influence and awakening a sense of responsibility which was dormant. The labourer's horizon has widened; he is no longer content to plod on as before; there has quickened in him a laudable ambition to improve his condition; desires have awakened in him for a higher standard of living, better cottages, more leisure for self-improvement, and some surer provision against sickness and old age.

The supreme achievement of the Union, its culminating point as it were, was the franchise for the agricultural labourer. When that was obtained the Union was no longer politically necessary, and it died a natural death. Should there be agricultural labourers' unions in the future, they will probably be of a purely local kind.

The labourer has now political power; it remains for him to use it wisely. The legislature, moreover, has placed local machinery at his command whereby he can benefit himself in divers ways. He needs guiding to use this machinery aright, and those who are in a position to do so, should help him by throwing the weight of their local influence into the local scale. It is their duty to help him to help himself and others, to respect himself and others. He must be helped to develop himself on his own lines, and to develop the material resources at his disposal. Adequate education, elementary and technical, is what the agricultural labourer now needs most of all. With education he can equip himself and his children for their lifework and so take a place in the community and fill it—not mis-fill it. Help the square peg to the square hole; the round peg to the round hole. In the average labourer's family there will generally be found some children who are fitted by nature for work other than that of cultivating the land; this being so, give them a chance of developing for right use any natural gift or faculty they may possess. Those who have local influence should see that an efficient technical school is within reach of these children, be they boys or girls. Many of course will drift away from the villages to the large centres of population; many to London. This is inevitable; but, if they are equipped with a good education, they will play their proper part in the struggle of life, and will become useful and self-respecting members of the community, whether their lot be cast in town or country.

I have noticed that a curious jealousy exists among some agricultural labourers against machinery. But education will bring about a proper adjustment between the agricultural machine and the agricultural labourer. The man will learn how to utilise the machine to the utmost for his own benefit; with a fuller knowledge he will make it co-operate with him, instead of allowing it to compete with him. Education, technical education, will also teach the labourer to make use of other means of improving his position, which now too often are lying idle by his hands; and it is here that the local owners and occupiers of the land can help him too. Allotments, small holdings, dairies, poultry-yards, gardens, bee-keeping, pig-keeping, and so forth, as well as various local industries and crafts, should be fostered. The housing of the labourers also, alas! too often needs improvement. Village shops might be developed into co-operative stores. In short everything which tends to make the village a centre of wholesome life should be heartily encouraged. Co-operation, on the basis of mutual good will, is what is wanted, for in this way we may come to a better understanding of each other's needs, know one another better and help one another more.

I am all in favour of fostering the local spirit. Make a man proud of, and interested in, his birthplace or locality—make him feel he has a part in it—and you have started him on the road to good citizenship. Some will remain strongly local all their lives; others will broaden and widen from the local basis. The right and natural development is from home to neighbouring homes; then to the homes of the parish, the district, the county, the country, the empire, the world. But everything depends on individual effort; the man must help himself if he is to help others. Surely the career of Joseph Arch, who fought his way up from the plough-tail to a seat in Parliament, is an apt illustration of this truth; and he won his fight, be it remembered, without any of the advantages which surround the agricultural labourers nowadays, and which he was so largely instrumental in securing for them.

I have said there are some expressions of opinion in this book with which I do not altogether agree, though I respect the honest spirit which dictated them. One of them refers to the somewhat sweeping strictures on the country clergy. What they may have been in the days of which Joseph Arch has written I have, of course, no personal knowledge; the dead hand was on the Church in those days, and sympathy with the people was certainly not a strong point with the clergy. As no less an authority than Dean Stubbs has put it: "Popular reforms in all ages and all countries, from the Prophet Amos down to Joseph Arch, have rarely met with much favour from the established authorities in either Church or State." * But it would be unfair to ignore the fact that this reproach has now been largely wiped away,

---

* "Village Politics," by the Dean of Ely.

and there exists no body of men more anxious to do their duty than the country clergy. There are many landowners, too, both great and small, despite the agricultural depression which has hit them hard, who are most desirous, and have always been desirous, to do all that in them lies to help their poorer brethren, and to sympathise with their needs and aspirations; and this in no spirit of patronage, but in the spirit of love. I believe this spirit is deepening and broadening every day, and in it may be read one of the most encouraging signs of the times. Whatever may be the immediate issues of the hour, social questions constitute the politics of the future. But these questions will never be settled satisfactorily until all classes of the community are willing to work for the common good.

FRANCES EVELYN WARWICK.

CONTENTS.

	PAGE
MY FOREWORD	1

CHAPTER I.
CHILDHOOD 3

CHAPTER II.
BOYHOOD TO MANHOOD 23

CHAPTER III.
WAITING THE CALL 42

CHAPTER IV.
THE CALL COMES 65

CHAPTER V.
FORMING THE UNION 93

CHAPTER VI.
PROGRESS OF THE UNION 117

Contents

CHAPTER VII.
THE GAME LAWS 145

CHAPTER VIII.
MY VISIT TO CANADA 174

CHAPTER IX.
MY VIEWS ON EMIGRATION 199

CHAPTER X.
MORE WORK FOR THE UNION 221

CHAPTER XI.
THE DAWNING OF THE FRANCHISE . . . 252

CHAPTER XII.
FOES FROM WITHIN 274

CHAPTER XIII.
THE LAND AND THE LABOURERS 300

CHAPTER XIV.
THE CAUSES OF AGRICULTURAL DEPRESSION . 323

CHAPTER XV.
I ENTER PARLIAMENT 346

CHAPTER XVI.
AT THE END OF THE DAY 378

JOSEPH ARCH:
The Story of His Life.

MY FOREWORD.

ALTHOUGH it has been frequently suggested to me that a review of the chief events in my chequered career, during the greater part of which I figured prominently before the public, would prove of interest to those whose lot it is to labour and to toil, and perhaps even to others, I never until now seriously entertained the idea of attempting to write a book. When, however, the illustrious and noble lady whose name adorns the title-page did me the great and unexpected honour to come forward, and most generously offer to edit the work, I could no longer resist.

I am in the sere and yellow leaf; my race is nearly run; my work will soon be over: I may therefore be pardoned for pleading at the outset that a kind and indulgent reading public will view with tolerant eyes such faults and failings as must necessarily appear in the following pages.

It is the life-story of an English agricultural labourer,—of a man who has undergone many and varied experiences, who has borne severe toil, privations, and hardships, and who was blessed with few social advantages or privileges, yet who was endued by Nature with a robust, healthy, and sturdy constitution, a dogged determination, and a steady, plodding perseverance, which culminated eventually in more than ordinary success. Should the perusal of such a "plain, unvarnised tale" act as a spur to effort, or should it encourage the young man reader in a worthy ambition to improve his condition socially, mentally, and morally, this unpretending volume will not have been written in vain.

CHAPTER I.

CHILDHOOD.

I WAS born at Barford, in Warwickshire, on November 10th, 1826. This village, situated on a bend of willow-fringed Avon, possesses a fine old bridge of grey stone, and in its straggling street there are houses still in existence, with peaked gables and projecting frames and eaves of darkened wood, which William Shakespeare may have seen, and even entered. Warwick Castle and the county town are within three miles, and Stratford-on-Avon lies not quite seven miles away; so my country—and I am proud to say it—is Shakespeare's country, and my home, and what was the home of many of my forefathers as well, lies right in the very heart of old England.

Three generations of Arches sleep the sleep of the just in Barford churchyard. They were, every one of them, honest, upright, hardworking children of the soil; good men and true, ancestors any man might be right proud to own. Some of my Warwickshire forbears fought with Cromwell at Edgehill, and in other battles of the Civil War, against tyranny and oppression and for the liberty of the people. I expect that is where I get my fighting propensities from; fighting was in the blood, and I just harked back to those old Roundhead ancestors of mine, who struck many a brave and sturdy blow on the right side.

Within a stone's throw of the graveyard, and nearly opposite the parish church with its fifteenth-century tower, stands the homely cottage in which I first saw the light. It has been in the possession of the Arch family for a good hundred and fifty years. Though repairs and alterations and improvements, including a new slated roof and the addition of a small greenhouse, give it a modern appearance, the open chimney and the black beams in the ceiling of the living-room show its true age plainly enough; so do the black beams of the gable at the back, which overlooks my workshop and my half-acre of garden. My grandfather bought the freehold of the cottage and little garden from a man named Thomas Ashley, for the sum of thirty pounds.

This grandfather was a famous hedger and ditcher in his day, a man who did with all his might whatever he put his hand to; and judging from all accounts he must have put his hand to a lot of things from his youth upwards. He came to hold a very good and responsible position under one of the Earls of Warwick. My grandmother was also employed by the same earl. They lived for several years at the Lodge, Warwick Park. They were a thrifty, hard-working couple, respected and looked up to by their neighbours. It was while they were living at the Lodge that they contrived to save up the thirty pounds. Little by little, coin by coin, they stored up the hard-earned money in what I may call the poor man's Post Office Savings Bank of that day—a stocking.

Well, I have good reason to remember that same old stocking with gratitude—and I do—for out of it came forth, as it were, the cottage and bit of land I call mine to-day.

My grandmother was one of a strong, well-grown stock, born and brought up in Oxfordshire. She certainly was a remarkably fine old woman, standing six feet four inches in height, and she had three brothers to match her; each of my great-uncles stood well over six feet four. She was long-lived, being nearly ninety when she died, and she kept her faculties up to the last. Although I was only about six years old, I can recall some of her sayings and doings clearly, and very quaint they were.

My father was a Barford man, and my mother was a Warwickshire woman, so I come directly of Warwickshire stock on both sides. My father was a shepherd when he married and brought my mother to the cottage where they lived and died, and where their four children were born—two boys and two girls. My elder brother died young; if he had lived he would have inherited our cottage. My father was a sober, industrious, agricultural labourer, steady as old Time, a plodding man, and a good all-round worker, who could turn his hand to anything, like his father before him.

He was quiet and peaceable by nature, no fighter; he did not agree with those who were ready to pick a quarrel and stir up strife for a trifle; on the contrary he was too much inclined to let people take advantage of him. But he could be independent and show a stiff back if it came to a question of principle; and he had no mind to bend his neck to squire or parson for the sake of their doles, when they wanted him to do what he thought was wrong. Quiet man though he was, he had his opinions, and he could stick to them on occasion. He showed that, to his cost and ours, when he refused to sign a petition in favour of the Corn Laws.

This petition was properly hall-marked by the local magnates; they sanctioned it, and they put their signatures to it; but my father was a staunch Repealer, and would have nothing whatever to do with such a document. He was made to pay, and we with him, for his honest adherence to principle. Because he dared to speak out and assert what he believed to be right and true; because he, a poor labourer, stood firm for Repeal; because he held on to his opinion, he was a marked man for the rest of his life. He did not turn aside for that though, and try to put matters straight for himself again by currying favour with the magnates; he just plodded steadily on, doing his own work day by day, rearing his family without reproach, on low wages, and in hard times.

My mother, whose first husband had been a coachman in a gentleman's family, was of a different character. She was shrewd, strong-willed, and self-reliant; always able to hold every inch of her own with anybody with whom she came into contact. In personal appearance she was a fine, big, stout, healthy-looking woman, and I am as like her as two pins. The following anecdote will serve to show my mother's strength of will and determination of character.

In our village we had a most despotic parson's wife, a kind of would-be lady pope, and one day she took it into her head to issue a decree. She gave out that all the girls attending school were to have their hair cut round like a basin, more like prison girls than anything else. My mother put her foot down, and said she never would allow her daughters to have their hair cut in such an unsightly way. When she heard this, the parson's wife became very nasty; and she could be uncommonly nasty when she chose. She proceeded to make things very uncomfortable for my mother; but she had met her match, and more, in the agricultural labourer's wife. My mother fought it out inch by inch, and though she had a tough fight of it she won in the end. But the parson's wife never forgave her for it. My father, if he had been left to himself, would have given in at once, for the sake of peace and quietness —he was against offending the "powers that be" in a general way—but my mother pulled too strong for him. She went out and did battle, but from that time my parents never received a farthing's-worth of charity in the way of soup, coals, or the like, which were given regularly, and as a matter of course, from the rectory to nearly every poor person in the village.

But though this was an unfair deprivation and a real hardship besides, with wages at nine shillings or, at the very most, twelve shillings a week, my mother would not let it trouble her; she was too independent for that. There was no cringing, no time-serving, and no cant about her. If ever there was a practical, just, devoted, and good woman she was; but cant and talk for talking's sake she could not abide. She did not hold with quarrelling for quarrelling's sake either. She always used to say to me when I got into a bit of a quarrel, and that was not seldom, "Oh, my boy, that won't do; he who would have friends must show himself friendly"; and all through my later life I have never gone anywhere without making friends, simply by following out her teaching.

There was another principle which she fastened on my mind, and that was self-reliance and self-help. Over and over again she would say to me, "What you can do for yourself, my boy, when you grow up to be a man, never let anybody else do for you"; and I have kept that advice before me all my life. She was a fine woman, and if ever a man truly loved and admired his mother I did! The training I had from her—the teaching, the example, and the advice—was the training that made me, and shaped my life.

She was a great admirer of Shakespeare. She used

to talk about him very often, and she was well versed in his works. She would read bits aloud to me of an evening, and tell me tales from the plays. On Sundays she used to read the Bible to me in the same way, and tell me stories from it. Shakespeare and the Bible were the books I was brought up on, and I don't want any better. I have heard and read a good deal since then, but I have never come across anything to beat them.

She was also a splendid hand at writing letters. A great many of the poor people who had children and relatives away from home, but who could not write to them, used to come to my mother and ask her to write their letters for them. She did it with pleasure; she was always willing to help her friends, and even her enemies if they wanted help. There was nothing vindictive or mean about her, she had too large a heart for that. A more upright, capable, kindly, and motherly woman never drew breath; her heart was full of sympathy, and her brain of resource. You might count on her giving the right kind of help at a pinch; if you were in a difficulty she was always ready to come to the rescue; and if you happened to be in a tight place she would generally manage to find a way out.

Before her marriage she had been in domestic service at Warwick Castle; she was a first-rate laundress and an excellent nurse, and she did not hide these talents in a napkin.

I may truly say that my sisters and I owed our lives

to her twice over, for she saved us from being starved to death one winter. It was 1835, the winter of the Repeal of the Corn Laws. I was about nine years old. I well remember eating barley bread, and seeing the tears in my poor mother's eyes as she cut slices off a loaf; for even barley loaves were all too scarce, and especially with us just then. Because my father had refused to sign for "a small loaf and a dear one," he could not get any work whatever for eighteen weeks. He tried hard to get a job, but it was useless; he was a marked man, and we should have starved if my mother had not kept us all by her laundry work.

It was a terrible winter. No one who has not gone through it, or has not witnessed something similar, can realise *how* terrible it was. The scenes I witnessed then made an indelible impression on my mind. I have often told the Tories, "You caused the iron to enter into my soul very young, and you will never draw it out. It will remain there till I die." That barley bread got into my vitals.

There was corn enough for everybody—that was the hard, cruel part of it—but those who owned it would not sell it out when it was so sorely needed. They kept it back, they locked it up; and all the time the folk were crying out in their extremity for bread,— crying out to men who hardened their hearts and turned deaf ears to the hungry cries of their starving fellow-creatures. To make as much money as they could, by letting corn rise to famine prices, was all the owners of it cared about. "Make money at any price" was their motto. They belonged to the class of men who always try to turn to their own profit the miseries, the misfortunes, and the helplessness of their poorer neighbours. They grew fat at the expense of their fellows. Those who ruled in high places, and had the making of the laws in their hands, were chiefly rich landowners and successful traders, and instead of trying to raise the people, create a higher standard of comfort and well-being, and better their general condition, they did their best—or worst—to keep them in a state of poverty and serfdom, of dependence and wretchedness. Those who owned and held the land believed, and acted up to their belief as far as they were able, that the land belonged to the rich man only, that the poor man had no part nor lot in it, and had no sort of claim on society. If a poor man dared to marry and have children, they thought he had no *right* to claim the necessary food wherewith to keep himself and his family alive. They thought, too, every mother's son of them, that, when a labourer could no longer work, he had lost the right to live. Work was all they wanted from him; he was to work and hold his tongue, year in and year out, early and late, and if he could not work, why, what was the use of him? It was what he was made for, to labour and toil for his betters, without complaint, on a starvation wage. When no more work could be squeezed out of him, he was no better than a cumberer of other folk's ground, and the proper place for such as he was the churchyard, where he would be sure to lie quiet under a few feet of earth, and want neither food nor wages any more. A quick death and a cheap burying—that was the motto of those extortioners for the poor man past work.

Being a little chap at the time, I did not realise all that—it was not likely—but I remembered what I saw with my own eyes and heard with my own ears. About the time of the Repeal things had got so bad that they could hardly be worse. The food we could get was of very poor quality, and there was far too little of it. Meat was rarely, if ever, to be seen on the labourer's table; the price was too high for his pocket,—a big pocket it was, but with very little in it; next to nothing most days, and sometimes nothing at all! In many a household even a morsel of bacon was considered a luxury. Flour was so dear that the cottage loaf was mostly of barley. Tea ran to six and seven shillings a pound, sugar would be eightpence a pound, and the price of other provisions was in proportion. If fresh meat is still scarcer than it should be in the labourer's cottage to-day, he can at any rate get good wheaten bread and plenty of potatoes; but in the twenties and thirties he had neither wheaten bread nor a plentiful supply of potatoes to fall back on. In the country districts generally potatoes were exceedingly scarce. In our own neighbourhood there were none to speak of; only one man near us grew them, and he hoarded them up. With corn at a prohibitive price, with fresh meat hardly ever within their reach, with what potatoes there were hoarded up and not for their buying—you see, that potato-hoarder was only following the wicked example of the corn-owners!—what, in the name of necessity, were the people to do? They could not grow potatoes; they had no allotments then, they had no hope of them, and the bulk of the labourers had no gardens.

Well, these people—people, mind you, who were clearing and planting and tilling the land, who were putting their very lives into it—in order to keep body and soul together, and some kind of roof other than the workhouse over their miserable heads, were driven to steal the food they could not get for love or money. Yes, would-be honest Englishmen were forced to become common thieves. They stole turnips from the fields, potatoes when they could get them, and any other edible thing they could lay hands on. You see, they were ravenous; they were starving. I have no doubt that if our Warwickshire earth had been eatable some of these poor sons of the soil, like the Andaman Islanders, would have tried to nourish themselves on it, so hard pressed were they. They were rendered so desperate through hunger that they defied the law and its terrors every day.

As they were unable to procure fresh meat honestly, they stole that as well. Poaching became so prevalent that it is hardly an exaggeration to say that every other man you met was a poacher. It is my deliberate opinion that these men were to some extent justified in their actions; they had by hook or by crook to obtain food somewhere, in order to enable themselves, their wives, and their children to live at all, to keep the breath in their bodies. Necessity knows no law but its own. I have always been one for keeping the laws of the land and upholding them as far as possible; but how can I blame these men because they would not sit still, and let the life be starved out of them and theirs? They would not; so they risked their liberty, the next dearest thing they had—though it was a poor enough liberty at the best—in their endeavours to obtain food. The horrors of those times are clearly and vividly before my mind's eye even now. It is as if they had been burned and branded into me. I cannot forget them.

There is one thing, however, for which I shall always be thankful, and the thought of it is like a bright spot in that dark, black time. I am glad to say that, even when things were at their very worst with us, my father was never obliged to go out and steal food. We grew carrots and turnips in our garden, and we had not to pay anything out for rent. There was always some money coming in. There was my father's wage, which varied from eight to ten shillings a week, and during those eighteen weeks, when he was without work, my mother, as I have already said, turned to and managed to earn sufficient to keep our heads above water—above ground rather! No, though it is true that things were as bad as bad could be with us, all through that bitter, hard winter my parents remained both honest and independent. They had a long, tough fight of it, but they kept their heads up bravely; they stole from no man, nor did they take alms from any one; they never sank down to the level of the thief and the pauper. It had never been my mother's policy to take alms. She was always willing and ready to accept a kindness and to return one, but she did not wish any one to help her while she was able to help herself; and when she had finished her work she wanted to draw her money, and spend it at her leisure and as she liked, without interference from anybody.

Numbers of people used to go to the rectory for soup, but not a drop of it did we touch. I have stood at our door with my mother, and I have seen her face look sad as she watched the little children toddle past, carrying the tin cans, and their toes coming out of their boots. "Ah, my boy," she once said, "you shall never, never do that. I will work these fingers to the bone before you have to do it!" She was as good as her word—*I never went to the rectory for soup.*

My mother, as might be expected, was not in favour at the rectory from the first. She did not order herself lowly and reverently towards her betters according to the Church Catechism. She had no betters for the matter of that,—not in Barford. She would not duck down to the rector's wife just because she happened to be the rector's wife, and she was not properly and humbly thankful for coals and soup. She showed plainly that she put a value on herself as a free and independent woman, and she would not stoop to beg favours of any one, let it be squire or parson or rich farmer. Threatening and bullying would not make her budge an inch—just the contrary. She had a good sound head on her shoulders, and when once she had thought a thing out and made up her mind about it she would stick to her opinion through thick and thin. The lady-despot at the rectory did not want to have anything to do with a woman of that kind; a woman with grit, and a good stiff backbone, had no business to be in the village at all, she thought. That a labourer's wife should ever have dared to stand up against her sacred authority was gall and wormwood to her.

Of course, if my mother had been a strong churchwoman, and a regular churchgoer, things would have been all the other way. If she had been ready to conform to the Church as by law established, the rector and his wife would have put up with a good deal of independence, and would have overlooked a lot of plain-speaking about other matters. But she was not appealed to by the Church service, and she did not hold with the Church teaching. It was not that she was an irreligious woman—very far from it; but there seemed very little practical religion in the Church in those days, and it was quite enough for her if preaching and practice did not go together. All men are equal in the sight of God, but if the parson preached that doctrine he did not act up to it in God's House. In the parish church the poor man and his wife were shown pretty plainly where they came among their fellow-creatures and fellow-worshippers—men and women of the same flesh and blood, and of like passions with themselves, however superior they might seem to be in the eyes of the world because they were rich and high-placed. In the parish church the poor were apportioned their lowly places, and taught that they must sit in them Sunday after Sunday all their lives long. They must sit meekly and never dare to mingle with their betters in the social scale. It was an object lesson repeated week after week, one which no one could mistake, and it sank deep into my mind.

I remember a thing which made my mother very angry. The parson's wife issued a decree, that the labourers should sit on one side of the church and their wives on the other. When my mother heard of it she said, "No, 'those whom God hath joined together let no man put asunder,' and certainly no woman shall!"

I can also remember the time when the parson's wife used to sit in state in her pew in the chancel, and the poor women used to walk up the church and make a curtsey to her before taking the seats set apart for them. They were taught in this way that they had to pay homage and respect to those "put in authority over them," and made to understand that they must "honour the powers that be," as represented in the rector's wife. You may be pretty certain that many of these women did not relish the curtsey-scraping and other humiliations they had to put up with, but they were afraid to speak out. They had their families to think of, children to feed and clothe somehow; and when so many could not earn a living wage, but only a half-starving one, when very often a labouring man was out of work for weeks at a stretch,—why, the wives and mothers learned to take thankfully whatever was doled out to them at the parsonage or elsewhere, and drop the curtsey expected of them, without making a wry face. A smooth face and a smooth tongue was what their benefactors required of them, and they got both. It was only human nature that the poor "had-nots" should look up to the "hads" and be obedient to their wishes; especially when the "hads" gave to the "had-nots" out of their abundance, dropped a few pence into the wife's hand when the husband's pocket was empty, or sent the family enough for a bite and a sup when the cottage cupboard was as bare as Mother Hubbard's.

With bowed head and bended knee the poor learned to receive from the rich what was only their due, had they but known it. Years of poverty had ground the spirit of independence right out of them; these wives and mothers were tamed by poverty, they were cowed by it, as their parents had been before them in many cases, and the spirit of servitude was bred in their very bones. And the worst of it was the mischief did not stop at the women—it never does. They set an example of spiritless submission, which their children were only too inclined to follow. Follow it too many of them did, and they and their children are reaping the consequences and paying the price of it to-day.

I can remember when the squire and the other local magnates used to sit in state in the centre of the aisle. They did not, if you please, like the look of the agricultural labourers. Hodge sat too near them, and even in his Sunday best he was an offence to their eyes. They also objected to Hodge looking at them, so they had curtains put up to hide them from the vulgar gaze. And yet, while all this was going on, while the poor had to bear with such high-handed dealings, people wondered why the Church had lost its hold, and continued to lose its hold, on the labourers in the country districts! It never had any hold on me—in that, I was my mother's son also. I never took the Communion in the parish church in my life. When I was seven years old I saw something which prevented me once for all. One Sunday my father was going to stop to take the Communion, and I, being a boy, had of course to go out before it began. I may here mention that the church door opened then in a direct line with the chancel and the main aisle, so that anybody looking through the keyhole could easily see what was going on inside. The door is now more to the side of the church, and out of direct line with the chancel. I was a little bit of a fellow, and curious. I said to myself, "What does father stop behind for? What is it they do? I'll see." So I went out of church, closed the door, placed my eye at the keyhole and peeped through, and what I saw will be engraved on my mind until the last day of my life. That sight caused a wound which has never been healed. My proud little spirit smarted and burned when I saw what happened at that Communion service.

First, up walked the squire to the communion rails; the farmers went up next; then up went the tradesmen, the shopkeepers, the wheelwright, and the blacksmith; and then, the very last of all, went the poor agricultural labourers in their smock frocks. They walked up by themselves; nobody else knelt with them; it was as if they were unclean—and at that sight the iron entered straight into my poor little heart and remained fast embedded there. I said to myself, "If that's what goes on—never for me!" I ran home and told my mother what I had seen, and I wanted to know why my father was not as good in the eyes of God as the squire, and why the poor should be forced to come up last of all to the table of the Lord. My mother gloried in my spirit.

I have heard, difficult as it is to believe, that much the same thing goes on in several villages even now, notably in Wiltshire. Perhaps the difference between the rich and the poor may not be driven home in so marked a manner in country churches as it was in the thirties; but if it is not, it is because they are afraid of us now, and dare not show up in their true colours. The dragon of caste is only scotched, not killed; he is a tough, scaly old monster, and many a sturdy blow will have to be struck at him yet, before he wriggles his last. He has been wounded in the fight;

we have fought with him, and some of the life blood has flowed out of him, but he is only lying low; his mouth is there and his teeth are ready, and if we give him the chance, he will turn and bite as hard as ever he did.

My father was a very regular churchgoer. Wet or shine he would be in his place of a Sunday; he went as regularly and as steadily as a wound-up eight-day clock. I used to puzzle my little head over it. I used to say to myself, "Why ever does father go and put up with such treatment?" I suppose he kept on going because he had been brought up to it. To church he had always been accustomed to go, so to church he went. And there were other working men like him in that.

My mother was different. To do a thing just because she had done it before was not her way; her reason, her judgment, and her will were always active. She did not agree with Church teaching, and she did not hold with parsons' ways. She did not say, "Whatever is, is right"; she thought that a great deal of what was, was wrong. She was a dissenter by nature and by conviction.

There was no chapel in our village, but when I was about fourteen years of age some dissenters began to come over from Wellsbourne. They used to hold meetings in a back lane. When the parson got wind of it, he and his supporters, the farmers, dared the labourers to go near these unorthodox Christians. If we did, then good-bye to all the charities; no more soup and coals should we have. And it was no idle threat. If that was not religious persecution I should like to know what was! They knew they had the labourers under their thumbs, and so they put the screw on when it pleased them. Of course we had long ago seen the last of the soup and the coals; they had been stopped when my mother fought over the hair-cutting. I well remember going with my mother to listen to these dissenters. They used to preach under an old barn in the back lane. Rough and ready men were they, dressed in their fustian coats, earnest and devoted to the truth as they saw it, good men all—they have gone home now. God rest them!

CHAPTER II.

BOYHOOD TO MANHOOD.

WHEN I look back to the days of my boyhood and live them over again in memory, I can see what a lot of truth there is in the well-known saying, "The hand which rocks the cradle, rules the world." It is my opinion, however, that pretty nearly everything depends on the kind of rocking. If the hand which rocks is a weak and unsteady one, why, then the poor babe will be jerked and shaken, and his walk through life will most likely be jerky and unsteady too; he will be more or less of a wobbler and a shirker, he will not march straight and steady to his mark. There will not be much of the ruler about him; he may reckon on being trodden down, and other folk will rule him.

They used to say and believe that fairies, good and bad, came to the cradle of the new-born babe with gifts. Well, I don't think there are many who believe that nowadays, but like all those old tales there was some sort of a truth behind it. My mother was my good fairy, in a manner of saying. She gave me the right-down good gifts of a healthy body and a strong brain, and she passed on to me some of the qualities for which I can take no particular credit to myself, such as sympathy with my fellow-creatures, integrity, and steadfastness of purpose. She rocked her cradle so firmly and so well that she rocked in as much of the good as she could manage, and she rocked out all the bad she could get at, and she got at more than a little. All her life she taught my sisters and myself by her precepts and her example; she educated us in the true sense of the word. She did her part towards making fair scholars of us by supplementing what instruction we got at the village school, and she continued to teach me in my spare time after I left. At that time a child was not qualified to begin his schooling until he was six years old; there was no such blessed thing as an infant school. A child could run loose about the village in " poverty, ignorance, and dirt," till he reached the regulation age; and after that also. There were no Board Schools, with their sixth and seventh and eight standards; there were no School Board Inspectors and grants, then. A village boy was given the bare chance of picking up a few scraps of rudimentary knowledge—the three Rs, as we used to say—or of going without. He could take it in or leave it out; and, knowing what stuff the ordinary village boy was made of, he did what any one might have expected—any one, that is, with an ounce of sense in him—he either left the little learning out, or he more often than not took it in all wrong. The teaching in most of the village schools, then, was bad almost beyond belief.

"Much knowledge of the right sort is a dangerous thing for the poor," might have been the motto put up over the door of the village school in my day. The less book-learning the labourer's lad got stuffed into him, the better for him and the safer for those above him, was what those in authority believed and acted up to. I daresay they made themselves think somehow or other—perhaps by *not* thinking—that they were doing their duty in that state of life to which it had pleased God to call *them*, when they tried to numb his brain, as a preliminary to stunting his body later on, as stunt it they did, by forcing him to work like a beast of burden for a pittance.

These gentry did not want him to know; they did not want him to think; they only wanted him to work. To toil with the hand was what he was born into the world for, and they took precious good care to see that he did it from his youth upwards. Of course he might learn his catechism; that, and things similar to it, was the right, proper, and suitable knowledge for such as he; he would be the more likely to stay contentedly in his place to the end of his working days.

The majority of the schools were parsons' schools; we call them voluntary now, but parsons' they are still, and they will remain so to the end. I should like to see them swept away from off the face of the country. I hope I shall live to see that day; but as they seem to have had a new lease of life given them lately there is not much chance of that! I never had any sympathy with this kind of school, and it is not in me to have it.

The school in our village was one of the parson kind, but luckily for us youngsters it was a downright good one. For that we had to thank our master; it was entirely owing to him. I can truthfully say that our master all those years ago was, master for master, a better one than the man they have there now. Our man was sensible and practical above the common, and he had the true interests of his scholars at heart. He knew how important it was that during the very few years of schooling we could have, we should be taught what would prove of most use to us in everyday life. He flatly refused to waste his time and ours over the catechism and other useless educational lumber of the same sort, to the exclusion of what it was so much more necessary for us to know. He was determined that he would make boys fit to do something to earn their living when they left school; and he stuck manfully to that determination. He was as excellent a teacher as a poor boy could wish to meet with, and I shall never forget what I owe him. It would have been difficult to beat him at reading, writing, spelling, arithmetic, and mensuration. I was only able to pick up the rudiments of these with him, but I picked them up so thoroughly that I never let them drop again. My master saw to it that the foundation was well and truly laid, and I was thus able to build up, later on, safe and sure, and by degrees, a solid little structure of knowledge on the top of it. I began to attend when I was six, the eligible age, but I was obliged to leave before I was nine, so that I had barely three years of regular schooling to start me on my way in life. But if the dark doom of the labourer's child fell up on me betimes, I did not let the black cloud of ignorance settle on my faculties. I started right away, not only to keep what knowledge I had gained, but to add more to it. I bought books, and studied hard, and educated myself, when I came home of an evening from the fields, or from following the plough; so that with the help of my mother and my books—books purchased out of my scanty wage—I managed to pick up piecemeal what was then considered a fair education. I was wonderfully fond of my books and my writing. I did not want to go into the street and play with the other boys; I stayed indoors and stuck to my self-set lessons. My mother would set me copies, give me writing tasks, and sums to work out. She was always ready to help me, willing to explain a difficulty, or smooth out a knotty point, if she could. She was as anxious that I should get on as I was myself.

I was a youngster of nine when I began to earn money. My first job was crow-scaring, and for this I received fourpence a day. This day was a twelve hours one, so it sometimes happened that I got more than was in the bargain, and that was a smart taste of the farmer's stick when he ran across me outside the field I had been set to watch. I can remember how he would come into the field suddenly, and walk quietly up behind me; and, if he caught me idling, I used to catch it hot. There was no sparing the stick and spoiling the child then! This crow-scaring was very monotonous work, and many a time I proved the truth of the old adage about Satan finding mischief, for idle hands. My idle hands found a good deal to do, what with bird-nesting, trespassing, and other boyish tricks and diversions. But if those days spent in the fields were rather monotonous, they were at any rate wholesome, and I throve apace. I had fresh air to breathe, plenty of room to stretch my young limbs in, and just enough plain food to nourish a growing boy. Had I been a miner's son, I might have been in those days slaving my wretched little life away in the depths of a coal mine, breathing foul air, herding with other children of my own age or younger still, dragging load after load of coal up ladders, or sitting behind a door in the pitch dark for fourteen hours at a stretch. I knew nothing of such a cruel, brutalising, demoralising child's life as that. I had the sky over my head, and if there came wind and rain and stormy weather, there came sunshine too. And I had the trees to look at and climb, hedgerow flowers to pluck, and streams to wade in. "Nature's feast of changing beauty" was always spread out before me; and, though I did not think much about it in that way, still I was taking it all in without knowing it.

I must admit, however that, if this sort of work did not prove harmful to robust boys with a sound constitution like myself, it played havoc with the weakly ones, and set loose all too soon the sleeping dogs of disease, the fell dogs of consumption and bronchitis and rheumatism, which devoured them wholesale when they should have been in their manhood's prime. If I had been cursed with a rickety body, if I had been ill-nourished and insufficiently clad, and had been obliged to stand in a new-sown field shivering on an empty stomach, while the cold wind blew and the chill rain poured down in torrents and soaked me to the skin, I should probably not be living to tell this tale to-day. If I had survived, ten chances to one, it would have been in the shape of a crippled martyr to rheumatism or a wheezy victim to bronchitis: I should have been a broken-down, doubled-up, worn-out old man. The sickly son of an agricultural labourer had as little chance of growing up to a healthy manhood as had the sickly son of a miner or a mill hand: it was a regular case of extremes meeting in a vicious circle. If he got past the bird-scaring stage he had the carter and the ploughman to contend with, and their tenderest mercies were cruel. They used their tongues and their whips and their boots on him so freely, that it is no exaggeration to say that the life of poor little Hodge was not a whit better than that of a plantation nigger boy.

I kept at crow-scaring for about twelve months, during which time I worked for several farmers. My first employer was a big, burly man, fairly well-to-do. He came to grief, however, through his extravagance. He did not look after his business properly, and, to make matters worse for himself, he married a London lady who would be very gay, would have everything after the London pattern, so she very soon brought him down. Here I may say that this is but one instance out of many which have, from time to time, come under my notice. There were too many farmers and farmers' wives of this sort in my youth, and it is my candid opinion that there are more of them about now than ever there were, and no one has any kind of use for them. Farmers' wives nowadays are ashamed to go to market to sell their eggs and butter as they used commonly to do. They want to play the piano, dress fine, make calls and ape the county gentry, and of course the farms will not stand it. How can they? And the farmers too want to hunt, and shoot, and play the fine gentleman at ease. Then, when these would-be swells find their cash run short, they cry out that it is the labourers who are extravagant and thriftless, who want too high a wage, who do too little work, and are bringing the land to ruin!

Why do not these farmers, with their wives and families, draw in, and turn to, and live according to their means, instead of being above their trade? Let the farmer give up his hunter, let his wife doff her silken gowns, her furbelows and her fal-lals, let his daughters drop their tinkling accomplishments, and let them give their time, their attention, and their money to the farm, as it is their clear and bounden duty to do. If they do not give the farm their care and personal attention, the farm will give them up. That is a dead certainty. This was what happened to the first farmer I worked for. My father, by the way, worked for this same man.

From crow-scarer to ploughboy was my next step, with an accompanying increase in wage of twopence a day. Three shillings a week was that amount better than nothing, but it was a small contribution to the common family fund; it was not sufficient to keep me, let alone buy clothes. We should have been in a very bad way if my mother, by her laundry earnings, had not subsidised my father's wage. My clothing was of the coarsest. I had to go to school in a smock-frock and old hobnailed boots, and my work-a-day garb was the same. The sons of the wheelwrights, the master tailor, and the tradesmen were just becoming genteel, and used to dress in shoddy cloth. These peacocky youngsters would cheek the lads in smock-frocks whenever they got the chance, and many a stand-up fight we used to have—regular pitched battles of smock-frock against cloth-coat, they were, in which smock-frock held his own right well. The lot of the ordinary ploughboy was not an enviable one, and I, in common with the other lads at the plough tail, had a rough time of it. Some of our carters were brutal bullies; and they liked to make us dance a quickstep to the tune of the stick and the whip—cutting capers in more ways than one! The head carter was so fond of this kind of tune and caper-cutting that he would be at it on the smallest provocation. He was a cruel flogger, and the very sight of him was enough to set some of the lads shaking in their hobnailed boots. Many a time and oft in the dark and early hours of the morning has little Joe Arch, the ploughboy, trudged up the lane, "creeping like snail unwillingly to work," with his satchel on his shoulder, containing, not books, but his food for the day. This would be a hunch of barley bread, with occasionally an apple baked in paste of coarse wheat-meal. Apple-dumpling day was a red one in my boy's calendar. When I had such a dainty bit in my bag it seldom stayed there many minutes. Although I had despatched a hearty breakfast before starting, out would come the dumpling. "Just to have a look at it, and to see if it is so big as mother generally makes them," I would say to myself. Then I would turn it about and admire its size. From handling the dainty to tasting it was a sure process. "I'll have one little bite—only a nibble," I would say. When I had got my tooth into that dumpling Adam with his apple wasn't in it; it was a case of "once bitten soon gone." Then I would hurry on to make up for my dawdling, with only the hunch of barley bread in my wallet, the joys of the dumpling behind me, and before me the day's drudgery with perhaps a thrashing thrown in.

When I was between twelve and thirteen years of age I could drive a pair of horses and plough my own piece. It was a proud day for me when I drove my first pair and got eightpence a day wage. This kind of work is generally called "gee-oh-ing."

I quickly became an efficient geeoher, and proved then, as I have often done since, the truth of the old saying, "Where there's a will there's a way." I geeohed with a will, so the way of promotion was not long in being reached. There was a wealthy banker and Justice of the Peace in the village, a great hunting man, who kept six or seven horses. I began to drive a pair of horses at plough for him; and after a bit, thinking I suppose that I was a smart, likely lad, he took me into his stables, made me a sort of stable-boy, and gave me eight shillings a week to start with. Here was a rise for a lad, who was set on rising as fast and as much as he could. In time my wages went up to nine shillings a week, and I was able to be a real help to our little household, and lighten somewhat the burden of care resting on my mother's shoulders. But this was the high-water mark; and if my wages were higher than they had been, my working-day was a longer one. I had to give my money's worth, and I gave it, good measure, as I have always done. I would stick like a limpet to my books of an evening. "Not an idle minute" was my rule. There were no slack half-hours for me, no taking it easy with the other lads. To make more money, to do more, to know more, to be a somebody in my little world was my ambition, and I toiled strenuously to attain it. There was not much in the way of amusement going on in the village to distract my attention, and draw me outside our home. The village lad had two kinds of recreation open to him. He could take his choice between lounging and boozing in the public house, or playing bowls in the bowling alley. That was all. There were no cricket or football clubs, no Forester's meetings. When they did start a sick benefit fund, of which, by the way, I am still a member, the parson, the farmer, and the leading men of the parish did their very best to put it down, to stamp it out with their despotic heels. The parson refused point blank to preach a sermon in aid of funds for it. His parishoners had no right to start such a club, he thought; it was a sign that they were getting too independent, that they were learning how to help themselves, which was the very last thing he wanted them to do, whatever he might say and preach to the contrary. That a labourer, who had fallen out of work through illness, should be supported, even for a time, from a common fund over which the rectory had no direct control, was gall and wormwood to the parson. Worse still, the labourer's wife would not be so ready to come to the rectory back-door, humbly begging for help. Worse and worse still, she and the children might slip out of the yoke of Church attendance altogether, if rectory charity were no longer a necessity. No; this sick club was the thin end of a bad wedge, and it must be pulled out and broken up without delay.

We labourers had no lack of lords and masters. There were the parson and his wife at the rectory. There was the squire, with his hand of iron overshadowing us all. There was no velvet glove on that hard hand, as many a poor man found to his hurt. He brought it down on my father because he would not sign for a small loaf and a dear one; and if it had not been for my mother, that hand would have crushed him to the earth, maybe crushed the life right out of him. At the sight of the squire the people trembled. He lorded it right feudally over his tenants, the farmers; the farmers in their turn tyrannised over the labourers; the labourers were no better than toads under a harrow. Most of the farmers were oppressors of the poor; they put on the iron wage-screw, and screwed the labourers' wages down, down below living point; they stretched him on the rack of life-long, abject poverty. I can remember the time when wages were so low that a man with several children was allowed parish relief. He was forced to accept this degrading kind of help, for he could not have brought up his family without it. Let him work as hard as he would, he could not earn the wherewithal to do it. The labourer who had a big family was blamed for it, and treated accordingly. I know for a fact that, when some of the men had a large number of children and were unable to keep them, the parish authorities used to take several of them away and put them in the workhouse. It was a disgraceful state of things, from which there seemed no loophole of escape. Parents pauperised because of their children, children pauperised from their youth up because their fathers, however willing, were not able to feed and clothe them. Is it to be wondered at that the people, more often than not, flung prudence, and thrift, and steady industry, and good conduct to the four winds? Who dare blame them and cast it in their teeth? The poor man who accepted the sop of parish help, which was cast to him as a bone to a dog, felt that life's heavy burden had been made lighter; he was relieved from sickening worry, he was no longer obliged to watch his children fading out of life before his miserable eyes. And so it was that men, born to be free, and willing to be independent, were turned into parasites. If a man was sober and prudent and industrious, what reward had he? What return did he see for the exercise of such difficult virtues? Why, even if he had managed, by the most strenuous efforts, to keep himself afloat on life's stream, he was almost bound to see his little raft of independence slowly, surely drifting on to the mudbanks of pauperism at the close of his voyage. Yes, after all his labour and toil, that was to be the end of him; there he would be stranded, there he would die, there would be his grave. Could a freeborn, self-respecting Englishman meet with a more bitterly cruel fate than this? The mere prospect of such a fate was enough to drive many a man into a downhill course of thriftlessness, recklessness, and hard drinking. What did he care then, if at the end of his rollicking road the poorhouse door would be yawning wide to receive him? He couldn't help that, he had given up trying. He drowned the thought in his glass, and chalked up his score with a laugh, and went down a bit faster.

Some of the farmer's wives were in sympathy with the people, but only a very few of them. I will not condemn the lot wholesale, for some of them were kind, especially to the labourer's wives when they had babies. All the womanhood in them came well to the front at such times; they would give milk, and nourishing food, and clothes, and they gave with a kind hand and a warm heart. I wish I could say as much for their husbands. They must have had their good points like other men; but what kindliness they possessed was like the other side of the moon in relation to the earth, it was always turned away from the agricultural labourer. The picture of them, which was bitten deep into my memory when I was a growing lad, is a bitter, black one. They impressed themselves on me as taskmasters and oppressors, and my heart used to burn within me when I heard of their doings, and when I saw how the men who toiled so hard for them were treated like the dirt beneath their feet. I observed, and listened, and remembered, and stored it all up for future use.

I went on working in the stables until I was about sixteen, and then I started mowing for the same banker. He used to pay me eighteenpence a day for what he would have had to pay another man half-a-crown. I knew this well enough, and the thought of the extra shilling which should have been in my pocket and was not, rankled and continued to rankle, though I kept pretty quiet about it at the time. In the succeeding summer I joined a gang of mowers, all in the banker's employ; we worked from five o'clock until seven, but not a farthing's increase on my wage did I get, though I was now as expert with the scythe as the best mower among them. I felt the injustice of this treatment more and more keenly, but I dared not speak out,—the time for *that* had not come, and I could not risk the loss of my earnings, for my father was in receipt of only eight shillings a week just then. We had to practise the strictest economy in order to keep the wolf of hunger at bay. That wolf is the poor man's familiar; he would be on the prowl round the labourer's humble home from Monday morning until Saturday night—ay, and on Sunday too. He was a ravenous, profane beast, having no respect for the Sabbath day to keep it holy. He was always snapping, and snarling, and growling round the corner. Because we had no rent to pay we fared better than many, but manage as my mother might, we seldom got a taste of fresh meat more than once in the seven days.

It was at this period that a crushing blow fell upon our little family: my mother died. It was an irretrievable loss, a terrible grief to me. Mother, teacher, councillor, guide, and familiar friend—she was all that to me, and more. Oh, if only she could have lived to see me in Parliament, what a proud and joyful day it would have been for her! This sad event took place in 1842.

I stayed on in the old home for a while and took care of my father, but I was more than ever bent on improving my condition and earning a better wage. A man from another part of the kingdom introduced a new style of hedge-cutting into our county. I very soon found out that he could make a tidy bit of money by it, so I set to work at once and learned how to do it. The banker in whose employ I still was let me try my prentice hand, and I practised this new style on his hedges, improving steadily year by year. Then hedge-cutting matches were instituted—"hedging matches" they called them. The first time I competed I gained a prize; the second time I again won a prize; and the third time I carried off the first prize. Then a championship match was arranged, all the head prizemen for many miles round being asked to compete. I entered the lists and won the first prize of two pounds, a medal, and the proud title of "Champion Hedgecutter of England." I had made up my mind that I would master everything I took up, and I was determined to take up everything which would further the one aim and object I had in life then—*i.e.*, the bettering of my own position by every honest means in my power. The winning of this championship is an instance of how I succeeded. Soon after this "glorious victory," I went into different English counties, and also into Wales, hedge-cutting. I got good jobs and very good money, and was in great request. Not only was I a master of this branch of my craft, with men working under me, but, as I had taken to mowing when sixteen years of age, I had now become a master hand at that also, and had almost invariably a gang of from twenty to twenty-five men under me in the field. This was my reward for having caught slippery old Father Time by his fore-lock. I made some very good mowing contracts with large graziers; they would give me six and seven shillings an acre. The farmers were not so liberal by half, as they seldom paid more than three shillings an acre. Still, taking one contract with another, I did well and could put more money into my pocket than I had ever done yet.

The Midlands and South Wales was my beat, and I kept my eyes and ears wide open, while going my hedge-cutting and mowing rounds. I saw that there was a smouldering discontent among the different classes of agricultural labourers with whom I was brought into contact, but they did not make any effort to improve their position. I would ask the men who worked under me, whether they were satisfied with their condition, and their answers were almost without exception in the decided negative.

But there it ended. Discontented as they were, they lacked the energy to better themselves. They would grumble and complain by the hour, but they would not budge an inch from the place and position in which they found themselves. The fact was, very few of them could write a letter, so the majority were afraid to go from home, because they would not be able to communicate with their friends. This inert mass of underfed, overworked, uneducated men was stuck fast in the Slough of Despond. Practically, they were voiceless, and voteless, and hopeless. I realised this, and I pondered over all I saw and heard as I ranged far and wide over the country on Shanks' mare. I laid it up in my heart against the day of wrath to come; the day, still far distant, when I should find my voice and make of it a trumpet, wherewith to sound forth through the length and breadth of the land, the woes and the wrongs of the agricultural labourer.

I now worked my way back to Barford, and at last found myself once more in the old cottage. I had gained both money and experience, I had travelled over large tracts of my native land, I had been tried as a labourer and had not been found wanting; as a mower, as a hedger and ditcher, I had more than held my own with the best. Wherever I had worked I had given proof that I was not one of the hopeless, helpless nobodies. I was conscious of increased strength, and vigour of mind and body; I had learned where I stood among my fellow-workers, and consequently I was more than ever determined to carve out an upward path for myself, and be a somebody in the world of working men.

CHAPTER III

WAITING THE CALL.

IT was early in the forties when I made my way back like a homing pigeon to the old Arch rooftree. I was now a stalwart young man, nearing the end of my teens, a true chip of the old block. There was nothing of the shamefaced prodigal son about me when I set foot in my native village once more, and returned to my father. I had not been wasting my wages in riotous living, and then been reduced to feed on swine husks because I had not a penny piece left to my bad name. No; it was young Joe Arch the worker, not Joe Arch the wastrel, who tramped home from his travels with money in his pocket, money enough to have bought and paid for a fatted calf on his own account, wherewith to give his father a treat. I had been journeying to and fro on the face of a fine broad bit of English earth, seeking what wages I could earn, what work I could get, and what facts I could devour. I found, I got, I devoured, every morsel which came in my way. I read, marked, learned and inwardly digested, as the prayer book says somewhere, all I could lay my hands or ears or eyes on. At the same time I was taking in a supply of facts which would not be digested—tough facts about the land and the labourer, that accumulated and lay within my mind, heavy as a lump of lead, and hard as a stone. No matter what I did, whether I was working with my hands or my head, that mass of indigestible facts was always in the background, worrying and bothering me. I got no peace; it worried and bothered me more and more as each year went by.

When in Wales, I remember comparing the condition of the Welsh agricultural labourer with that of his English brother in the Midlands, and especially in Warwickshire. It was all in favour of the Welshman. He could obtain a decent cottage at a low rental, and as a rule he could get a strip of garden with it. Fruit was plentiful, and you could get as much good cider as you wanted to drink at about a penny a quart. The majority of the men owned at least half a score of prime apple trees, some had more, and occasionally you would see a little orchard containing as many as forty trees in full bearing. There was no doubt about it, and I saw it with a heavy heart, the Welshman had a better time of it, a more hopeful lot, than his English brother.

There was another thing which my travels showed me plain as a pikestaff, and that was the real value of our little freehold property. I had been proud of it before, now I was thankful for it as well. In one

English county after another I saw men living with their families—if *living* it could be called—in cottages which, if bigger, were hardly better than the sty they kept their pigs in, when they were lucky enough to have a young porker fattening on the premises. These garnished hovels, for such they were with their outside trimmings of ivy and climbing roses, were garnished without, but they were undrained and unclean within, so that the seven devils of disease and vice had possession, and flourished like weeds on a dunghill or toadstools in a cellar. And these precious hovels would be the property of a farmer, or a squire, or some other Dives of the neighbourhood. Even if a labourer did scrape enough money together to buy the roof over his head, he very soon found out that the roof was not for sale—not for him, at any rate, the privilege of owning a bit of house property. Oh, no; the labourer might live in his garnished hovel on sufferance, he might bide there at Dives' good will and pleasure, or he might be kicked out bag and baggage, at a week's notice, if Dives so chose. Try as he might, the labourer could not get at the land either. In parish after parish he could not lay so much as a little finger on one rood of it; he could neither buy nor hire it. Landless, and all but roofless, these men were, hundreds and hundreds of them. When I used to see how terribly bad things were with them I would say to myself, "Well Joe, you have something to be thankful for, when all's said and done. You mayn't be the young Queen Victoria in her palace, nor the Earl of Warwick in his castle; but your father is king of his cottage and lord of his mite of land, as his father was before him, and as you will be in your turn, please God."

By the way, if a poor knight of labour had the right to carry such a useless article as a coat of arms, I would have an old stocking figuring on it, fine and large!

Glad as I was to get back home, the old place did not seem the same without my mother. We missed her badly at every turn. I learned then that the workingman's home is no home at all, if there is not a good housewife within doors. Let his wife be a slattern, and a wilful, careless waster,—well, then, before very very long, there will be woeful want stepping in, bringing angry words and worse behind, and driving love like smoke up the kitchen chimney; let his home be hugger-mugger, and it is only a man in a thousand who will not step down to the public-house for an hour's comfort and enjoyment after his day's labour is over. Who will cast the first stone at him for doing it? Not I—though neither my father nor I went that way. We put up with inconveniences of all sorts, and tried to get along as best we could, rather than run the risk of having dishonest people about us, plundering right and left when we were safe away in the fields. I worked at hedging and ditching and draining, at fence and hurdle making, at any and every job which would bring in good money: it was all in the week's work, and in the evening I would keep pegging away at my books.

When I was in my twenty-first year a gentleman, who was going to travel abroad, asked me to accompany him as his servant. I jumped at the offer. I was eager to go, I wanted to see more of the world and what life was like in foreign parts, and I might not have such a chance again. But when I told my father about it he implored me not to leave him; he said he was getting old and feeble, and that he had nobody but me in the world to look after him. I could not forsake the old man after that; it would have been a cruel thing to do; and I thought too, that, if I did go abroad, it was more than likely that I should not get the comforts I was able to get at home. So I said, "All right, father, I won't leave you in the lurch; I'll stay." There was nothing for it then but to marry and settle down, for we could not go on as we had been doing. It had been a makeshift kind of a life at the best. So it came about that, in 1847, when barely one-and-twenty years of age, I took unto myself a wife. She was the daughter of a Wellesbourne mechanic; she was in domestic service in the village when I met her. We soon settled down comfortably in the cottage, where seven children were born to us, six of whom are still living.

My wife was not the woman my mother was. She was no scholar, and she did not think over questions and have a firm opinion about them as my mother did; and I felt the difference almost from the first.

She was a good, clean wife, and a good mother; she looked after my father well; she was always attending to her home and to her family; but she was no companion to me in my aspirations. My father noticed this, and often used to say, "Joe, she is hardly a companion for you." She had not any idea of rising in the world; she wished to stop in the place where it had pleased the Lord to call her. She thought, "As it was in the beginning, is now, and ever shall be, world without end. Amen." Those were not my mother's sentiments, and they were not mine. Then, she never could bear my going away from home to work. Over and over again I used to say to her, "What on earth is the good of my stopping in the village earning nine shillings a week with four or five little ones to keep, and bread eightpence-halfpenny a loaf, when by going away I can earn forty shillings a week, and can send you home twenty-five shillings?" But, oh no, I must stop at home with her. It was natural enough I suppose, but it was foolish. We never could convince her that I was right in going, though we tried very hard to make her see as we did about it. Of course, she was never alone; she had her children to look after, and father, who was at work close by, used to come home to his meals regularly. She taught her children how to work, and in this respect she taught them well; but she could not train them for better positions in life. What extra education they had I gave them myself; she could not. She meant well, and she did well, as far as she was able; she was a good, honest woman, who acted up to what lights she had. She was a Nonconformist, and on that point we were at one. I flung Churchgoing over early in life, from religious conviction. I did not believe in Church doctrine, as preached by the parson. I did not believe either in ordering myself "lowly and reverently to all my betters," because they were never able to tell me who my betters were. Those they called my betters I did not think my betters in any respect. Like my good mother before me, I was a Nonconformist by nature and by conviction. I began to be in open sympathy with them from the time when I went with my mother to hear the Wellesbourne men preach in that old barn up the back lane, which I have already mentioned. A chapel was built in the village in 1840. The Wesleyans happened to get hold of a piece of ground, on which an old butcher's shop had formerly stood; they built a chapel on the site of it, and there it stands to this day. It was supplied by local preachers. Very soon after my marriage I began to take an active part in local preaching, and other doings of the Nonconformist community. My religious views are strong ones. I cannot bear cant—I despise it. I believe in practical Christianity. I would not deceive a man, if I knew it; and as for wronging a man, I can say with an easy conscience, if I were going to die the next minute, that I have never wronged a fellow-creature intentionally, in my life. Yes, my religious views are strong ones; but I don't want to talk much about them, for I hold that a man's religion should be more in his life than on his lips. If it is in his life, it will take him the best part of his time to live up to it; and if he feels a strong call to preach, as I did, there is the circuit open to him, and the chapel pulpit of a Sunday.

By this time I had formed my political opinions. When I was only about eighteen years of age, I made up my mind to be a Liberal, and I have stuck to the party ever since. I expect the Tory barley bread I had to feed on got into my bones and made me a Liberal! It has had that contrary effect on more than one man I have come across. Then, as a lad, every time I earned a penny by doing odd jobs or running an errand, I would buy some old papers. These were originally published at fivepence-halfpenny. I used to read Gladstone's and Bright's speeches in them, and from these I formed my opinions. But it was a case of like to like; I got what I wanted in the speeches, they gave me reasons for feeling and thinking in the way I already did. I should have been a Liberal, even if there had been up to then no such word in the language. I should have thought and felt as I did, even if I had never heard of Gladstone and Bright. I could not help being one. Liberalism was in me to start with.

The stage of my life on which I had now entered was a busy, a varied, and a trying one. I had a young and increasing family to provide for. Though my habits were frugal, and my wife showed herself a marvel of economy and good management in the house, I very soon saw that I must put my best foot foremost, and tramp farther afield than Barford. My wife objected, but I was determined that my children should be brought up decently; that they should have plenty of plain wholesome food; as good an education as I could get them and give them; and a fair start in life. If they did not have this it would not be my fault, but my misfortune. So off I set on my travels. Hard work, good wages, rough quarters, strange companions, long journeys and long absences—such was the programme. When in Wales I would preach in chapels among the mountains, and more than once I have 'held forth' in my everyday clothes. The Welsh cotters gave me a warm welcome and the right hand of fellowship wherever I went. Many a little token of their hearty good will have I carried off with me. Working, preaching, and reading whatever books or papers I could pick up, I would find my way home and settle down for a while to much the same kind of life in the village.

My mother had fought a good fight with the "powers that be." It was my turn now to stand up for my rights, and those of my children. I had some tremendous fights, especially in connexion with the schooling of my children. I remember well the following incident:—One day my second daughter went with me to Warwick. I went to do some marketing and to buy some new tools. While there she saw a hair net studded with white beads. She took a great fancy to it and said, "Father, do buy that net for me." I saw no harm in it, so I bought it for her. It cost ninepence. The little maid was only about nine years old and was therefore naturally very proud of her hair-net. On the Monday morning nothing would suit her but she should put this hair-net on to go to school in. Off she trotted with it, as pleased as Punch. Well, the parson's wife went down to the school that morning and saw my child with her hair-net on. Up she marched to the child and said, "I shall not allow you to come to school with a hair-net on—we don't allow *poor people's* children to wear hair-nets with beads, and, if you dare to come to school this afternoon with that trumpery on, I shall take it off and teach you a lesson." I happened to be working close at home just then, and when I came in to dinner I found my child crying. I asked her what was wrong and she told me what the parson's wife had said. It made my blood boil. Tradesmen's children were to be allowed to wear buckles on their shoes, and feathers and flowers in their hats, while the poor labourer's child was not to be allowed to wear a hair-net with a few beads on it! My wife was for giving in to the parson's wife, because she did not want to have any bother and unpleasantness; but I happened to be made of sterner stuff. I told the child then and there to keep her hair net on, and I took her back to school myself. I saw the schoolmistress, and I said to her "Mrs. —— what's the matter with my children?" "Matter, Mr. Arch?" says she; "there's nothing the matter, there are no better behaved children in the school." "Then," I said, "what is the meaning of this?" and I went on to tell her about the net. She said she had never made any such rule, it was the parson's wife who had made it. Then I told her to tell the parson's wife, if she came into the school that afternoon, that if she dared to take the hair-net from off my child's head I would summons her at Warwick, as she had no more right to take the hair-net off my child's head than I had a right to steal my neighbour's goods. This settled the lady; for when she came into the school that very afternoon the schoolmistress told her what I had said. "Oh," said the parson's wife, "that Arch is a horrid man. He is a firebrand in the parish," but she never attempted to touch my child.

They had a very bad system, which I later on was instrumental in breaking up. When a father had a boy old enough to go to school, he had to go to the parson and get a ticket before the boy was allowed to enter the school; and the mother had to go to the parson's wife to get permission for the girls to enter. This was another of their numerous dodges to keep up the power of the parson. But I upset that. I had a little grandson up from Wales. I got my wife to clean his boots and trim him up nicely, and then I told her to take him to school without first obtaining a ticket. To the school she took him right away.

"Have you a ticket?" asked the schoolmaster. Said my wife, "Oh, my husband said I was not to get one." "Then I cannot admit the boy," said the schoolmaster. My wife brought the boy back and told me what the schoolmaster had said. Here was my opportunity. I knew the Act, I had read it through and through. The Act said to me, "You must get your boy educated." Said I to the Act, "With the greatest of pleasure, and whatever is due and required to be paid I will pay; but to go to the parson to ask whether I may carry out the provision of the law I never, never will!" So I just told my wife to take the boy to the school again on the following Monday morning and to tell the schoolmaster that, if he refused the child admission, I would at once write to the School Authorities and ask them to summon me before the Bench at Warwick. My wife went down and told him this. "Oh," said he, "that will never do. I will accept the boy on my own responsibility. He can come in now." After that we were not troubled very much about tickets. They knew better than to fight it out. They knew they were in the wrong, that they had not half a leg to stand on; so they kept quiet. They would have dearly liked to drive me out of the parish, neck and crop.

I had another tussle with the parson. There was a sort of village charity, the outcome of an agreement made many years ago with one of the Earls of Warwick. There used to be a right of way across the park; it was the shortest cut to the town, and the Earl offered to give two hundred-weight of coal every year to each working man in the village. This was to buy us out. The villagers agreed to it, so it was a fair bargain. My birthright was sold long before I was born; still, the coals were there to claim if I chose, and I did choose. For two or three years I did not have any, but one day when they were distributing these coals I happened to be at home, and I thought I might just as well go for my two hundred-weight. So I got my barrow, and went to the man who was giving them out. "I have come for my coals," I said.

"Oh," said he, looking at me, "have you?" "Yes," I said, "and I mean to have them too." He looked at his list. "Your name is not down on my list," said he. "Oh," said I, "it's not, is it? Who makes out that list, I should like to know?" "The parson," said he. "I thought so," said I. "Well I have come here to do business, let there be no sort of a mistake about that. It is now about a quarter past one—if I do not receive an order to fetch my coals by three o'clock, I am going across the park; and, if they summon me, I will tell the reason why. All the world hereabouts shall know why I went." I said no more, but went off. I had said quite enough, however, for before three o'clock had struck, up comes a lad with a message, "Please will you come down and fetch your coals." Down for my coals I went, and had no more bother about it.

My fights for the liberty of the subject and my struggles to preserve the freedom and independence of myself and my family did not stop at the parson. I had four pitched battles with the Bench at Warwick over the vaccination of my children, and I beat them every time. I defended my own case, for I knew the Act pretty well and so had no need to employ a lawyer. I remember the Bench remitted the fines, but

I had to pay seventeen-and-sixpence costs. The fines amounted in all to about four guineas. The Chairman of the Bench was a rigid Tory, and he knew I was a labourer; so I had nothing very nice to expect from him. The doctor used to attend at the village school, and the women were in the habit of carrying their babies there to be vaccinated. I put my foot down over this vaccination business, and said straight out that I did not intend to have my children treated as if they were cattle. Every time I was summoned the Court was crowded; sometimes the Chairman had a job to keep order, for there was so much feeling stirred up. The Bench adjourned the first time, and set the policeman and the registrar to make enquiries as to whether anybody else in the village resented the law. I was not going to be behind-hand in the matters and I also got a friend to go round making enquiries. We found out that there were a hundred and twenty-five children not vaccinated, yet I was the only criminal. It came out afterwards that this was one of the parson's tricks. He knew my children had not been vaccinated and he could not let pass such a chance of having a dig at me. I must have walked two hundred miles over that case. I was then working about twenty-five miles from the Court, and I did the journey eight times—four times to the Court, and four times back to my work.

The second time I came up before the Court the chairman said, "Why have you not had your children vaccinated?" I said, "Because my children are healthy, and no hereditary disease can be traced in their ancestors for many generations, and I am not going to have their blood tainted now by the filthy matter which is too often used for vaccination purposes." I then asked the chairman, as he said the law compelled me to have my children vaccinated, whether my children belonged to the law or whether they belonged to me, and whether, if the law were that their ears were to be cut off, I must needs obey? Said I: "If I do have my children vaccinated, and if they become ill from the effects of it, and become disfigured for 'life, as many a poor child does, will the State maintain and keep them?" The answer was "No." "Then," I said, "I shall certainly not allow my children to be vaccinated." "But," said the chairman, "you are the only one in the village who will not have it done." "Who told you that?" I asked. "The registrar," he said. "Perhaps," said I, "you know how the registrar does his business. If not, I will tell you, because it is quite time you did know. That man goes to a public-house keeper, and asks him to find out all the children that are born, and what their names are to be. When the registrar has obtained this information from the public-house keeper, he enters the names of the children in the public book. I do not allow my wife to lower herself, by going to a beer-house to inform them she has a baby, nor do I intend to so lower myself. If my wife has a baby, it is the duty of the registrar to keep a record of the fact. It is not the duty of a father or a mother to go down to a public-house and inform the keeper of it, so that the registrar may save himself any trouble." Well, the chairman had nothing to say on this point. It was a crying disgrace that such a state of things should be permitted.

Of course, all this disputing and contending with the high and mighty ones helped to spread my name abroad, and there was not a parson or a squire in the countryside who loved the sound of it. If they could have stuck a gag in my mouth, gagged I should have been in a jiffy. If they could have clapped a muzzle on me, muzzled I should have been before I could say "Jack Robinson!" But they could neither gag nor muzzle me. They gave me the bad name, but they couldn't hang me. They, and others of the same kidney, wrote me down a contentious brawler, a dissenting wind-bag, and a Radical revolutionary; but not one of them could say I was an idler who neglected his family, and left them to shift for themselves. The fact of my being a steady, industrious, and capable workman was a stumper for them; they could not get over that. My little house and garden were kept in good order—apple-pie order, I might say. The garden was choke full of fruit and vegetables in their season, and I raised as many flowers as I could find room for. When my father died, in 1862, I took off the old thatched roof of the cottage, and replaced it with one of slate, put in windows, and made it as smart and comfortable as it is to-day. I had to wait until his death to make these improvements, because the old man would not have it touched. He used to say, "You may do what you like to the old place, Joe, when I am gone, but while I'm above ground it must stay as it is." He could not bear to see the things about him altered, and I respected his wishes.

Every year now my interest in politics, and in all that had to do with the land and the labourer, was growing stronger and stronger. I remember that we had no election contests at first, but at last a candidate of the right colour came along, and there was a bit of a commotion; our rural waters were troubled; but not to much purpose then, for the Tories beat us by a fifteen-hundred majority. Still, the fight had begun, and what Liberals there were had waked up, and were pulling together. At the next election we decided to put up two men. Before, it had been a sort of three-cornered fight; two on the Tory side, and one on the Liberal. We ran our men in by twenty-seven votes. I stumped the country for our side, and took an active part in the Liberal cause. The squire I mentioned was a Tory, and he came and asked me to vote Tory, but I absolutely refused to do it. I thought to myself, "You little know Joe Arch, if you think he's going to play the part of a political Judas for any master born." But he had not done with me. This great squire—he was a very rich, influential man—sent for me to go down to his house when my work was over, in order to canvass me. I went down, and after some talk he said to me, "Do your Liberals find you employment?" "What has that to do with my vote?"

I said. "I sell you my labour, but not my conscience; that's not for sale."

"Oh!" said this big, strapping, six-foot man.

"Now look here, sir," I said; "I sat second horse behind you for several years, and I have worked in your stables, but since I have been out of your stables have you ever given me a sovereign without my having given you a sovereign's worth of good labour? No! You know I have always given you a sovereign's worth of labour for every sovereign you have given me, and therefore why should I give you my vote because I sell you my labour?" "Then," said he, "Sit down, Joe, and have a glass of sherry." Down I sat accordingly, and drank sherry until I could hardly see my way out, for I was not used to such drink at that time. As I was going out of the room the squire said to me, "Let's shake hands." So we shook hands. Then he said, "Arch, I admire you; you can be trusted anywhere, and with anything. I knew that before to-night, but I thought I would canvass you. I told the lawyer I was going to canvass you, but I expected this result."

We had open voting then, and the following day I went to poll behind the man for whom I was then cutting hedges; he was a farmer. The Conservative candidates were not liked by the farmers, for they were landlords of a bad kind. When my employer met me outside the Corn Exchange, he said:

"Which way did you vote?"

"Liberal," said I. "And how did *you* vote?"

"Oh, Tory," said he.

"Now look here," I said, "you would have liked to have gone my way only you dared not. And, though I have voted Liberal, you dare not sack me; because you cannot get anybody else to do my work."

He said nothing then—they were a couple of home truths he had to swallow as best he could. But the next day he confessed to me that I went to poll a political free man whilst he went as a political slave. "I should have lost my farm," he said, "as, being open polling, it would have been noted if I had voted Liberal as my conscience directed me."

Here was a nice state of things. I thought to myself, "Yes; every word of it's true, and I wouldn't be in your shoes—they cost more than mine, and it's a kind of price I wouldn't pay if I had to go barefoot." This happened during the election of 1868. At that time, such was the strength of Tory tyranny and terrorism, very few of the farmers or the labourers dared serve on the Liberal Committee; they were afraid, and with reason, that they would lose their farms or their work, if they did. But I never troubled myself on that score, I continued to take a prominent part in local politics, and I have been ever since in connection with the organisation of the Liberal party in that part of the country.

By this time I had got a great deal of influence in the village. The big-wigs found out that I was a labouring man they had to reckon with; that, if they tried to tread on my toes, I trod back with my hob-nail

Waiting the Call

boots; that I had a voice and a hand and a head which matched, and more than matched, theirs. My neighbours found that I was no cracked bell; that, whenever I was hit, I rang true for liberty and the rights of the people. They knew that, though I preached on a Sunday, I was no humbug on a week-day. If I told them in the chapel pulpit that I hated shams and loathed oppression, that I earnestly believed in the higher destinies of man in this world as well as in the next, and that I had a deep and tender sympathy with the sorrows, the struggles, and the aspirations of my fellow-men,—if I told them all this and much more, in the pulpit, each working day made it clear to them that these words did not come glib from my lips, but warm from my heart. I knew their difficulties and the hardships of their lot, because I had shared that lot and faced the same difficulties. Yes; I tried to practise on a week-day what I preached on a Sunday to my brother labourers.

Times and again I have had as many as from twenty-five to thirty men working under me, and have had to pay them their wages. Never once did I stop any of their pay for being late, although by doing so I could have made a fair amount of money. During the whole of my labouring career I discharged only one man. If a man did not do his work properly I used to say to him, "Look here old chap, you couldn't get these wages elsewhere, so set to work and learn to do it properly"; and to do them justice they generally took my advice in the right spirit, and put in much better work from that time forward. A wise word spoken in time makes the working wheels go round; and a wise word will be a dam to stop a flow of foolish ones, if you know just when to say it. "Waste words, and you waste time; waste time, and you waste wages," I used to say. When a gang of men are bark-peeling, one man chattering will put all the others off work; and that means a biggish loss of money in a short time. When I undertook a lot of contracts for the Government for oak felling, peeling and squaring, I was in honour bound to see that it was not defrauded; and also, as I had to pay the men their wages, it was to my interest to see that I got a fair day's work for a fair day's pay. So I used to put it to them this way: "The man who wastes his time, and the time of his mates in idle chatter plays the fraudful fool; he cheats the Government, he cheats me, and he cheats himself." They knew I spoke the truth. They could never say that I shirked while they worked. I would do my share of timber squaring with the best man in the gang; very few could beat me with an axe, for I could cut almost to a hair's breadth anywhere I liked. The men respected me accordingly—I was a master at their own trade. They saw too that I had their interests at heart; I proved it to them by the way in which I treated them.

By the end of the sixties and the beginning of the seventies, I had bettered my position as a labourer all round. I did not work then for farmers at ten shillings a week! I used to obtain large ploughing jobs at from two shillings to three-and-sixpence a day; but the farmers would cut me down to the two shillings whenever they could. I did not see the force of that, and I let them know it. I used also to get work as a carpenter's labourer from a friend of mine, who was a builder and carpenter. He is alive now, and is one of my greatest friends. He used to send for me when he got very busy coffin-making, or putting on roofing, or making church work. I could do very useful work for him, for which he always paid me well. Then my skill at hurdle-making and gate-hanging would come in handy at odd times. Being a good all-round man I was never at a loss for a job.

But, if things were going well with me at the beginning of the seventies, they were going from bad to worse with the agricultural labourer generally. In our part of the country his poor little tide of prosperity was at its lowest ebb. Things were so bad with the men that they were beginning to grow desperate. The trodden worms, which had so long writhed under the iron heel of the oppressor, were turning at last. The smouldering fire of discontent was shooting out tongues of flame here and there. The sore stricken, who had brooded in sullen anger over their wrongs, were rising to strike in their turn. The men were murmuring and muttering the countryside round, but they wanted a voice; they spoke low among themselves, but they were afraid to speak out. They were sick of suffering but they had no physician. I took note of it all; I had been taking note of it for years;

and I had thought out the remedy. There was only one remedy, and that was *Combination*. The men were weak—if they would be strong they must unite. I saw the day drawing steadily nearer and nearer, when the wretched units of labour would be forced to unite, driven to combine. I saw the time surely coming when, as one man, they would waken to the fact that "Union makes Strength." When that day came I would be ready to help them, willing to speak for them. So I bided my time; I knew it must come.

In 1872 that time came, and it found me ready.

CHAPTER IV.

THE CALL COMES.

WHEN 1872 began I was in my forty-sixth year, an experienced agricultural labourer in robust health, active in mind and body, master of my work in all its branches, in full employment and earning good money. The house I lived in was an English working man's castle of the right sort—it was my own, every stick and stone of it. No lean minion of the law had the right to lay so much as the tip of a parchment-finger on it, and I had no horse-leech of a mortgage fastened on to me draining the blood of manliness and independence out of me. The bread I earned by honest sweat was, crust and crumb, my own; and I could stand up and look the whole world straight in the face, for I owed no man anything, not so much as a copper farthing. My plot of land was no waste field either; it was a fruitful garden if ever there was one; every square foot of it was tilled, planted and watered, and I raised more fruit, flowers, and vegetables off it than I had any use for.

Inside my house I had a good wife to keep it clean and neat, to cook the victuals, which, if homely, were plentiful, and to attend to my wants and make me comfortable. Outside it I had earned the confidence of men in my own walk of life; they knew me for a fellow-labourer with a plain-speaking tongue in his head, a heart in the right place, and a good will towards them, and the day was now close at hand when they would make proof of me. I had earned the distrust and dislike of my so-called betters, but I did not care one jot or tittle for that. I knew I was as bad to their taste as a dose of bitters or a jorum of Epsom salts, and when I thought of that I chuckled. One old farmer used to say I was the most dangerous man that ever went on a farm, as I was always talking about combination to the labourers, and spreading discontent far and wide. So I was, and the farther I could spread it the better I was pleased. I would speak a few words to this man and a few to that, trying to stir them all up, and make them see where the only remedy for their misery lay; in season and out of season I was at them, dropping in the good seed of manly discontent; and I made sure, too, that most of it was not cast on to stony ground. I daresay the employers likened me to the enemy who came by stealth and sowed tares; but that was not my view of it. I considered that I was sowing seed which, if properly looked after, would sprout up into the bread-yielding wheat of Union.

Although I had reached a pretty prosperous condition of life in 1870 and 1871, things were still going from bad to worse with the bulk of the labourers in our neighbourhood; in fact, they had got so bad that they could hardly get worse, and I knew that the men in other parts of the country were in the same plight. After the harvest of 1871 had been reaped, and the winter had set in, the sufferings of the men became cruel, and when the new year of 1872 opened there seemed to be only two doors left open for *them*: one was the big door of disgrace which led to a life of degradation in the poorhouse; the other was the narrow door of death, which perchance would lead to a freer and happier life beyond the grave. When such a choice as this was all that was left for many an honest labouring man, who will dare to blame them because they refused to make it! Their poverty had fallen to starvation point, and was past all bearing. They began to raise their heads and look about them; and they saw that if they would keep life in their bodies, and rise out of their miserable state, they must set to and force open a door of escape for themselves. Oppression, and hunger, and misery, made them desperate, and desperation was the mother of Union.

I had spent years thinking the matter well out; I had pondered over it when at work in the wood and the field; I had considered the question when I was hedging and ditching; I had thrashed it right out in my mind when I was tramping to and from my day's toil; and I had come to the conclusion that only organised labour could stand up, even for a single day, against employers' tyranny. I told many a man that, in the course of talk, but I was determined not to make any attempt to start the Union myself. I saw it was bound to come; but I also saw that the men themselves must ask me to help them. My part was to sit still and wait; about that I was clear; so I waited.

I had heard that some few men were stirring at Willey and Weston, and that one or two of them had asked for higher wages, saying they meant to have better pay, as it was their right. Many a time I had cried out within myself, like the souls under the altar mentioned in the Book of the Revelation, "How long, O Lord, how long!" When this good news reached me I said to myself, "It won't be long now. They are raising their voices at last! the day is at hand." And it was so.

The day was February 7th, 1872. It was a very wet morning, and I was busy at home on a carpentering job; I was making a box. My wife came in to me and said, "Joe, here's three men come to see you. What for, I don't know." But I knew fast enough. In walked the three; they turned out to be labourers from over Wellesbourne way. I stopped work, and we had a talk. They said they had come to ask me to hold a meeting at Wellesbourne that evening. They wanted to get the men together, and start a Union directly. I told them that, if they did form a Union, they would have to fight hard for it, and they would have to suffer a great deal; both they and their families. They said the labourers were prepared both to fight and suffer. Things could not be worse; wages were so low, and provisions were so dear, that nothing but downright starvation lay before them unless the farmers could be made to raise their wages. Asking was of no use; it was nothing but waste of breath; so they must join together and strike, and hold out till the employers gave in. When I saw that the men were in dead earnest, and had counted the cost and were determined to stand shoulder to shoulder till they could squeeze a living wage out of their employers, and that they were the spokesmen of others likeminded with themselves, I said I would address the meeting that evening at 7 o'clock. I told them that I had left nine shillings a week behind me years ago, and as I had got out of the ditch myself, I was ready and willing to help them out too. I said, "If you are ready to combine, I will run all risk and come over and help you."

I remember that evening, as if it were but yesterday. When I set out I was dressed in a pair of cord trousers, and cord vest, and an old flannel-jacket. I have that jacket at home now, and I put a high value on it. As I tramped along the wet, muddy road to Wellesbourne my heart was stirred within me, and questions passed through my mind and troubled me. Was it a false start, a sort of hole-and-corner movement, which would come to nothing, and do more harm to the men than good? If a Union were fairly set afoot, would the farmers prove too strong for it?

Then I thought of what I was risking. If I were a forward figure in this business, and things went all wrong it might be the ruin of me. I remembered the Labourer's Union in Dorsetshire, started in the thirties—what had become of that? Poor Hammett had had to pay a heavy price for standing up with his fellow-labourers against the oppression. He and five others had been tried in 1834, and sentenced to seven years' transportation. The law had said that, when forming their little Agricultural Labourers' Union, they had administered illegal oaths. The plain truth of it was that, for daring to be Unionists they had been sent to the hulks in Australia. What matter though such a storm of anger had been raised by the shameful punishment that a free pardon had been granted them after about two years. They had been terribly punished. The disgrace and the indignities they had been obliged to put up with could never be wiped out. They were martyrs in a good cause, and I honoured them; but I did not want to be a martyr, I wanted to win alive and kicking. The law could not send me to the hulks; but there are more ways of torturing and ruining a man than one, and I knew that if the law could catch me anyhow it would. Those brave Dorsetshire labourers had paid a heavy penalty; they had suffered bitterly; that little Union had fallen to pieces, and the last state of the poor labourer had been worse, far worse, than the first.

What if the Union we meant to start in this corner of Warwickshire to-night should fall to bits like a badly made box? There was no saying what might happen. The men might be in earnest, but could they stay? Could they stand it out? Had they grit enough in them to face the farmers as freeborn Englishmen demanding their just dues, when they had been cringing to them so long? And what was a handful of poverty-stricken, half-starved, agricultural labourers going to do against so many of these powerful employers and rich oppressors! No Union I was sure could do any real good, or make any lasting improvement in the men's condition, if it was to be confined to a few men in one county. It would have to be a thumping big Union, with hundreds in it heartening one another for the glorious struggle before them. It would have to be a Union whose members were drawn from every county in England, and bound into one great unit by a common desire and a common hope.

The off chance of failure was present with me, as I trudged forward through the slush that chill February evening. But soon my spirits rose again. Was not the time fully ripe? Yes, I knew it was. In my heart I felt surely, surely, that the time of harvest was come. Those three men who had tramped to Barford that morning, and had called me to come over and help them, were but the firstfruits of it. Oh, there was going to be a grand reaping, and a glorious gathering in—the grandest, the most glorious the agricultural labourer had ever put his hand to in England for ages.

Why then should I despond and be cast down? Why should my soul be disquieted within me? Was I not marching on my way to lead my fellow-men out of the house of bondage, to deliver them from the hand of the oppressors? What if the beginning were small—would it not swell and grow greatly? What if the labourers were weak as bruised reeds? They should band together and bind themselves round with the strong steel of Union, so that they should stand up as one man in their strength to confound the mighty. Shoulder to shoulder they should go forward to strike a blow for freedom, to fight a good fight for life and liberty. When thoughts such as these burned in me like live coals, I said, "Joe Arch, what you have got to do is plain, and there must be no skulking and running away from the work which has been set you to do. You mustn't play the coward, you must play the man. You have got to trust in the Lord and in the power of His might, and speak out strong for Union." At that I took courage, and went forward with a bold heart.

When I reached Wellesbourne, lo, and behold, it was as lively as a swarm of bees in June. We settled that I should address the meeting under the old chestnut tree; and I expected to find some thirty or forty of the principal men there. What then was my surprise to see not a few tens but many hundreds of labourers assembled; there were nearly two thousand of them. The news that I was going to speak that night had been spread about; and so the men had come in from all the villages round within a radius of ten miles. Not a circular had been sent out nor a handbill printed, but from cottage to cottage, and from farm to farm, the word had been passed on; and here were the labourers gathered together in their hundreds. Wellesbourne village was there, every man in it; and they had come from Moreton and Locksley and Charlecote and Hampton Lucy, and from Barford, to hear what I had to say to them. By this time the night had fallen pitch dark; but the men got bean poles and hung lanterns on them, and we could see well enough. It was an extraordinary sight, and I shall never forget it, not to my dying day. I mounted an old pig-stool, and in the flickering light of the lanterns I saw the earnest upturned faces of these poor brothers of mine—faces gaunt with hunger and pinched with want—all looking towards me and ready to listen to the words, that would fall from my lips. These white slaves of England stood there with the darkness all about them, like the Children of Israel waiting for some one to lead them out of the land of Egypt. I determined that, if they made a mistake and took the wrong turning, it would not be my fault, so I stood on my pig-stool and spoke out straight and strong for Union. My speech lasted about an hour, I believe, but I was not measuring minutes then. By the end of it the men were properly roused, and they pressed in and crowded up asking questions; they regularly pelted me with them; it was a perfect hailstorm. We passed a resolution to form a Union then and there, and the names of the men could not be taken down fast enough; we enrolled between two and three hundred members that night. It was a brave start, and before we parted it was arranged that there should be another meeting at the same place in a fortnight's time. I knew now that a fire had been kindled which would catch on, and spread, and run abroad like sparks in stubble; and I felt certain that this night we had set light to a beacon, which would prove a rallying point for the agricultural labourers throughout the country.

The news of the meeting soon spread like wildfire, and publicity gave great help to the cause. The result was that, when I got to the chestnut tree on the evening of February 21st, a fortnight later, I found a bigger crowd than before, and I think we had nearly every policeman in the county there as well. They thought there would be a disturbance, but they need not have troubled themselves on that score. I have always preached restraint, and advocated keeping within the law, if possible. Now, more than ever, did I feel called upon to plead for moderation, and I told them in the plainest terms that, if they had recourse to violence and riot and incendiarism, or if they wantonly destroyed any kind of property, they must not look to Joseph Arch to lead them. I would be a peaceable Wat Tyler of the fields, but I would be no rioting leader of the riotous. Neither I nor they should wear handcuffs and see the inside of a gaol, if I could help it. We had come there to strike off the rusty old fetters that had crippled us, and our fathers before us, not to forge new ones for ourselves. We had come there to gain our freedom by lawful means, not to lose what little we had by lawlessness. We were going to stand up for our rights, we were going to ask for our just dues, and we were resolved to have them; but from first to last we were going to act as law-abiding citizens, not as red-handed revolutionaries.

That meeting was as orderly a one as any man could wish to take part in who respected himself and others, and the police had nothing to do but look on and listen, while an agricultural labourer hit the nail of tyranny on the head with unsparing blows. Many a nail was hammered hard and fast into oppression's coffin that night!

A lot more joined after the meeting, and in my opinion these horny-handed sons of toil who gave in their names for Union were like the old Barons at Runnymede, for they put their sign and seal as best they could to the Magna Charta of the English Agricultural Labourer. How my heart glowed and swelled with joy as the men came in to us! Here were some hundreds of my despised, crushed and downtrodden fellow-workers daring to stand up at last like independent men, and pledging themselves to look the farmer fair and square in the face and say: "Give us a fair day's wage and we will give you a fair day's work; if you won't pay fair, we won't work; if you starve us, we will strike." And any one who saw their faces and heard their words would never have had a doubt but that they meant to strike a stout blow for the cause, and not one blow either. "Dogged does it" and "strike or die" were their sentiments, and I rejoiced to know it.

We let neither grass nor weeds grow under our feet after this, I promise you. A small committee was got together, a secretary was appointed, and we set actively to work. Notices were served upon the farmers asking for sixteen shillings a week, with a week's notice if refused. We first thought of asking eighteen shillings; but from an average wage of twelve shillings to one of eighteen shillings was too much of a jump up, and no farmer would be likely to fork down another six shillings every week for the asking. An average increase of four shillings a week was more reasonable, and more likely to be granted when the farmer found he would lose his men if he did not give it. But it soon turned out that they would not hear of the sixteen shillings either; for, when the men went for their wages on the Saturday following, the farmers refused to grant it, so the men came out on strike. The shepherds and waggoners who were engaged by the month, and who had a shilling a week more than the ordinary labourer—they worked a seven days' week for it—did not come out. It was the twelve shillings a week labourer who struck; twelve shillings was the average, but there were men getting nine and ten shillings; and some were earning on an average not more than eight.

In a very short time there were a hundred men out in Wellesbourne alone, and nearly another hundred from the neighbouring villages. On the Monday after, there was hardly a labourer in Wellesbourne who went to work as usual. Men who for forty and fifty years had never known what it was to have a free day, hung about idle, and did not know what to do with themselves. These poor fellow-workers of mine did not know what to do with a holiday when they had taken it. All work and no play during a lifetime had turned Jack, the agricultural labourer, into a dull John Bull. But, dull as he might be, he had sense enough to know that once out he must bide out till the employer came to terms with him. Many a man and woman that Monday morning felt that there was a grim struggle before them; that they and their children might have to suffer pangs of hunger even worse than those they had endured in the past; that things might go so badly with them, that they would be driven from their homes, and have to be like wanderers on the face of the earth, seeking work and perhaps finding none.

But every man who had put his hand to the Union plough meant to stick to it till the Union work was done. Not a man Jack of them would yield and turn back now. That was the stubborn spirit abroad among them. There was not a pound's worth of silver among the lot who came out on strike in Wellesbourne, and till funds could be collected for their support, they had to get credit from the shop for the barest necessaries. Kettle broth, and tea made from crusts burnt black and scraped into the pot to give a little colour to the " water bewitched," was no new food and drink to the half-starved labourers; it was what they and their children had been fed upon year in and year out; but the bit of bacon could be no longer counted on. A rasher of bacon at the middle-day meal would put some heart, if not much strength, into a man; now he had to go without, or borrow it from the shopkeeper. The worst of it was, that owing to the miserable wages paid the men they were nearly always in debt to the shop a week a-head—this system of dealing was called "one week under another," and it meant that the greater part, if not the whole, of the labourer's wages were spent each week before they were earned. How could a man in such a bondage of debt as this call himself free, or feel free? No, there was always a little millstone of debt hanging round his poor weak neck, and he was a very lucky man who could rid himself of it before death took him. But they had struck for freedom now, and more were striking every day.

I was going from place to place as hard and as fast as I could, addressing meetings and forming branches of the Union. All that stirring time I felt as if there was a living fire in me. It seemed to me that I was fulfilling a mission; that I had been raised up for the work. Had not the vision of it been before my eyes for twenty years! There was a strength and a power in me which had been pent up and had been growing, and now it flowed forth. The people responded nobly to the call. I declare that, as I look back on those days, the only words which properly describe them are the words of the prophet Ezekiel when he speaks of his vision in the valley of dry bones: "So I prophesied as I was commanded: and as I prophesied, there was a noise, and behold a shaking, and the bones came together, bone to his bone. And when I beheld, lo, the sinews and the flesh came up upon them, and the skin covered them above: but there was no breath in them. Then said he unto me, Prophesy unto the wind, prophesy, son of man, and say to the wind, Thus saith the Lord God; come from the four winds, O breath, and breathe upon these slain, that they may live. So I prophesied as he commanded me, and the breath came into them, and they lived, and stood up upon their feet, an exceeding great army."

The people seemed to me to rise up like that when I went and spoke to them at this time. At one place forty-five men gave in their names, and a branch was formed in less than five minutes. Branches were formed at Barford, and Radford, and Cubbington, and Fenny Compton, and many another village and township in the neighbourhood. Then the movement spread on and on, into no less than eight counties. The men of Oxfordshire, Herefordshire, Leicestershire, Somersetshire, Norfolk, Northamptonshire, Essex, and Worcestershire rose to their feet in their valleys of dry bones, and stood up for Union. Then the whole country was aroused and was ringing with the news. All the leading papers took note of this strange thing; they could no longer ignore the fact that a great moral and intellectual awakening was in progress among the down-trodden peasantry of England.

There was anger and amazement among the powers of the land—the lord, the squire, the farmer, and the parson—when they saw these serfs of the soil girding on their manhood, and heard them refuse to starve any longer on nine and ten shillings a week. Toilers in the north and in the south, in the west and in the east, stood still to watch and listen. Here were the lowest of their brethren, those who had been dumb with fear and stricken to the earth with want, holding themselves like men, and bracing themselves together for battle with the powers of darkness seated in high places. Their voice was gone abroad with no uncertain sound, and the noise of their moving was heard afar off. The grand day of awakening had fully come.

Then the employers took counsel together; they were beginning to quake in their shoes. They tried threats first; threats had served their turn in the past, when a labourer here and there had opened his mouth to ask for more wages, threats would soon cow the labourer and teach him that his right place was to sit quiet and be thankful for what he had. The peasant might mop and mow before his lord like a monkey, but he stood up as a man at his peril. Yet the peasant continued to stand up, his poor, bent back growing stronger and straighter every day, and the high and mighty employer glared at the astonishing spectacle in powerless wrath; he got as mad as a hornet, and as savage as a bull of Bashan. These fine gentlemen had not a single serf to bully and crush, and dance a devil's dance on now; no, they had combined men to reckon with, men who, in union, were strong with the strength of a giant.

It was not very long, either, before the employer found that, when he had done his worst, he was but a poor sort of giant-killer; for the more blows he showered on him, the more that terrible Union giant thrived and waxed strong. To his terror, he learned that the giant would not be propitiated by false oaths, and deluded by lying promises into laying down his arms; that he could not be lulled to sleep by specious words and smooth speeches, so that he might be throttled and killed; but, that on the contrary, this redoubtable giant had his eyes wide open, that his cudgel was grasped firmly in his mighty hand, that he was ready to strike blow after blow for freedom with it, and that his teeth were sharpened for a bite at the hand which had starved him, and which was now stretched out to bestow on him a treacherous caress. Though the employer approached him softly, with honey on his tongue, the giant knew there was poison as of asps underneath it—yes, this new son of man turned with loathing from the Judas that would have betrayed him with a kiss.

And the powerful ones talked with one another about this new thing. The lords of the land, the hostile lords of Brobdignag, eyed it superciliously through the microscope of their own self-importance, and said, "What strange creature is this? Ah, some miserable little insect. It may do damage. Some one should kill it." That was how the lords looked at the Union man in those days.

Said the squire, swaggering up to it, "What new

vermin is this? A dose of rat-poison's the thing. Bury it out of sight and make manure of it," and swaggered away again. Said the parson, "Surely it is an evil spirit or a devil, let us flee from it"; and the parson fled as fast as his black coat would let him. Said the farmer, "We can't take stock of this thing anyhow. It's a breed we've no use for—it's dangerous. Catch it and knock it on the head"; and he stood growling. These lords and squires and parsons and farmers could not kill the Union giant; they could not even scotch him; but they tried hard to put a quick end to him.

By the beginning of March, the farmers all about were grumbling and growling at the top of their voices. Spring work had been delayed on account of the continuous rain; the weather was now fine and dry, but the men were got so fine and small, that the farmer could not see them on his farm. Out they were, and out they would stay till they had the wage they wanted.

The employers thought that, when they refused the sixteen shillings, the men would be starved into submission. It was soon evident that they had made a mistake in their tyrannical calculation. Day followed day, and the men did not come creeping humbly back like whipped curs to heel. Then the employers laid their angry heads together—they were as hot as red pepper with rage—and they declared that, if the men would not bend they must be broken. One of their schemes was to discharge the whole of the labourers in the district. "For," said they, "if all are out they will be in such a state of distress that they will not be able to help each other as they are doing now. The men who have not yet struck are contributing to the strike fund out of wages given by us—well, we are going to put a stopper on that little game. Lock out the lot, and then they will have to knuckle under."

But things did not turn out as the farmers thought they would; they could no longer work their wicked will unchecked on a miserable handful of labourers who would sink unnoticed in a local struggle. Hodge the Unionist was up for a bout with Jack his master, and the ring looking on was as big as all England. The press gave tongue, and then there was a hue and cry all over the country. The *Daily News* did us yeoman service by sending down Archibald Forbes, the famous war correspondent, to collect information and write up the subject. He went round to several of the villages with me to see the condition of things for himself, and when the first of his powerful articles appeared he came to me with a copy of the *Daily News* in his hand, and said, pointing to the article, "Now you won't want for money."

He spoke the truth too; practical sympathy was stirred by them, and the money we sorely needed flowed in from unexpected quarters. The *Daily News* has been a true and staunch friend to the labourer all through, and I should like to put it on record here that I consider we owe the paper a debt of gratitude for the service it rendered the Agricultural Labourers'

Union in 1872. Those articles opened the eyes of a large section of the public to the gravity of the struggle going on in South Warwickshire at that moment, and materially helped to turn the scale in our favour at a critical time.

The strike was now in full swing. The farmer had beckoned to the labourer and patted the hard bed of servitude in vain; all their patting and wheedling could not persuade the men to come back and lie down on it. Skin and bone had had enough of flinty couches. Said the labourer, "Give me the sixteen shillings a week and I'll make my humble bed my own way. It won't be a bed of luxury, but it'll be a bed I can rest my aching bones on. If you don't I'll walk off to where I can get what I want."

Then the farmer began to hit out right and left with his arbitrary fist, and the word was passed round among them that every Union man was to be knocked flat and jumped on. At Radford and Wellesbourne and other places near, they were turned out of their cottages; about Harbury and Snitterfield, they were discharged, and the masters all over the neighbourhood followed suit. One well-known gentleman who occupied an influential position in the county, made his agent serve notices on all his Union tenants about Walton and Wellesbourne. He also called a meeting in the interests of the employers. These kind gentlemen agreed among themselves that the Union fostered a spirit of discord, and that the demands of the strikers were excessive; and it was resolved that in the interests of the men themselves, they should be dissuaded from joining the Union, and that those of them who had been foolish enough to join, should be strongly advised to withdraw. Spoil the Union piecemeal was their policy; but they found we were wide awake, and declined to be spoiled. Some employers said they would advance wages from twelve shillings to fifteen shillings; but they did not wish to give the additional shilling, because it would look as if they had been forced to it by the Union. One landlord, Lord Leigh, granted an advance to fifteen shillings, and a good many offered fourteen shillings. The question now was, " Is it to be fifteen or sixteen shillings ? "

Canon Girdlestone wrote in a friendly spirit advising compromise and conciliation. He said the Warwickshire labourer was already better off than many of his kind. We did not dispute the fact that the bulk of the labourers in Devonshire got only eight shillings a week, that few or none got more than nine shillings, and that bad cottages and high rents were the rule there. It was all too true ; but to our thinking, this only showed that the sooner they had the Union all through Devonshire and such benighted regions the better for Hodge.

The London Trades Council took up our cause. It offered help, and it called on workmen of all classes to support us. It was pointed out to the artisan that by assisting his brother-toiler to stay in the country on better conditions, he would then not be so likely to crowd into the towns, and his purchasing power would most probably be a good deal higher. "Help your brother and you help yourself" was the moral of it.

On the Good Friday of 1872, about six weeks after the formation of the Union, we held a great demonstration and tea meeting in the public hall, Portland Street, Leamington. It made a tremendous stir, and people came flocking and streaming in from miles round. Crowds of poor labourers with their wives and children marched into the town, headed by their village fife and drum bands. Leamington had never seen such a sight in all its born days; and those who saw it and took part in it are not likely to forget it. Wellesbourne was to the fore as usual. John Lewis had seen to that. He was one of the very first men in the district to help set the Union going, and he was no laggard now. He sent messengers off to scour the neighbourhood, and he got a bell and went round like a town-crier, summoning the people to a tryst under the old chestnut tree at 8.30 a.m. on Good Friday morning. At the appointed time men and women came tramping up dressed in what of best they had. A poor best according to rich folk's notions no doubt, but smock frock and fustian jacket and shabby gown covered brave English hearts, beating high with hope of the good times coming. That little band of stiff and bent and battered men, stunted and toil-worn, with their thin and haggard wives, were no coneys—a sorry and a feeble folk. No; they were strong in Union as they took the road this March morning, with stout and trusty John Lewis at their head. They marched away, singing this rhyme as they tramped into Leamington:

> "The farm labourers of South Warwickshire,
> Have not had a rise for many a year,
> Although bread has often been dear;
> But now they've found a Union."

And so they had, as all the world was soon to know.

It was a busy day for me, if it was a proud one. I took the chair at the Organising Committee which sat in the room downstairs. They elected me organising secretary at a small salary, and Henry Taylor, a Leamington carpenter, was elected paid secretary, on the condition that he gave up any office he might hold in another Union, and joined ours. We wanted neither outsiders nor professional Trades Union men; we knew our own business and we were determined from the outset to manage it in our own way. "Hands off!" we said to any outside meddler who wanted to poke a finger into our Union pie. We then drew up the following Rules:—

1. The name of the Society shall be the "Warwickshire Agricultural Labourers' Union."

2. Its object is to elevate the social position of the farm labourers of the county by assisting them to increase their wages; to lessen the number of ordinary working hours; to improve their habitations; to provide them with gardens or allotments; and to

assist deserving and suitable labourers to migrate and emigrate.

3. In all questions of dispute about remuneration of labour, an attempt shall be made to decide such dispute by arbitration between the Union and the employers of labour.

4. The Board shall have power to make arrangements for arbitration as regards the price of labour; to take charge of all disputes between employers and employed; to make arrangements for supporting members when out of work; to help labourers to migrate and emigrate; to suspend, fine or expel any member who shall violate the society's regulations, and shall have such other powers as may be necessary to accomplish the objects of the Society, and shall avail itself of all requisite provisions under the Friendly Societies and Trades Unions Acts.

5. The Board shall hereafter decide how many hours, not exceeding ten, shall constitute a day's work, and all over-time shall be paid for at the rate of fourpence per hour, and all Sunday work shall be paid for as overtime, except in such cases as the Union shall direct.

6. Labourers' work shall cease by four o'clock on Saturdays, except in such cases as the Union may direct.

7. The Board shall consist of one delegate, elected by each branch numbering not less that fifty members, and three members of the Leamington Trades' Union; but the last-mentioned members shall not have the power of voting.

8. The Board shall meet monthly at Leamington to transact the business of the Society, and special meetings may be convened by the secretary and chairman jointly at two days' notice; nine delegates to form a quorum.

Rule 9 provided for the election of a chairman, secretary, treasurer (who must find security), two trustees, and a professional auditor.

Rule 13 provided that there should be a yearly meeting at Leamington, at which the Board shall submit a report and balance sheet (audited) for approval.

The contributions to the Union were fixed at sixpence entrance fee, and twopence per week subscription.

We had got through a good afternoon's work by the time all was settled, and we had the evening meeting still before us. Oh, what a meeting that was!

Many of the Trade Unions took part in it, and nearly every tradesman in and around Leamington was there. The gentlemen of Warwickshire were conspicuous by their absence, but the people had been pouring in, and pouring in like a flood, till the hall was as full as it could hold; and then they overflowed into the street, and thousands more joined the overflow. They called for me to come out and address them; so out I came, and Forbes took the chair and we held a meeting there. When I stood up in my moleskins, I faced such a crowd of my fellow-creatures as I had never before set eyes on. It was a flood-tide of humanity which swayed and heaved as far as I could see in the gas-light; it extended right away down Windsor Street.

The spectacle of those waiting thousands was enough to touch the heart and fire any man not made of wood and stone. It fired me so that I felt I had got the strength of ten men in me. My heart went out to every listener there, and that made my voice reach them too. I told them what a struggle I had had, how I had fought my way up, bit by bit. I wanted them to know that I had been through what they were suffering now; that I was no professional agitator, but a working agricultural labourer, who was acquainted with their griefs from personal experience, and who was convinced that their one chance of social salvation lay in Union; that if they meant to have a living wage instead of a starvation one, they must combine and unite to get it. It was their due; for when a man gave his master honest work, he had a right to honest money in return. It was no matter of compliment or favour between master and man, but of fair dealing and bargaining. I wanted the men to act rightly by themselves and their wives and little children.

Years ago, when I was a young married man, my master had said to me, "Eighteen-pence a day is all I'll give you." I had a wife and two children, and I knew my duty to them before God, because of the vow I had made to her at the altar, to be, to do, or to die, to keep them. I knew that eighteen-pence a day would not keep them, and I struck. I knew I got into bad report for that, and in consequence I had to put on clothes on Monday morning, and never took them off again till Saturday night, and I went where I could get higher wages. Sometimes I could not get anything but straw to lie on, and once I slept for nights on corded wood. The Union offered the men a shorter way to a living wage than the slow road I had been forced to take. And why? Because I was single-handed. I could never have gone as far as I had done, if I had not had a great deal in my favour. I put it all before them, and I urged every working man and woman present to join the Union. Through it and through it only would labourers' right prevail against employers' right. While I spoke I felt I was carrying the people along with me. It was a splendid meeting.

Inside the Hall the people heard capital speeches from gentlemen who were in sympathy with the cause. Among the principal speakers were Sir Baldwin Leighton, the Hon. Auberon Herbert, Mr. E. Jenkins, M.P., Dr. Langford of Birmingham, and Jesse Collings. A labourers' friend at Birmingham sent us a donation of £100, through Mr. Dixon, M.P. When this was announced there was a tremendous outburst of cheering, and when a note from this unknown friend was read out the cheering was louder than ever. He wrote to us, "The right to form the Union must be fought for to the death." The people caught up those words like a battle cry. It was just what we were all feeling that night inside the hall and outside it. With one voice we shouted, "The right to form the Union must be fought for to the death!" The labourers of Warwickshire who had assembled in Leamington on that Good Friday evening tramped back to their poor homes strong for Union. Yes, the dumb had found a voice at last; the despairing were filled with hope; the downtrodden slave had become a man again. Their forefathers had stood up for the threatened liberties of England, and with scythes and pitchforks and clubbed muskets had beaten back the King's Life Guards till the cannon mowed them down. The men of Warwickshire, in the year of grace eighteen hundred and seventy-two, meant to stand up like soldiers, and fight or die for the Agricultural Labourers' Union.

CHAPTER V.

FORMING THE UNION.

THE Leamington meeting was a startler to those gentry who had blinded themselves with blinkers, and made themselves hard of hearing with cotton wool, and had sat at ease in the lordly chair of the scornful. It burst like a bomb among these proud lollers and made them jump with rage. There was a fine clattering and chattering from one end of the county to the other; such a noise and a to-do as if the skies were falling in on them, and the ground was crumbling away under their feet. In a manner of speaking the ground they trod on had become alive, and had risen up against them, and given them earthquake shocks, each stronger than the last, till after the big one at Leamington they stood up shaking. But we were not idling our dear-bought time away, listening on our doorsteps to the hullabaloos: not a bit of it; for they might clatter and chatter till their tongues ached, as long as they left us free to finish the work we had set our hands to. Six weeks we had been at it almost night and day, and we were hard and fast at it now, pushing ahead at racing speed, covering the ground on our own conveyances as if we were walking and talking for a wager. So we were; we had staked our little all—our widow's mite—on the Union, and it was fight or fall with us. We did not mean to fall and lie flat; we meant to stand up and wrestle and strain every sinew till the day was ours. "More money and men for the Union!" was our battle cry now.

We had made an appeal to the country for funds; we now sent out circulars to all members of Parliament, and to the Trade Unions throughout the country as well. In a very few days cheques ranging from £50 to £100 began to come in. The response was quick as it was generous. That golden stream caused fresh life to flow through our veins. When the lock-out commenced we had only five shillings in hand and that was in coppers, pennies and half-pennies contributed by some of the labourers; most of them had not a farthing to their name.

I remember once, after a meeting under the old chestnut tree—Archibald Forbes was there, also the Hon. Auberon Herbert and Mr. E. Jenkins—how we adjourned to John Lewis's cottage to transact business in those early Union days. We had a solitary light to lighten our darkness, and the committee stood on the stone-flagged floor. We had two teacups to hold the money. I and another member received the books from the local secretaries and advanced what cash was needed. The books contained the list of names of all the Branch members, also of those out of work, and a record of the number of days in the week on which any had got work. When this statement had been made in full the secretary received the total amount for his particular branch. We allowed about nine shillings a week for each family when we could. Well, such was the staunch feeling for the Union among the members, that those who had been fortunate enough to get work in the second week of the strike and lock-out, paid in something for the others, though they were not bound by any of our rules to do so. That is but one example of the self-sacrifice and brotherly kindness which prevailed amongst us. Yes; we were strongly knit together by loyalty and good will, so it would have been a strange thing if we had not won.

I remember, too, a stirring meeting at Southam early in April. I addressed upwards of three hundred labourers and their wives on the bowling green there. It was a good place for the unskilled labourers to be drafted to, as there were stone quarries and lime works in the neighbourhood. At that time I was all for migration, from one part of the country to another. I did not want to see our best men taken out of the country. I knew that there was room and work for all, if only some gumption and common-sense were exercised by the labourers and their leaders in settling and arranging with the right masters in the best places. I believed that work could be found then, without much difficulty, for six or seven hundred men at wages ranging from twenty to twenty-five shillings a week. If the worst came to the worst we could send as many out of the country. Emigration agents, with the best intentions no doubt, were prowling around, picking and choosing the most likely, and tempting them across the sea. I set my back stiff against the emigration door as long as I could, but men were slipping through, for there was hope on the other side of it; land and life and liberty might be theirs in the colonies, and the mother country had given them stones for bread, and for drink the cold water of workhouse charity.

Some of the discharged men were migrating to other localities. Gentlemen came in search of hands for the cotton mills, and others wanted labourers on the railway works. The North Eastern Railway offered work for drivers and horsekeepers at one pound and twenty-three shillings a week A good many went North and some emigrated to New Zealand. The labourer, through the Union, was now able to break the chain of poverty, fear, and debt, which had tied him by the leg to one place. He would hobble off elsewhere, and soon he would learn how to walk erect—a free man. The employers kept locking-out the men and refusing to come to terms with those who had asked for the rise. There were some two hundred men on strike in the Leamington district alone. But I should like to honourably mention one employer who was a noble exception to her class in our neighourhood. Miss Rylands, a Wellesbourne lady, took the better part; when she received notice from her labourers she sent for a gentleman from Birmingham, asked him to arbitrate, and on his award she increased their wages without more ado.

I was holding meetings wherever I could get men together, and we met mostly out of doors. I remember addressing over four hundred in an orchard at Harbury. Sometimes we gathered under a tree, sometimes in a field; now it would be in an orchard, and the next might be by the roadside. We met by sunlight and moonlight and starlight and lantern light—the sun in the sky or the farthing dip—it was all one to the Union man at that time. When we were assembled we often led off with a song or Union ballad such as the following:—

STAND LIKE THE BRAVE.
(Adapted by G. M. Ball.)

O workmen awake, for the strife is at hand;
With right on your side, then with hope firmly stand
To meet your oppressors, go, fearlessly go,
And stand like the brave, with your face to the foe.

    Stand like the brave, stand like the brave;
    Oh, stand like the brave with your face to the foe.

Whatever's the danger, take heed and beware,
And turn not your back—for no armour is there;
Seek righteous reward for your labour—then go
And stand like the brave, with your face to the foe.

The cause of each other with vigour defend,
Be honest and true, and fight to the end;
Where duty may lead you, go, fearlessly go,
And stand like the brave, with your face to the foe.

Let hope then still cheer us; though long be the strife,
More comforts shall come to the workman's home life;
More food for our children; demand it, then go
And stand like the brave, with your face to the foe.

Press on, never doubting redemption draws near—
Poor serfs shall arise from oppression and fear;
Though great ones oppose you, they cannot o'erthrow
If you stand like the brave, with your face to the foe.

We would start that to a rousing tune, and sing it with a will all together. There was another which was a great favourite; it was called "The Fine Old English Labourer," and it went to the tune of "A Fine Old English Gentleman," as follows:—

Come, lads, and listen to my song, a song of honest toil,
'Tis of the English labourer, the tiller of the soil;
I'll tell you how he used to fare, and all the ills he bore,
Till he stood up in his manhood, resolved to bear no more.
  This fine old English labourer, one of the present time.

He used to take whatever wage the farmer chose to pay,
And work as hard as any horse for eighteenpence a day;
Or if he grumbled at the nine, and dared to ask for ten,
The angry farmer cursed and swore, and sacked him there and then.

He used to tramp off to his work while town folk were abed,
With nothing in his belly but a slice or two of bread;
He dined upon potatoes, and he never dreamed of meat,
Except a lump of bacon fat sometimes by way of treat.

He used to find it hard enough to give his children food,
But sent them to the village school as often as he could;
But though he knew that school was good, they must have bread and clothes,
So he had to send them to the fields to scare away the crows.

He used to walk along the fields and see his landlord's game
Devour his master's growing crops, and think it was a shame;
But if the keeper found on him a rabbit or a wire,
He got it hot when brought before the parson and the squire.

Forming the Union

But now he's wide awake enough and doing all he can
At last, for honest labour's rights, he's fighting like a man;
Since squires and landlords will not help, to help himself he'll try,
And if he does not get fair wage, he'll know the reason why.

They used to treat him as they liked in the evil days of old,
They thought there was no power on earth to beat the power of gold;
They used to threaten what they'd do whenever work was slack,
But now he laughs their threats to scorn with the Union at his back.
    This fine old English labourer, one of the present time.

If a squire or a parson or a farmer had passed by on the other side while we were singing this song or others like it, his ears would have told him that the English labourer was awake to his wrongs, and meant to have his rights at last. Yes, poor Hodge was sitting up and rubbing his eyes after his long sleep, and he was getting on to his feet and shaking himself and pulling himself together, and was walking about and was talking over things with his mates. "We won't be worms much longer," the men were saying, not under their breaths as if they feared stone walls might betray them, but they were using the manly voice their Maker had given them.

The movement was flowing over the country like a spring tide. The men of Denham in Buckinghamshire joined in hundreds. There was agitation in Norfolk, where the men struck for shorter hours; there was a lock-out at Long Sutton Marsh, and very soon the wages in that district advanced to two shillings and threepence and two shillings and sixpence a day. Men in Dorsetshire were striking; the labourers about Shaftesbury and Blandford came out asking for a rise to twelve shillings a week. The state of the labourer in that county was as bad as it could very well be.

The men of Gloucestershire and Worcestershire were moving and meeting. The wages there were from nine up to twelve shillings a week, and I daresay the average would be about ten shillings. Rents were high, from four to six pounds a year, and the accommodation was miserable. They worked very long hours all over this part. A man would start at five o'clock in the morning, and he did not leave off until dark; often he was at it till very late, and cases were frequent where the men had a day's work that went nearly round the clock twice over. Of course here, as in other places, the carters had a seven days' week; many of them having from five to ten horses to look after. For a man to be free of debt was the great exception, and not the rule. At one meeting I asked the men present who were not in debt to the shopkeeper to hold up their hands, and when I looked there was not one single hand held up. The curse of debt lay heavy on the agricultural labourer wherever I went, and who was going to blame them?

Take the case of a man getting what was at that time considered a good wage for the labourer in most places, thirteen shillings a week. A Barford man would have to pay for rent one shilling and sixpence, if he had something of a family and lived in a decent cottage. He would spend about nine shillings on bread, loaves being sevenpence-halfpenny each; potatoes were at the rate of four shillings and sixpence for eight gallons, flour about twelve shillings a bushel. If there were two children at school that would be a regular out-going twopence a week.

It is easy to see that a man's expenses were bound to be greater than his earnings. The family lived on potatoes, dry bread, greens, and herbs, kettle broth, and tea which was coloured water; there was a bit of bacon for the man now and then, but fresh meat would come like Christmas, once a year. Perhaps one of the boys might be earning about three shillings a week at ploughing, another getting a little for bird-scaring, and sometimes the wife herself would go into the fields, but she could only go if the family was small and running on its own legs—if there were several young ones and a baby in the cradle she was forced to bide at home. There was the wear and tear of clothes to be reckoned. In nine cases out of ten the bread bill had to wait for clearance till harvest bounty, when for about a month the man would earn about one pound a week. What chance had that family of being strong and healthy? Low living made poor blood and poor bones and poor flesh. If the father got a leg sore and was laid by with it—and that was no rare thing—the family would have to go on the parish till he could get about again. Many an honest striving man was no better than a wrung dishclout before he was half through his day's work. It was no uncommon occurrence for a decent, self-respecting labourer to find himself, after a working life of sixty years, brought down to parish help at the bitter end.

I knew of such men and their wives, who had worked early and late, toiling and moiling and patching and contriving, who had reared a large family of sons and daughters, who had kept themselves to themselves, and showed a brave front to misfortune, and had never had a farthing of parish relief the whole time, and yet who, in their honourable old age, were driven to go on the parish when they began to fail. The Union said, "We're going to stop this."

All through April the labourers were rising, and the farmers were standing out, and the clergy were taking the matter up. The Vicar of Harbury convened a meeting in support of the Union, and there was a parson here and there who went with us openly; but the majority were against us, and others blew now hot now cold, and flew round like weather-cocks as squire or farmer or villager grew strongest at the moment. These shining lights of the Church as by Law Established were but poor farthing rushlights to the agricultural labourer. The Farmers' Club threatened us, but the young Union had fastened its milk teeth in the farmers' jaws, and did not mean to leave go. Some of the farmers were all for advertising; they wanted to import Scotch and Irish labour at cheap rates, because the season was advancing, and our men were leaving the neighbourhood, and unless the employers granted the rise they were not likely to be such fools as to come back again.

Some of those gentlemen who had the good of the cause at heart warned me against having anything to do with professional agitators; Mr. Bromley Davenport, M.P., was one of those who cautioned us, and there were others who said, "Arch, don't let this movement be complicated by Trade Union interference." I had made up my mind to keep clear of them all; I was not going to let them have any control over our affairs if I could help it. Our movement was well started before they took any notice of us. When I met with one of the Trade Union men down at Whitnash I had already founded eight of our Branch Unions. Letters were now coming in by the gross from all parts of the country, asking for help and advice, and inviting me and Russell to come and start branch Unions. We found ourselves with an immense job on hand. I remember how our Executive Committee sat the whole day through—it was, I think, on April 10th—in the Primitive Methodist Chapel at Wellesbourne, settling what further organisation was necessary, and making plans for larger united action. We divided the country into two districts, North and South; a secretary was appointed to each, and a staff of speakers was told off to lecture and carry on the campaign. As thousands had joined us, and more were coming in every day, we felt that the time had come for establishing the Union on a wider basis.

It had grown to be a national movement and it was high time it had a national name. The idea was to concentrate and consolidate the County Unions somewhat on the lines of the Farmers' Agricultural Chambers, all of them to converge in one central body, which would assemble at some appointed place. We accordingly decided that we would call together a great congress to be held at Leamington towards the end of May, in order to establish a National Agricultural Labourers' Union. This was to take a mighty big stride forward, but we considered that facts warranted our making it.

Agriculturists were officially recognising an agitation which had been going on for two months. At a special meeting of the County Chamber of Agriculture, held at the Shire Hall in Warwick, the Earl of Denbigh advised employers to confer with the labourers, and see if they could not between them come to some satisfactory settlement; for, as it was, things were at a dead-lock. Some of the farmers now began to declare that the ground had been cut from under their feet by the labourers.

We knew nothing about that; but it was pretty plain we were making farmer and landlord sit up and take stock of us, and our doings and askings. They declared that they could not increase the men's wages to any extent, as rent depended on the value of the poorest land that could be cultivated profitably, and that the effect of any great rise in wage would be to throw the poorest land out of cultivation.

The employers were agreed that better dwellings should be provided, and that many of the cottages were not all they should be; but, said they, "Look at our side of the question; unequal local taxation prevents the landlord from investing capital in better cottages, and so improving his property." They talked away and argued and discussed, and said something must be done, but what that something was to be they did not exactly know. Others said that it was only to be expected that the labourer would ask for some sort of rise in his wage, because there appeared to be a general increase of prosperity in all kinds of trade throughout the country, and that the agricultural workman knew this, and wanted to share in it; also, that in some form, direct or indirect, he was bound to benefit with the rest, though the advantage might not be permanent. They asked us to send some delegates to a conference, but we declined. They proposed that the Union should appoint three representatives to meet three landowners and three tenant farmers. Russell wrote back that our executive committee would be glad to know a little more about the properly appointed representatives, and what qualifications they were supposed to possess. He wrote, too, that the resolution of the Executive Committee was, " That in view of the present incomplete state of the formation of the Agricultural Labourers' Union, this meeting is of opinion that the proposal should be postponed for the present." Russell's letter was dated April 29th, 1872. We were not going to be hurried into action to suit the convenience of the employers.

The County Chamber of Agriculture held another meeting at the Warwick Shire Hall early in May. Said they to themselves, "Something must be settled, and that soon, or where shall we be?" This labourers' agitation is really a very serious matter indeed. Look at this Union, its success is quite extraordinary, it has extended into all the adjoining counties, and in a few weeks it is to be expanded from a mere County Union into a National one, by means of a great congress of representatives. Owing to migration and the state of the general labour market, wages are still going up; they have already risen from twelve to fourteen and fifteen shillings; and this Union is insisting on having sixteen shillings, and it says that if the sixteen shillings is withheld the men can get twenty-three shillings, and even twenty-seven shillings by taking train to the North. This is terrible; if we delay, wages may go higher still. We must show the Union that we are willing to come to terms, that we even court reconciliation, but we must be careful not to pledge ourselves to particulars."

It was clear the employers meant business. Most of the prominent members of the Council were present, including about thirty tenant farmers and several influential landowners. They sent an answer to Russell's letter, saying that the Chairman and two other members of the Chamber of Agriculture would be willing to meet any three members appointed by the Committee of the Agricultural Labourers' Union as their representatives. The employers were all for conciliation now, and they went so far as to consider the labourers' feelings! They declared that the Wellesbourne farmers' resolutions placarded about the country, intimidating men from joining the Union by threatening to turn them out of their situations and cottages, was most illegal, inconsiderate and uncalled for.

Here was a change! The Chamber was now advocating piecework; and also payment of wages in coin, instead of partly in coin and partly in kind. Said these gentlemen, in their new-born consideration for the welfare of the labourer, "This practice of paying wages in kind prevents a just estimate of the value received by the labourer, induces unreasonable demands on the part of the employed, affords facilities for impositions by unscrupulous employers, leads to improvident habits, and increases intemperance."

All very true, but why did these gentlemen not find this out before; or if they had found it out, why had they not taken action? Such was their tender feeling for the labourer *now*, that they agreed to ask the farmers to pay the men their wages the day before the local market, so as to give them an opportunity of laying out their money to the best advantage. A new day was dawning for Hodge indeed!

Just after this I presided at the first meeting of our board of directors. It was held in the Temperance Hall at Leamington, and some five and thirty delegates from the county branches put in an appearance. Our chief business was to make all arrangements for the coming Congress. The Board was greatly assisted by the valuable counsel of Mr. E. Jenkins, of the Middle Temple, a member of our Finance Committee. I remember what cheering reports were put in. Contributions were coming in from every side, and the total amount already reached the figure of over £800.

About four thousand men were enrolled in Warwickshire alone; Lincolnshire had between three and four thousand in Union; Cambridgeshire had over two thousand, and Huntingdonshire the same.

It was resolved that a National Congress should be held at the end of the month. We decided to accept the offer of a preliminary conference with the representatives of the Chamber of Agriculture: I and two others to represent the Union. We appointed Jesse Collings, E. Jenkins, J. Arnold, and E. Haynes, Union trustees.

As there was now only a handful of labourers out on strike in the Wellesbourne district, we resolved that, subject to the necessities of the Warwickshire Labourers' Union, such subscriptions as came to hand should be held in trust to assist our brethren in other parts. We were of opinion that the Union funds should be for the general benefit of the agricultural labourers throughout the kingdom—those who were in the Union, of course—and we decided to take the opinion of the congress on the subject. It was certain that we ought to be regularly empowered to draw on our funds for general migration and emigration purposes when needful. The contributions were general, and the Union was becoming general too.

We meant to hold an evening meeting in the Temperance Hall as well, but so many wanted to attend that we decided to have it in the circus instead, where there were seats for about three thousand people. We sent out hasty announcements by handbill and crier, and in spite of the heavy rain there was a large gathering, and the meeting was a most enthusiastic one. It put fresh spirit into all of us. Later on in the month we had a good meeting at Buckingham. Then came the great day of the Congress—May 29th—when some sixty delegates attended. Invitations had been sent to every county in England and Wales, requesting the Unions to send up two or more *bona fide* representative farm labourers, that they might take part in forming a National Union, the aim of which was the general improvement of their brethren. Some of the delegates came very long distances, the expenses being borne by the local Unions. They met to discuss such points as the raising of wages, the lessening of working hours, the improvement of cottages, the securing of suitable allotments, and the aiding of emigration. Influential and experienced gentlemen were invited to read papers on the second day. We wanted high and low to join in throwing light on the subject, with a view to taking legislative action. "Act, act in the living present" was our motto.

G. Dixon, M.P. for Birmingham, was in the chair, and among those present on the platform were Sir Baldwin Leighton, Hon. and Rev. J. W. Leigh, Rev. J. J. Trebeck, Rev. C. F. C. Pigott, Dr. J. A. Langford, Rev. A. O'Neil; J. Campbell, J.P. (Rugby),

W. G. Ward, H. Pratt, Sec. of the London Executive Committee, Jesse Collings, and A. Arnold. Letters of sympathy were read from the Hon. Auberon Herbert, Professor Fawcett, M.P., Lord Edmond Fitzmaurice, M.P., Canon Girdlestone, and others.

Dr. Langford reported on the progress and condition of the Union. There had been some thirty village meetings, attended by a total of twelve thousand one hundred labourers and others; sixty-three branches had been formed, consisting in all of four thousand six hundred and seventy-two members. About a hundred and fifty men had been helped during the strike, and had been assisted to migrate. Some two hundred labourers had emigrated. It was calculated that in all there were between forty and fifty thousand in Union.

I should mention here that a Union movement had been started in Herefordshire in 1871, nearly a year before ours. It began in the village of Leintwardine and it was backed up by the rector. It spread over six counties in a very short time, and when our Congress sat it had been so successfully worked by T. H. Strange, the secretary, and by others, that there were about thirty thousand members in it. The watchword of the Herefordshire organisation had been from its commencement, "Emigration, migration, but not strikes." This West of England Union had sent surplus labour to Yorkshire, Lancashire, and Staffordshire, where the wages averaged sixteen and seventeen shillings; and some men, about forty, I think, had been emigrated to America. Before this movement began the average rate of wages in Herefordshire had been from nine to ten shillings; in Gloucestershire the average was nine shillings; often a man's wages did not amount to more than eight shillings; and that not for "wet or dry," so that his earnings might not reach seven shillings a week sometimes. No sooner had this Union caught on than wages in Herefordshire rose on an average two shillings a week, and all over the six counties there was improvement, though there was plenty of room for a great deal more. In Wiltshire and in Dorsetshire particularly, there was much more to be done in the way of a general levelling up.

Well, here we were at the end of May 1872 with a strength of nearly fifty thousand, and I consider such a splendid force of Agricultural Labourers, banded together in one common cause, justified us in putting on record the faith that was in us, which we did as follows :—" The Committee believe in the justice and righteousness of their cause, and have the firmest faith that Divine blessing will rest upon it."

Our delegates also proposed, seconded, and adopted the following resolutions :—

" That a complete list of the public subscriptions be printed, and that the hearty thanks of the Conference be hereby given to all who have contributed to the funds of the movement, or otherwise promoted it.

" That a National Union of Agricultural Labourers be formed in each county or division of county, and that the National Agricultural Labourers' Union shall consist of representatives elected by such district Unions.

"That the Council of the National Agricultural Labourers' Union meet at Leamington at least twice a year, and that the expenses of the representatives so attending be paid by the various district Unions.

"That the Executive or Managing Committee of the National Agricultural Labourers' Union shall consist of twelve labourers elected annually at a meeting of the Council of the National Agricultural Labourers' Union.

"That such Executive or Managing Committee shall meet at Leamington at least once a fortnight.

"That the following twelve labourers constitute the Executive of the National Agricultural Labourers' Union *pro tem*: J. Arch, E. Russell, G. Allington, T. Parker, J. Biddle, J. Prickett, J. Harris, E. Haynes, H. Blackwell, G. Jordan, B. Herring, G. Lunnon, and E. Pill."

In the afternoon we again met for further settlement of the constitution of the National Agricultural Labourers' Union, and the following were some of the resolutions adopted :—

"That a committee be formed of gentlemen favourable to the principles of the National Agricultural Labourers' Union, for consultation and advice, but without the power to vote; such committee to be invited to act by the Executive Committee.

"That the Executive Committee of the National Agricultural Labourers' Union be requested to draw up the rules of the Union, and obtain such aid as may be necessary, and submit such rules to the first general meeting of the Council for approval.

"That the Executive of the National Agricultural Labourers' Union be empowered to procure the necessary offices and paid officers, and other help for the transacting of the business of the Union.

"That Mr. J. E. M. Vincent be requested to act as the treasurer of the National Agricultural Labourers' Union.

"That the funds of the National Agricultural Labourers' Union be invested in the names of the following gentlemen as trustees:—

"Jesse Collings (Birmingham); E. Jenkins (London); A. Arnold (Hampton-in-Arden); E. Haynes (Ratley).

"That all payments made by the treasurer be based on resolutions of the Executive Committee signed by the chairman and one of the Committee members.

"That the repayment of money by the trustees to the treasurer shall be on authority of a resolution of the Executive Committee signed by the chairman and one other member of the Committee."

The Executive decided to select for a committee of advisers, such gentlemen from the London and Birmingham Aid Committees as they thought would be most useful.

Hodgson Pratt, secretary of the London Central Aid Committee asked us how his committee could best assist the movement; he, and indeed all those from outside who attended, showed a spirit of most hearty goodwill.

It warmed my heart when I saw the delegates come in. I was able that proud day to give the hand of fellowship and a true Union greeting to men come up from Herefordshire and Bedfordshire and Shropshire and Wiltshire, from Dorsetshire and Gloucestershire and Staffordshire, from Yorkshire and Norfolk and Suffolk and Bucks and Nottinghamshire, from Northamptonshire and Worcestershire and Huntingdonshire, and from distant Radnorshire. Never had there been a gathering like unto this. When I stood up there with all these brethren gathered together in Congress, while we sang Russell's spirit-stirring Union hymn as with one mighty voice, I said within myself, " Joseph Arch, you have not lived in vain, and of a surety the Lord God of Hosts is with us this day."

In my speech I told them that we must have frequent meetings for consultation and discussion, that we might keep up the spirit of good fellowship and put heart into one another. There must be no local jealousies, no self-seeking, no isolation; we must stand and act together, if we would not fall to pieces like a bundle of sticks without a binder. The Branches and Districts would work in concord through a common representative and Executive Committee. A Central Fund was the stand-by of the great trade societies, and so it would be of our National Union; we were bound to have a central common treasury. Every member was clearly to understand that the Branch was to remit its fund to the District; that each District would remit three-fourths of the receipts to the National centre; and that if any Branch or District failed to do this, it would have no kind of claim on the general resources of the Union. It was essential that money matters should be regularly organised on the soundest possible basis. The fourth part, which the Districts were to be allowed to keep back, was to be spent at the District Committee's discretion in meeting current expenses and promoting the general objects of the Union.

For the working expenses of the various Branches we recommended an Incidental Fund, which could easily be kept going, if each member would make a small payment. I urged all members to act with great caution and referred them to Rule 10 which ran like this:—"All cases of dispute between members of of the National Agricultural Labourers' Union, and employers must be laid before the Branch Committee to which such members may belong; and should the Branch Committee be unable to arrange the question to the mutual satisfaction of the parties interested, in conjunction with the District Committee, recourse shall had to be arbitration. Should the District Committee be unable to arrange for such arbitration, an appeal shall be made to the National Executive Committee for its decision. Any award made by the arbitration or by the decision of the National Executive shall be binding on all members of the Union; and in no case shall a strike be resorted to until all the above means have been tried and have failed."

That shows plainly how we felt and intended to act on the strike question. "Don't strike," I said, "unless all other means fail. Let peace and moderation mark all our meetings; let courtesy and fairness and firmness mark all our demands. Let us exercise patience in the enforcement of just claims; let us fraternise, let us centralise, and all will go well with us; and we shall surely prosper in the glorious work we have put our hands to. With brotherly feeling, with a united front, with every District welded into a great whole; with a common fund to which all shall contribute, and on which all shall have the right to draw, the time will not be distant when every agricultural labourer shall have what few have yet enjoyed—a fair day's pay for a fair day's work. Nine and a half hours, exclusive of meal times, as a day's work, and sixteen shillings a week pay are not extravagant demands. Brothers, be united and you will be strong; be temperate and you will be respected; realise a central capital and you will be able to act with firmness and independence. Be united, be sober, and you will soon be free."

United action for our common freedom—that was the sentiment of the Agricultural Labourers' Congress which sat at Leamington; and which, by its action in organising the Union on a national basis, marked an important epoch in the history of the movement, and started it forward on a fresh career of struggle and of triumph.

CHAPTER VI.

PROGRESS OF THE UNION.

THE May Congress which inaugurated the National Agricultural Labourers' Union was so much more of a success than any of us had expected that not a few were nearly carried off their feet by surprise, so to speak. It roused more feeling for and against us than ever. Our friends cheered us on with right good will; and I do not think I am using much of a figure of speech when I say that our enemies went about gnashing their teeth with spiteful rage, and grinning like the dog mentioned in the Psalms. They might run around grinning and gnashing and foaming as hard as they pleased as long as they did not cross our track; there were some of us who thought that if they did they would be served as the cow was by the engine, it would be a bad day for them; the big Union engine was now going along at full speed with plenty of fuel to feed it, and it would just run over them, and would never so much as know it had done it. But you may be sure we had no time to waste in cock-crowing when once Congress rose. We had got our work cut out for us on a large scale; there were no inches about it, miles made the measure.

We had listened to able papers from the united gentlemen, among whom were the Hon. Auberon Herbert, M.P., who gave us one on the Game Laws, which was growing a very hot subject; it had long been a sore one; Sir Baldwin Leighton who, though a Conservative landlord, treated garden and meadow allotments from a fair and liberal point of view; the Hon. and Rev. J. W. Leigh, who took co-operative farming as his subject; Mr. Butcher, of Banbury, who gave us a capital paper on co-operative stores; Jesse Collings, who took education; and Rev. H. Solly, who took village clubs and reading-rooms. We wanted to get all the information we could from trustworthy sources, and from friends who were honestly interested in the movement; but at the same time we did not mean to be led away into starting all sorts of schemes before our own proper work was done, and was securely established. I was not going to have the cart of agricultural reforms stuck before the Union horse; though from the time of the Congress onward there was a body of men inside and outside the Union who kept urging us to adopt such a topsy-turvy way of driving to destruction.

"No, thank you," said I. "I'm for reform as much as anybody, but it's got to be the labourer first, and reform all round after."

"Oh," said some, "but you can do both at the same time. You can raise the labourer and push forward reform—the one helps the other."

"Not a bit of it," said I. "Reform away as much as *you* please, but I'm a practical man, and I'm not such a fool at this time of day as to try sitting on two stools at once. And I'm not going to entice any fellow-worker of mine to play such a down-falling game either."

"Oh," said some, "but then the Union must not sink into a mere organisation for Trade Union purposes—this is a great moral uprising which promises to have the most beneficial result on the country at large."

"Very good," said I; "so be it, with all my heart. I hope it *is* moral, and I should be sorry if it did not have beneficial results on the country at large, but charity must begin its good work at home; when the home work is well done it may go and work abroad. It may work away then like one o'clock, and my blessing will go with it. But there's no blessing attached to those who try to run before they can walk. We've got to take a step at a time and that a steady one; we'll run on to reforms of law and land fast enough, and sure enough, when we're ready. It's a poor shoemaker who can't stick to his last. Well, to raise the wages, shorten the hours, and make a free man out of a land-tied slave is *my* last, and to that last I'll stick as tight as beeswax for the present. Raise a man's material condition to the level of self-respecting decency and the moral will rise too. Give the agricultural labourer the chance of making his home life like a well-tilled freehold plot, and the seed of morality will soon show its head above ground; and if well watered and tended, it will grow into a sturdy and thriving young plant, and no one need fear but that God Almighty will give the increase. But keep a man living like a hog and he'll have more or less the mind and the morals of a hog; and what's more, if you drive him hard, he'll be like an English Gadarenean swine; a drink devil will enter into him, and drive him down a steep place into the sea of death and destruction."

We had the Union plough well started, and the team was pulling straight and strong, and all together, and I should have been a queer kind of a ploughman if I had let half a dozen ploughshares be tacked on to mine. There were furrows in plenty to be turned over in the English agricultural field, and there was room for a dozen good drivers with teams and ploughshares to match.

Union meetings, meetings everywhere, was the order of the day, and we had to be on the sharp look-out to keep professional Trade Unionists from the towns in their own places. I was not going to have our folk made light-headed with wrong notions, so that they would be leaping over the hedge of the law into a jail. Said a good friend of the cause, "We must have a care that Hodge does not blossom into an Anarchist." I did not intend that he should, though.

I had no special fancy for fiery blooms of that sort. Wherever I spied out a blossom of anarchy and arson I said to myself I would nip it in the bud; and nip it I did, sharp as a November frost or a pair of scissors.

Of course I was called an agitator; so I was, because everyone who stirs people up to do things is an agitator, but those who so named me attached a bad meaning to the word. I was agitating for the right and not for the wrong; I was no "Arch Apostle of Arson," as some one chose to call me. The Bishop of Gloucester (Dr. Ellicott) was one of my worst enemies in the early days of the movement. He wanted me, and those like me, ducked in the horse pond. He was at a dinner one day and the question of our agitation came up. He did not say in so many words that I ought to be ducked in the horse pond, but he spoke in a sort of parable. If I remember right, he said with reference to me, "There is an old saying, 'Don't nail their ears to the pump, and don't duck them in the horse pond.'" The sentiment of his remark was a downright incitement to riot, in my opinion. I paid the bishop out several times over for that saying, for it was a wrong spirit for a bishop to show. I remember on one occasion, when I was at Gloucester, I said in the course of speech, "I have a good mind to lay a heavy indictment against the bishop. He appears to believe in adult baptism which is contrary to the doctrine of the Church of England." Unless I am mightily mistaken, Dr. Ellicott repented in episcopal sackcloth and Lenten ashes for that little speech. It was in the early autumn of 1872, I think, that he showed which side he was on. As to the parsons generally, I never expected them to have much sympathy with us. Their stock argument against the Union was that it was "setting class against class." This was their poll-parrot cry. "Oh yes," said they, "the men have a perfect right to try and improve themselves, and we will help them; but the Union is setting class against class."

It was in the autumn of this year that a considerable number of men emigrated to New Zealand on very favourable terms; they went out on railway contract work for the firm of Messrs. J. Brogden and Sons. The idea of emigration was taking more hold of the men than I liked. But migration was a different thing, though sometimes when I urged migration they would say, "We don't want to leave the old county, if we can find work and a living in it. We can't all migrate North, and to those places where the wages are good. If we do we'll have wages going down, or we'll be turned off 'not wanted,' and then where should we be? Wages are so low in most of the other parts of the country that, if we did move, it would not be to better ourselves." There was too much truth in it.

Early in December a great meeting in our favour was held at Exeter Hall. The citizens of London wished to publicly show their sympathy with us. Samuel Morley took the chair. He was a first-rate man and a substantial helper of the Union. He gave the first £500 cheque towards the support of the Warwickshire men. Among those present on the platform were, Sir C. Dilke, M.P., Sir C. Trevelyan, Sir John Bennett, Mr. Mundella, M.P., Archbishop Manning, and T. Hughes, M.P. I, and Ball, and Mitchell represented the town.

Charles Bradlaugh was there, too, and I should just like to say a word about him. I first came across him at a meeting in the Town Hall at Northampton, when I spoke. The next time we met was on this occasion at Exeter Hall. I got to know him very well and was very friendly with him. He was a fine statesman, and before he died he gave proof of it too. In his way he worked hard for our cause. His sceptical ideas went against him, and the majority of people were horrified at him. I was not; and I can truthfully say that, though he and I had many interviews and conversations, he never once broached the subject of religion, or aired his sceptical opinions to me. He always took care to keep them well in the background. Also, I never heard him allude to them on any platform. I honoured and respected Charles Bradlaugh; he had a great struggle all through his life, but he fought like a man for what he believed to be the right. He was a man of principle, a big-hearted man; and a good many of his traducers might have taken a few lessons from him with a great deal of benefit to themselves. In the course of my career I also met Mrs. Besant several times. When Bradlaugh held a great indignation meeting in Trafalgar Square to protest against the use of brute force, I went up to London to take part in it. Mrs. Besant was in the room where the committee were making all the necessary arrangements, and it was there I first saw her. She often spoke, and most eloquently, on behalf of our cause. At that time she held the same views as Bradlaugh. I think she lost a good deal of her influence when she took up with Theosophy, but I dare say she then influenced a different class of persons.

At this Exeter Hall meeting Cardinal Manning spoke up nobly for us. The testimony, at such a time and in such a place, of a man so respected, and who occupied such a commanding position in his Church, was of the greatest value to the Union. He said that the agricultural movement was not an act of insubordination, nor were the promoters of it mischievous agitators, and that the men who had asked him to speak at this meeting had said, "We are resolved to attain what is just, and we will attain it only in a God-fearing and law-abiding way."

I remember he told us that he believed he was the only man present who could say that he sat as chairman of a rural vestry in 1833—4, and saw doled out to the labouring man, the gallon of flour and the shilling a head, which was given according to the number of his family. He also told us that he had had an acquaintance with the labouring men of Sussex, extending over a period of seventeen years; and he remembered the first introduction of the New Poor

Law Amendment Act, with all its precipitate applications, which had caused untold misery and suffering. Yes, Manning, both as Church of England parson, and as a Roman Catholic priest, ever proved himself the working man's friend. He was a practical friend to us, for he sent us a subscription of £10 in 1878, and again one of the same amount in 1879. He also publicly testified to my good faith and was a true friend through thick and thin.

There had been an electoral reform conference held at St. James's Hall in November, at which I was present. Joseph Chamberlain presided, and the voteless condition of the agricultural labourer was discussed. It was again mentioned at this December meeting. I believed the vote was as certain to come as sunrising, but we had not made it a plank in the Union platform yet; the time was scarcely ripe for it. When we three labourers stood up to speak in our turn, we stuck pretty close to our subject—the labourer. I remember how Ball, who was a Lincolnshire man, told them that as a child he had worked for twopence a day, and that he had been obliged to go to work hundreds of times on a breakfast of bread and hot water, and as for dinner —well, a herring and a bit of bread had to do duty for *that*. Owing to the Union, things were looking a little brighter in Lincolnshire at the end of 1872; wages had risen, which was something to the good; but on the other hand, cottage accommodation was very bad. The small holdings were being broken up, for the small holders generally were in a ruinous condition.

Then the cottages fell into the hands of bigger proprietors. When a man was put into a cottage the farmer of whom he rented it, or the landlord of whom he held it, would say to him, "If you live here you work for me, and if you work for me you will have to take what I choose to give you." If the man was not told this in so many words, it practically came to the same thing. There was no doubt that the whole land question wanted a thorough overhauling; and many were convinced that the problem would never be solved till the day came when land would be owned in the same way that other property is owned, when it could be transferred and dealt with as easily as consols or railway shares.

Mitchell, who was a Somersetshire man, told them a little of his experiences, too; and they had been bitterly hard. He was frightened away from the plough-tail when he was about nineteen. He slaved at farm work from 4 a.m. till 10 p.m., and often longer, and frequently not more than two pennyworth of victuals would pass his lips the long day through. Slave as he might, his tyrannical employer was never satisfied. Wages would run in those parts from six to seven shillings a week and stop at eight or nine shillings. There were old men whose wages did not go beyond a miserable five shillings, and when they had paid one shilling and sixpence out of that for rent, they made a close acquaintance with half-starvation. One poor old man said he was so hungry most days, that he often did not know what to do to get along. The ordinary breakfast would be a tea-kettle broth—that is, bread in the breakfast pot with hot water poured on it; for dinner there would be a few potatoes, some bread, and occasionally a bit of bacon, but the bacon was most often seen on the father's plate while the rest had to feed on the smell of it; then for supper bread again, and perhaps a small bit of cheese. Here was high living for a working-man! The cottage accommodation was a disgrace to civilisation; and this, not only in Somersetshire, but all over the country. As many as thirteen people would sleep all huddled up together in one small cottage bedroom. A well-known country clergyman, the Rev. Mr. Fraser, afterwards Bishop of Manchester, who gave evidence before an Agricultural Commission held in the sixties—it extended, I think, over the years 1867-8-9—stated that it was impossible to exaggerate the terrible state of things then existing; they were so bad physically, socially, economically, morally, and intellectually, that it would be difficult to make them worse. Well, in 1872, at the end of that year of grace, this particular disgrace to Christian England was as rampant as ever it had been. And I think among the worst sinners in this respect I should name the class of small proprietors. Most likely they had not the money—in fact, we know that the bulk of them had not the wherewithal—either to improve and enlarge the cottages they owned, or to pull them down and build new and better ones. So the labourer and his family were forced to sleep in one room—it makes my blood run cold when I think of it—while squire and parson, and oftentimes farmers, had commonly more rooms than they needed—they had plenty of room at any rate for decent living. Spare rooms and suites of apartments, the squire, and the landlord, and the wealthy employer had at command, while the labourers on their estates were herded together like beasts of the field, or worse.

I gave the audience some of my early experience also; and I had something to say about the farmers as well. I was the candid friend of the farmer then, and in my opinion I have never been anything else. I knew well enough that many tenant farmers had injuries to complain of as well as the men, and I did not want to see the neck of the farmer under the foot of the labourer; not at all, there should be no neck and foot business about the relationship between the two. Farmers as a class had been fearfully oppressed. In my own country the custom was that the farmer should hold his land upon a twelve-months' notice. Say that a man rented a farm and improved it greatly during a five years' tenancy; would he be able to rest secure, and confidently reap the fruits of his labour? Oh dear no; soon would come the landlord, have the land re-assessed, and impose an extra five shillings an acre on it. The farmer had to pay this or go; and how, when he had been so fleeced, could he raise the labourers' wages when they asked him to give them a shilling or two more a week? He had to cut down his expenses to make good the extra iniquitous rent; and you may be sure that in this paring process the poor labourer got most of the cutting; he was shorn close to the skin.

Farmer and labourer had improved the land together, but the landlord took the increase thereof. And now the farmers were so bat-blind to their own best interests, that they were trying to crush out the Union. It was a foolish and short-sighted course they were taking; but the majority made themselves deaf as adders then, and for a long while after. Indeed, I might say that at this present time too many of them are bat-blind and adder-deaf still.

Over and over again I have tried to show them that here in England the interest of labourer and farmer is at bottom one and the same—is, was, and ever shall be, while the land system continues on its present basis, and there are such men on the earth as landlords, farmers, and hired labourers. I say that the farmer and labourer are the Siamese Twins of the agricultural world, and he who would tear them asunder and put them apart is their most deadly enemy. Every farmer, who by word and deed denies this vital fact and cuts himself off from the life interests of the labourer, is his own assassin; he will very soon find that he has dealt himself a suicidal blow. To commit suicide is the act of a fool or a madman; every one in his senses will agree to that I should think. Well, not only have scores and scores of farmers in the past behaved like fools and madmen, but they are behaving so still. By stopping up their ears, which were dull enough before, so that they became deaf to the voice of reason and common-sense, they made themselves no whit better than the horses and mules without understanding; they turned themselves into their own worst enemy, and it served them quite right when they had to pay through the nose for their folly. They paid in the past, they paid in the early years of the Union, they have kept on paying ever since. They do not seem able to learn a simple lesson—simple as A, B, C, or the multiplication table. I said at that meeting:

"The farmers are afraid of the labourers combining, but they are not afraid of our strong arm when they want us to work, nor of the blessings of life we have toiled to procure them. I do not wonder at the kicking of the landlords, who see where all this will push them by-and-by; but I am surprised, very much surprised at the poor farmer. I pity his poor brainless head. I say to the farmer, 'The labourers are your best friends, yet you take them by the neck and bundle them into the street, and the landlord pats you on the back and says, "Oh, you have done it so nicely, do it again," and you go away and do it again.'

"I warned the farmers ten years ago, when they formed their Chamber of Agriculture, to take care and see what they were about, and they pooh-poohed me as only an agricultural labourer, who could not possibly know anything of the farmer's business. Well, now they are finding themselves in the ditch. We will try and pull them out by means of our much despised Union. But I would have farmer and landlord take heed of a labourer's warning. The Union will prosper and the Union will win, and woe be to them who oppose it. Our motto is, 'United to protect, but not combined to injure'; but we will fight tooth and nail for the Union, if we are driven to it by those who, in their own interests, should be on our side. If things go on as they seem to be going now, Lord Derby will not prove to have been so far out, when he said there would be two masters to one man. I say, 'You will get your toes pinched as sure as you are born, if you don't keep a sharp look out, and mind where you are walking.'

"I speak from an honest and manly heart to landlord and farmer on this question. I am not one who strokes a man down the back because he is a gentleman, nor do I speak evil of him when he is out of hearing after giving him a mouthful of smooth words. I'm no back-biting cringer, nor do I cherish bitter feelings against any—there is no dumb, black dog in me—so I say right out here and now to the landlords of this country and to the tenant farmers, that if they continue to make our Union men suffer in the way they have done, if they mean to turn them away from their employment, starve them, and drive them into the streets, leaving them without shelter or with only 'the hillside for their bed, and the broad canopy of heaven for their curtain,' then landlord and tenant farmer will live to rue the day on which they were born.

"What have we to thank our country and its

Government for either? Parliament spent some twenty millions of money to wipe out slavery in the West Indies, but how about the slaves at home? We who have been white slaves, and those of us who are white slaves still, are driven to desperate remedies. I say that, if our country means to go on treating us as mere machines in the hands of a money-mongering few, we will leave her, let her fate fall how it may. Waves of men have rolled from her shores to foreign strands, and waves of men will follow. Yes, the tide of labour will ebb away from these island shores, and agricultural England will be left bare. Those who have toiled in the sweat of their brow to make her fruitful will leave her to barrenness. They will forsake in sorrow and anguish of spirit her who has been to them no nursing mother; they will go from her, they will depart and will return no more."

Emigration was beginning to stare us full in the face, but I wanted to keep it in the background as a last resource. I remember we passed a resolution at this meeting declaring the present condition of the agricultural labourer to be a national disgrace, inimical to the best interests of the nation. That resolution was nothing but God's own truth.

At the end of December the Warwickshire Labourers' Union was formally affiliated with the National Agricultural Labourers' Union at a meeting held at Leamington, when Mr. G. H. Ward of Perriston Towers presided. There were some sixty-nine or seventy delegates present. They represented the branches of the Warwickshire Union, which consisted of about six thousand two hundred members. The reports were cheering, for wages had been raised one, two, and, in some cases, three shillings above the average wage given before the Union made its power felt; the farmers were giving in. Still there was more to be done in this direction, for the highest wage seldom reached fifteen shillings; it was sometimes fourteen shillings, but the average was thirteen shillings; and there were still far too many places in which the average wage was eleven shillings; occasionally it was down at ten shillings, and even nine shillings.

Since May we had forwarded some two hundred and fifty men to other parts; some had been migrated and were working at more remunerative employments, some had emigrated, and thus the so-called surplus labour of the districts on this side of England had been reduced. But in spite of improvement, cases such as these were all too common.

A carter would come and say: " My wages are twelve shillings but I have no perquisites; I have to work fourteen hours a day six days out of seven, and on Sunday I have to put in half a day's labour."

A shepherd would say: " And look at me, I got ten shillings for a week of seven days, and I lost time in bad weather; out of this I had to pay one and sixpence rent for a cottage with two bedrooms, and now here I am, sacked because I've joined the Union."

A farm labourer would say: " My poor wages are

seven shillings a week, and I lose money on bad days; my rent is one shilling and threepence, and I have to pay out one shilling and threepence halfpenny a month for club money; how is a man to keep alive and going on it? I'm most always hungry, and I can't keep decent clothes on my back, not even of a Sunday, and my family has to make the best shift it can. 'Tisn't life at all, and I often wish I was out of it."

What man, with no better chance before him than dragging out a miserable existence like this, would not have wished the same?

We had done wonders in 1872. When I look back now on that first year of our Union's life, I see clearer than ever what a grand start we had made in less than twelve months; but as I reviewed our progress then, when '72 was nearing its end, and considered that there were still many hundreds of our brethren scattered over the land who could cap and match these tales of grinding misery, it seemed to me we had done next to nothing. We would have to be up and doing in 1873, and I said to myself that the motto for the coming year must be, "Press forward, push onward, rise upward without ceasing."

The New Year which dawned on the first of January 1873, brought stormy times along with it. Early in the year some labourers held a meeting in the village of Littleworth, near Farringdon, in Berkshire. An ill-conditioned farmer made a fuss, and so three leaders of the meeting were summoned before the Bench for having caused obstruction on the Queen's highway. This was all nonsense, and only a pretext, because the Primitive Methodists had been in the habit for years of holding meetings on the very same spot. The three men were convicted, and there was a to-do all round the neighbourhood.

"Oh," said we, "this is too much; we are not going to let the right of meeting together in the open be taken away from us without a struggle. This is a case for the Union to take up and fight out. We will call a test meeting, and if we are summoned for obstruction, so be it. We will go before the Bench and conduct ourselves as law-abiding, peaceable citizens should; but we will have the best legal advice at our backs, for we have Union funds to pay for it. The Bench will find we are no longer poor, ignorant, unprotected labourers, to be browbeaten and bullied and put upon; we will give them a Queen's Counsel to tackle, and we will stand by to see what they make of the job."

So we arranged to hold a test meeting towards the end of March, and it was a tremendous one. On the appointed day the big Market Place at Farringdon was more than half-filled with labourers. John Charles Cox, J.P. (he is now a minister of the Church of England), took the chair, and upheld us splendidly. Mackenzie and I, and also two or three well-known gentlemen, were in a waggon drawn up by the side of Cox. Very soon after the proceedings commenced, the superintendent of the police appeared on the scene, just as we had expected he would. He asked us to break up the meeting and disperse, as we were causing an obstruction; but we were doing nothing of the sort, for we had taken particular care to keep the crowd all round us compactly, so that people could walk or drive about easily. He said our meeting was illegal and must be dissolved at once. We civilly refused to go; thereupon he asked for our names and addresses, which we of course gave, and when he had taken them down we were allowed to finish our meeting without further molestation.

Two or three of the magistrates down there, however, were very bitter against me—I believe they would have hanged me if they could—so but a few days were allowed to pass before they sent me a summons to appear before the Bench. Cox and Mackenzie had summonses served on them also. Off we went to Farringdon on the morning of April 15th, to get our case tried. We had Fitzjames Stephen, Q.C., to defend us; Mr. E. Jenkins, our constant friend, was retained, and the case was entrusted to Messrs. Sheen & Roscoe, London. As I was entering the Court, the superintendent of police, a regular old Dogberry said to me, "You will catch it hot this time; they mean to give it you stiff." "Well," said I, "let them; but if I am convicted I am not going to leave the Court unless I am handcuffed. If I've got to go, I go as a felon. You can take me to Reading gaol if you will, but before I go there I shall telegraph to the House of Commons."

By one o'clock on that Tuesday morning the Court was packed. The trial lasted over an hour, and then the magistrates retired to consider their decision; but might have saved themselves the trouble of going through that piece of formality, for we had won the day. We had got a surveyor to make out a plan of the Market Place, and the boundary line of the space covered by the crowd was plainly marked on it. The surveyor proved beyond dispute that there was plenty of room for anybody to walk or drive round the crowd, so they could not obtain a conviction on the ground of obstruction in fact.

There was one particular magistrate who hated me and the Union and all its works, and he was as mad as a hatter when he saw how things were going. Then Fitzjames Stephen proved that we had a parliamentary petition down for consideration on our meeting programme; and as the Bill of Rights protects from imprisonment all assemblies of English citizens who meet for the purpose of petitioning the House of Commons, this settled the matter. We could not be sent to prison; but of course I did not know what trick the Bench might not have up its sleeve. I knew that the magistrate I have mentioned would convict by hook or by crook if he could. I heard afterwards that he did stick out against us as long as he had a leg to stand on, but he was compelled to climb down at the finish. When the magistrates returned to the Court, the Chairman said, "We have decided not to convict you this time, but you will be bound down to hold no more meetings in Berkshire."

"I shall not accept that decision," I said. "I am going to hold a meeting to-night about three miles away."

The magistrates did not know what to say, and finally they dismissed the case, and I held my meeting that night without let or hindrance.

While we were in Court there were about four hundred labourers outside armed with sticks; and although I begged them to keep quiet and not to strike a blow, they said that if the police brought me out in handcuffs, they would go for the policemen and smash them. I am certain they would have done it too, for there was very hot and bitter feeling aroused among the men. The magistrates dared not leave the Court by the front entrance; they slipped away by the back door, and in that they showed their wisdom, for if the men had caught sight of them there would have been a row on the spot.

The Union won a great victory and we exulted over it. We had good reason to rejoice, as every public building in those parts was closed against us. It was a decision which strengthened our position very much and cleared the ground for us in more senses than one.

Then there was the shameful Chipping Norton affair, which roused the indignation of the whole country, as well it might. Sixteen respectable English working women were committed to prison with hard labour. It happened this way.

At Ascot, in Oxfordshire, some men were locked out. At this time there were small strikes going on here and there in the county. Some Union men working for a farmer or two would ask for Union wages. They would give notice on the Saturday that they wanted the rise the next week. If the farmers held out and refused it, the men would leave on the following Saturday. There was a small local strike on at Ascot, and the carter of a farmer there, named Hambridge, joined the strike without giving the usual notice. Hambridge summoned him and got the costs. Then Hambridge called in outside labour, got over, I think it was, two men, from a village in the neighbourhood. Of course this made the bad feeling ten times worse; it was not dropping oil on troubled waters anyway. These Ascot women, who had husbands out of work, thought they would drive the men away when they came. It was but natural that they should object to outsiders slipping into their husbands' shoes, and they wanted to show the farmers that Ascot folk, women though they might be, were not going to stand by and see their bread and butter pass to strangers without some sort of protest. So when the men came in, out marched the women and mobbed them. The women dared them to enter Hambridge's field. The only blows that they struck were tongue blows, though I heard that some of them carried sticks. Hambridge took the matter up, and the women, seventeen of them, were summoned before the magistrates at Chipping Norton.

The presiding magistrates were two clergymen—squarsons, as they called them. In their evidence the labourers, who were strapping men and not likely to be frightened and hurt by a parcel of women, gave evidence that, so far from being set upon with sticks, they had been invited by the women to come back to the village and have a drink. In fact it was plain enough to any unprejudiced person that no physical injury was attempted; at the most there might have been a little hustling, but these stalwart labourers after saying "No, thank you," to the offer of a drink—it was the poor women's tempting bait—went to work on Hambridge's farm under the protection of a police constable.

Of course the women pleaded "Not guilty," and the reverend magistrates retired to consider and consult. They were a very long time about it. Then they came back into Court and passed sentence on sixteen of the women; seven were to be imprisoned with ten days' hard labour, and nine were to have seven days' hard labour. Here was a sentence to be passed by clergymen of the Church of England, on respectable working women, some of whom had children at the breast!

We had been prepared for the infliction of a fine, and one of our men was in Court with the necessary money all ready. He thought he would only have to hand over the sum named by the magistrates, and the women would be free; but imprisonment with *hard labour* was what none of us had bargained for. When this scandalous decision was known, Chipping Norton was turned upside down; and as Holloway—he was chairman of the Oxford district of the National Agricultural Labourers' Union—said, "If I had not been present, violence would have been committed." The people were raging, for no one had the least idea that such a law existed as was now brought to bear on them with such terrible force. It fell on them like a thunderbolt from the blue. There was a riot in the town that evening, and I believe the police there had to telegraph for assistance not knowing how far the people might go. The authorities thought discretion the better of valour, for instead of waiting till the morning as was usual, they had the women driven to Oxford in a brake, and they were locked up in Oxford Gaol at about six o'clock in the morning.

The press took the matter up, and the action of the Bench was unanimously condemned. One pressman who was sent down by a leading London paper to inquire into the matter said, " Act 34 and 35 Victoria, c. 32, which is an act to amend the Criminal Law relating to violence, threats, and molestation," did not allow the option of a fine. The magistrates might have allowed the women to stand out on their own recognisances, binding them " to come up for judgment when called upon," or they could have left out the hard labour.

The feeling was intense; we were roused to a man; petitions for the immediate release of the women were sent up to the Home Office, and our Leamington Committee acted at once. I, and also Attenborough, issued an appeal to the county and the public. The result was subscriptions amounting to eighty pounds came in—five pounds of the sum in pence—and we arranged that the sixteen women should have five pounds apiece presented to them on their release from prison. When their sentences had expired we got two brakes with four horses in each and went to meet them as they came out of Oxford Gaol, and took them right into Ascot, headed by a band of music. When we arrived in front of the house of the ringleader of the farmers, I gave each of the women five pounds.

I remember we had a crowded meeting at Chipping Norton—there were nearly three thousand around the waggon; and there was an indignation meeting held in the evening, when we declared that we must have (1) extension of the franchise; (2) repeal of the Criminal Law Amendment Act; (3) appointment of stipendiary magistrates. It was high time that the clergy should be removed from the bench. The resolution carried was, "That clerical magistracy is most unsatisfactory; and in order to secure a better administration of the law, it is considered absolutely necessary to establish a stipendiary magistracy, on account of class influence on the present administrators."

I had long been of this opinion. I had seen too

much of this class influence on the Bench and had felt it too. I heard that the parsons' friends got up a kind of counter demonstration to express their sympathy with the poor persecuted prosecutors. Well, it was the opinion of every right-thinking person at the time that these clerical magistrates had thoroughly disgraced themselves, and had shown what spirit they were of. By their decision they lowered themselves in the opinion of all Christian people; and those of us who had felt bitter against the parson and all his works, felt more bitter than ever; we said, "Not a single solitary parson shall sit on the bench to deal out left-handed judgment, if we can help it."

It was a bad and a discreditable day's work those parson-magistrates did at Chipping Norton, both for themselves and their like; and those responsible for it were down in our black books for many a month, aye and many a year after. What man among us, let alone our wives, could forget that sixteen honest and respectable labourers' wives had been cruelly sentenced to imprisonment and hard labour? We said, "An insult has been passed on every working man and woman in England. Would such a punishment have been meted out to sixteen of the farmers' wives in the neighbourhood? Never; the parsons would not have dared to do it. These Church of England gentry have too often trampled ruthlessly on the labourer in the past; but we had our own Union now, and they could trample on us no longer. I held then, as I hold now, that clergymen have no business on the Bench, and I am glad to see they are becoming fewer and fewer. It is a matter of common knowledge that clerical magistrates are always the hardest and most severe, and yet they call themselves ministers of One Who always tempered justice with mercy.

CHAPTER VII.

THE GAME LAWS.

IN the May of 1873, I gave evidence before a Select Committee on the Game Laws. Sir Michael Hicks Beach was present, and George Ward Hunt was in the chair. I suppose they had me up before them as being a representative man of my class. Well, on that occasion, I made myself the Agricultural Labourers' mouthpiece, and they got more home truths than some of them liked to swallow. I remember that they tried to find out what the labourers thought on some other subjects. Owing to the Union, Hodge had grown to be something more than a nonentity in the landlord's eye; his poor poll had popped up above the employers' horizon, and they were beginning to get very curious about him. This Hodge had feelings and opinions of his own, no doubt; perhaps they had better know just what they were in good time, and so be prepared for the evil day, which might come all too soon, when Hodge would have a *vote*. Then he would no longer be only a dumb, human man, a son of Adam on a level with the earth he tilled, and with no more voice in the ordering of affairs than the horses and sheep he tended. He would be a political man with a voting voice; and what was still more dreadful, there would be a great many of him.

Yes; this Hodge was growing up fast now to political manhood, and the landlords must examine the creature and see what stuff he is made of; how much blind side he has got and how much right side, so that they might be sure of catching hold of him, and gripping him well, and then bringing a little paternal pressure to bear on him—all for his own good, of course.

Said the Tories, " If Hodge will not sit quiet and be paternally governed by us, he will have to be paternally persuaded; but rule himself he cannot, and must not. What with the Elementary Education Act of 1870, and the Ballot Bill of 1872, we shall have to look sharp after him and his ways; and if he gets the vote he will be kicking over the traces altogether, so we must take him in hand in good time, and train him in the way he should go, that he may vote as we wish, because of course *we* know what is best for him."

I had taken notice of what landlords had been saying and doing for many a year; I do not say that all the landlords were cast in the same mould or made of the same metal—no; there were some who were our true friends, who were no wolves with a sheep-skin thrown over them—but the majority of them were against us in their hearts, and a number of them showed openly that they were all for their own class,—that they and their kind came first and second and third, and Hodge nowhere. I knew the class pride and the pocket pride of them, so when I came up before the Committee I had made up my mind that I would not be drawn. I was determined to keep to the Game Laws, and they pretty soon found out that evidence on that head was all they were going to get out of me. I could speak, but I knew how to keep my mouth shut and my teeth locked up tight. Teeth-locking was a trade I had learned early in life. If I had been a weak and fearful man, like scores of my class, I might have got lock-jaw when in the presence of my "betters," and "the powers that be." The timid labourer did, and his masters thought that he was so dull and slow that he had next to no wits, and so had nothing to say. That might have been so with many—and small wonder at it—but there were hundreds who could speak out and up when they were by themselves, but who had learned the trade of mouth-shutting and teeth-locking as soon as they could talk, and before they knew what bird-scaring was. A man with the weight of many masters on him learns how to be dumb, and deaf, and blind, at a very early hour in the morning.

I gave the Committee what information I could on the subject they were there to inquire into. I repeat it, with additions, because a good deal of it holds equally good now. I told them that the agricultural labourers strongly objected to the Game Laws. I said, " We think such laws are a great scandal to the nation; we feel very hot about it and it is spoken of at all our meetings; I and others have spoken very strongly against them lately, whenever we have had the chance. The day that the Poaching Prevention Act of 1862 became law was a black day for the labourer; from that time onwards he might at any hour be subjected to the indignity of being assailed and searched by the police officer."

I remember that, when the Act was first brought to bear, I myself was compelled to make a definite and positive agreement with my employer, in regard to perquisites I had when I was at work. When wood-felling and timber-cutting I always liked to have a basket of chips and dead wood to carry back with me; it was a customary perquisite. I understood that the new law allowed a police officer to seize me and search me, if he saw me after dark with anything which aroused his suspicions. As I did not give over work while it was daylight in the short days of winter, that of course exposed me to the chance of being way-laid by a police officer and being searched for game. The very thought of such an indignity made me, and the other labourers as well, exceedingly angry, and I determined to take what steps I could to prevent myself getting into trouble. I made this wood perquisite a matter of bargain between me and my employer, so that I took it as a legal thing. I knew well enough that the word of a police officer is generally believed before a working man's: that I couldn't help. I knew too, that if an employer thought well to prosecute a man with wood found on him he could do so, unless there was a thorough understanding between man and master. That thorough understanding I took care to have wherever I went.

Two women in my village suffered through this matter of perquisites. It has been the custom in our neighbourhood, ever since I was a boy, that if a woman was cleaning turnips in a field she might take two or three, once or twice in a week. Farmers did not object, as a rule, and I have often seen women when turnip-cleaning put some into their aprons before the employer's face; it was an understood thing. Farmers have made such offers of turnips to me, and of course I have taken them; I no more thought of refusing them than I would have thought of refusing to put my week's wages in my pocket. After the Act came into operation the police set upon these women—respectable, honest, married women—searched them, brought them before the magistrate at Warwick, and charged them with stealing turnips. The police prosecuted and gave evidence, and the women were fined. It was a very great shame, and the village people were very bitter and sore about it. If tidy, decent, hard-working mothers of families were not safe, who could be? Before this Act passed a working man might trudge home at night in peace, carrying his little basket or his bundle of perquisites; but after it became law the insulting hand of the policeman was hard and heavy upon him. 'Twas as if so many Jacks-in-the-Box had been set free to spring out on the labourer, from the hedge, or the ditch, or the copse, or the field.

There was a man arrested in 1866, within forty yards of his own house. He had got two or three sticks which he had picked up in the road going along. They had been blown out of the hedge and lay on the highway, so he put them in his inside pocket, for they were only bits. A policeman jumped out on him and caught him by the collar and said, "I have a strong suspicion that you have game." The man said, "I have no game."

"What have you in your pocket then?" said the policeman.

"You can soon see what I have got," answered the man, and he showed his inside pocket in which were the few sticks.

The policeman then said, "You must go along with me; I must lock you up."

At that the man began to be a little bit resolute. He felt as I should have felt when the police officer said he would lock him up, and they had a little bit of a tussle in the road. After that I suppose he was charged with resisting the police. They took him off and locked him up that night. He had his hearing the next morning and the case was adjourned to the following Saturday; but there he was kept two or three days, and was not bailed out. Our blood was up at all this; so we collected evidence in the village, and employed a solicitor for him—we found the money to do it—and the man was discharged. I knew him well and had worked with him, and I had never known him dishonest in my life. The whole affair was a burning shame. And it was not the only case of the kind that came under my own notice.

There was the case of my own brother-in-law. He was walking home from Warwick to Barford, a distance of about three miles, along the highroad. It was near Christmas time, and he had been to buy the week's groceries. He was a bit late, which was only natural and to be expected; for I daresay he had not got home from work till six or half-past six—the usual time—and when he had had a wash and a cup of tea it would be something after seven in the evening. Then he would have to walk into Warwick, and do his business, so he would be on the road home about ten o'clock at night. Well, as he was walking innocently along, a policeman stepped out of the ditch and laid hold of his collar, and said, "What have you got in your pockets?" My brother-in-law said, "I have nothing there but what is my own. I have been in to Warwick to buy the week's groceries." The policeman let go, but of course my brother-in-law was very angry, and so were we all at such an indignity. This was what a decent, law-abiding man was exposed to when walking along the Queen's highway on his own private business. How were we to know that we had a legal remedy for such treatment as this? We were ignorant of the law, we feared the law, and

I think we had good reason to, considering the way it was often administered. We did not know that the law says if a constable stops a person when he has no reasonable cause to suspect him of having come from land where he had probably been in search of game, the man so stopped might county-court the constable for undue search. I did not know it myself till the Committee told me such was the law. But suppose my brother-in-law had county-courted that policeman for undue search, the chances are that the police or the magistrates would have found a way out, and the policeman would have got off scot free, while the labourer would have had a black mark against his name for ever after.

After a bit the police made so many mistakes that they grew a little more cautious. Lord Leigh, chairman of the bench at petty sessions, reprimanded them in one or two instances for bringing up cases where there was no real ground for suspicion. But there was, speaking generally, far too much partiality and strong prejudice and class feeling prevalent among the magistrates. I believe Lord Leigh and some others that sat upon our bench always did justice; those we knew, and we said among ourselves, "Oh, if I was to be brought before the bench I should prefer so-and-so, and so-and-so, to try us. Justice would be done; even if the day went against us, we should be sure it was the fault of the law and not of the way in which it was administered." Yes, we are not such fools as not to know a just man when we see him, whatever his rank and standing in life may be. And to a just man, who administers the law justly, I take off my hat.

Why, a policeman in the neighbourhood of Coventry told me, that if a certain gentleman was on the bench, he never dared to take a case of poaching before him unless the evidence was very clear. When that particular gentleman was not there he brought up several cases where there was only slight suspicion, but he got convictions. "We picked our customers in the magistrates," he said.

Then there was a case but last year in the county court. I know of a man who sued a labourer for damages because he did not fulfil his week's work; he had left it at a very short notice. Well, the labourer had to pay a certain amount for damages. But that very same master, only a fortnight ago, discharged a man at a minute's notice. The man sued his master for a week's wages, but the judge nonsuited him, and it was the same judge in both cases!

The only proper remedy for this sort of thing is to have stipendiary magistrates, for they could come and judge a case on its merits. What is a judge but a man after all? The county court judge makes but a very small circuit. He lives in the very centre of magisterial influence; magistrates are the friends of game preservers; and these game preservers are sure to be landlords, with a great deal of influence. If a county court judge gets his table well supplied with game from his preserving friends, he would be something more than human, I think, if he was not hand-in-glove with them. I don't wish to imply that they would judge unjustly of set purpose, or knowingly deliver wrong judgment, or go against the law of the land; but I do say that they would naturally favour their own class, and their own friends, where the law gave them a chance of doing so. I don't know much law, but I have had experience enough of it to be certain that there are plenty of loopholes of escape, which a clever and competent lawyer can slip through by the skin of his teeth, as it were. And the way they do slip and wriggle through astonishes a plain man. I should like to see the magistrates taking circuits, and knowing no game preserver, no landlord, no poor man, till the case is brought before him on the bench. I do not see, for my part, how we can have even-handed justice dealt out in any other way. When a poaching case comes up before them, some of the magistrates seem to lose their heads altogether.

There was a man who most brutally ill-treated his wife, and the punishment he got was a fine of ten shillings and costs. In the very same place, and just a week after, a man was brought up for poaching, and he was fined one pound and costs. He was charged, I think, with aggravated assault on the keeper as well; but, allowing for that, look at the difference—just double punishment in the poaching case! This is one instance among very many of a similar sort. We labourers notice it, and of course we are riled and sore; there is a lot of smothered anger among us at the present time, and there will be till the law is altered.

As to the prevalence of poaching since the Prevention Act came into operation—well, I do not profess to give an opinion.; generally speaking, I can only speak with knowledge of my own neighbourhood. When I was a lad, there used to be a gang of poachers in our village; they went out at night as regularly in the seasons as others went to their day's work and their harvesting. There were, I believe, four or five, or maybe more, of them. The gang broke up some years ago. One or two are still alive, and following constant work; the others are old, or dead. A professional or gang-poacher generally gave it up when he was about fifty or so, because he began then to get stiff, and lost his speed. Poaching means very quick work, and, to succeed at it, a man is bound to be a fast runner, agile, and quick-witted. A little poaching goes on still about my neighbourhood, I regret to say; some few men manage to work by day and poach by night, but such a burning of the candle at both ends quickly tells on them; some will do a bit of rabbiting, say two nights a week, so that they can do their ordinary work all right. I know of one man who did this, and he said he had bought his cow with the money he got for the hares and rabbits and birds he had caught. Still, the younger men now value their own manhood more; they think that a man should work by day and not prowl by night, and I quite agree with them. Times have changed since the thirties and forties and fifties, and men have changed with them.

The bitter, bad days of my youth are, I hope past

for ever; a man was often driven to poach, then, if he wanted to live; now, owing largely to the Union, the rate of wages in South Warwickshire—in what I call my corner of old England—has risen to fourteen shillings, fifteen shillings, and sixteen shillings; risen to a living wage, tight fit though it may be, if a man has a large family to provide for. I am most proud and thankful to be able to say that, for the last winter or two, we have not had a man out of employment the whole year through; every single one has been able to get a job here or there. Before the Union started, the general rule was, no constant employment, and an average wage of nine to ten shillings, sometimes eleven shillings. I have known of labourers who were in the habit of taking a gun with them when they went to work, and as they were going along the road, or perhaps crossing by a field path, if a hare or a rabbit came in their way they would shoot it and bring it home for the wife's cooking pot; and if they had not procured a little fresh meat for themselves in this way, they would never have tasted it at all. That was before the law was passed, forcing a man who carries a gun to take out a licence. If a labourer is bent on poaching now, he uses other weapons and instruments; but poach he will and can if he has a mind to. To my thinking there will be poaching till the Game Laws are abolished. They have done untold harm to the labouring man.

For instance, a farmer would sometimes say to me, "If you see any man setting snares, or in any way destroying game, and if you know who he is, and will report him to me, I will give you ten shillings." Such an offer as this was common enough, and it made tattlers and tale-bearers of the men who wanted to earn an extra ten shillings if they could. It was demoralising, because they had no sympathy with the law, but quite the contrary: I might say that their sympathy with it was limited to a chance of getting an extra ten shillings whenever they could spy on a brother labourer and report him. Then the keepers—who were often turncoat poachers themselves—would be quite ready to buy game eggs of a labourer. Some time since a keeper came to me—he had charge of a sort of preserve, not a regular one—and he said, "If you find any pheasants' eggs, bring them to me and I will give you one-and-sixpence. I will give you the same money whether you bring only half a dozen or half a score." It was a temptation, and this was by no manner of means a rare case; men were tempted like this here, there, and all about.

I remember I once had an opportunity of being a game watcher; but I refused the offer, because I like my bed, and it does not suit me to expose my head for the sake of hares and rabbits. There's far too much made of game, and a pheasant is more of a pampered creature than a peasant, any day of the week. If that isn't turning things backside foremost, what is? Game, game! We have heard too much about it, and had too little of it. Game and their keepers have been as bad as an Egyptian plague to many an honest man. Why I have been watched by a gamekeeper myself; regularly stalked I have been. After draining or hedge-cutting, when I have finished my work at night, he has gone right along my work and beyond, to see if I had put any game or traps there, and he has looked into every hole to see if I have committed myself. The keepers as a rule are men who want to get up cases, and they do not care where they get them from. That keeper, if he had put a hare in one of those holes beyond where I had not cut, and I had gone the next morning and begun my day's work and had unfortunately picked it up,—although I never put a wire there,—he might have watched and come down on me and prosecuted. Keepers have been known to play such dastardly tricks on labourers. I am of opinion that these men would be considerably better if they had hard work to do. They say the best poacher makes the best gamekeeper, and it is more than likely. But neither the police nor the keepers nab many poachers. Sometimes a farmer is reluctant to prosecute a man caught with a hare or a rabbit on him; but to a certain extent the police will compel him. There was such a case, where a man stepped out of his way and fetched a rabbit out of its hole. The police saw him and summoned him. The farmer who rented the land said, "I don't want the man summoned. You had better let it drop"; but the policeman said he should summon the man, and if he did not he should never bother about the hares and rabbits on his farm after.

I gave the committee, before mentioned, examples from my own knowledge of how labourers are made to suffer unjustly, owing to these laws.

"Last Thursday," I said, "I saw a man who was made to pay £1 9s. 6d. because he was getting some liverwort for his afflicted wife. He went into the wood where it grew; it grows by the sides of dykes in woods, and I have often got some of it myself, and other herbs which are very essential to the health of a growing family. I have always used them for mine for years. No doubt the man should have asked leave, I grant that, but I daresay he never thought about it; he only thought of the liverwort. He went just inside the gate and was picking the herb when up marches the keeper, apprehends him, and summons him for trespass in pursuit of game. On that charge the man was tried, and he had the option of paying, or going to prison for twenty-one days. Why, I myself would have got over a gate to procure adder's-tongue or a herb of that description if necessary, and that without a second thought. This man's case is only one of many, there are plenty such."

I said that, "An honest labourer would think nothing of knocking over a rabbit in the daytime, if he saw it and it came in his way, and neither should I. I don't see any harm in it, because in my opinion ground game is wild. The plain truth is, we labourers do not believe hares and rabbits belong to any individual, not any more than thrushes and blackbirds do. I should not inform against a man who knocked over a rabbit or a hare. Has the hare or the rabbit a brand on him for purposes of identification? If I found a stray loaf on the road it would be mine, and so with a rabbit or a hare. But if I found a loaf or a sheep, and they were branded, then of course I should take steps to restore them to their rightful owners."

One of the Committee raised the question of a likeness between game and spirits, and I said there could be no comparison between the two. "Who," I asked, "has ever seen game with a duty stamp on it? I suppose there is a Government stamp upon all spirits that duty is paid for; well, if a man defrauded the Government of the duty on certain spirits so stamped, he would know perfectly well that he was cheating the Government. The stamp would be there to point the moral. Then who ever heard of a cask of spirits running here and there and eating? A hare does though, as many of us have found to our cost. Such a hare may have gone and got his breakfast in my garden, and then after having a feed at my expense, and perhaps doing some damage as well, he may course off to my employer's farm and have another meal at *his* expense. That hare might go coursing and eating from farm to farm, and who is to know where he comes from and whose property he is supposed to be? All I can say is, if I could catch that hare and kill him, I would, and I would carry him home and jug him, and have a tasty meal off him."

To see hares and rabbits running across his path is a very great temptation to many a man who has a family to feed; besides, there is a propensity in every man to look at what he believes to be nice and tasty, let it be winged game or running. He does not believe, either, that it has been created exclusively for one class of the community; and so he may kill a hare or a rabbit when it passes his way, because his wages are inadequate to meet the demands on them, or from dire necessity, or just because he likes jugged hare as well as anybody else. If a man sees unstamped temptation running along before him on four legs he'll run after it on his two, and will knock it over if he can, and take it home and make a feast of it. I should not consider him a guilty person if he did, but he would be run in to prison and run up before the bench in no time, if the police officers or the gamekeeper caught him.

When a game preserver lays the charge, and a game preserver is on the bench, what chance has a poor labourer who has unfortunately stepped out of his way to kill a hare; what chance has he of getting off, poor fellow? Why, none of course. And it is a serious, a very serious, thing, because even if it is a first offence—it should not be counted an offence at all, I think—the man is looked on as a poaching vagabond by all the employing class round about. It is true that his neighbours do not desert him. I myself have taken such men along with me, as good men to work as ever took a tool in hand, but who after such a conviction could not get employment from the farmers. Well,

I have gone with them from one end of the village to the other, to farmer after farmer, but nobody would give them a job. They have not had a farthing in their pockets, and what were they to do? "Oh," they would say, "there's nothing for it but to go back to poaching, and we'll go the whole hog." If it is a first offence a man should be let off with a caution; but I don't see why he should be brought before the bench at all, though I suppose it is heresy to say so.

I remember taking with me on a contract job a man who had been up before the magistrate only once, and the farmer for whom I was working came up to me and said, "You must get rid of that man."

"Why?" I asked.

"Oh, the keeper has been round and I know he would not like to see him at work here. You had better get rid of him or it will cause a noise."

That man had to go then and there, though I was very reluctant to part with him. Even if a labourer does get employment after a poaching conviction, he is watched and suspected; he is looked on as a suspicious character, and the sooner he makes his exit from that village the better, because to live under such spying and suspicion is morally bad for the man; it makes him sour, or reckless and hopeless, and he says, "All right; if I'm to be a marked man I won't be a marked man for nothing," and he goes poaching, out of recklessness and devil-may-care misery.

There was a case which made me very angry. Some boys belonging to our village were going along together; there were two or three of them, the biggest lad a youth of about twelve. A leveret came through the hedge, and the lad took aim at it with a stone, and by chance hit it; it was quite a speculation. What should one of the boys do but run off to the farmer, who happened to have the shooting on his own farm. The boy sneaks to the farmer, who comes to the other lad and makes him give up the leveret. I don't complain of that; but that farmer was heard to say, "Ah, if that boy had been a bit older I would have sent him to Warwick for a month." Suppose the lad had been sixteen years of age, and had incautiously thought, "There is a hare, I'll have a throw at it," and had hit it and knocked it over; he would have been immediately apprehended, his prospects would have been blasted, and there would have been nothing for him left to do but to go away from his home and his parish. He would have gone with a cloud on him, and if he did not happen to be independent and resolute, he might be ruined in character as well. And what for? Surely a boy is of more account than a leveret!

I have worked, and I would work, with a man who has been convicted of knocking over a hare or a rabbit, but I should not care to go to work with a man who had taken a hen off a roost. If the poacher was a good workman, it would be all right in my eyes and in the eyes of the other labourers; but let a man who had stolen a hen off a roost be ever such a good workman, I should have nothing to do with him; I should keep clear of him and avoid his company, because he would be a felon. What is more; if I saw any man steal six-pennyworth from an employer of mine, I should at once report the man.

I have never poached myself, not once; but I take no particular credit to myself on that account. I am glad I can say truthfully, as I said to the Committee then, "Gentlemen, I never poached, but I don't glory in it." Why for should I? This I know: Suppose I am had up before the magistrates on some slight charge not in any way connected with game, and I see sitting on the bench in close proximity to the magistrates a certain squire, on whose property I had once happened to knock over a hare or a little rabbit. If that squire recognised me, as he would be sure to do, he would tell the magistrates, and they would be very likely to inflict on me the heaviest penalty in their power. The case taken on its own merits might have been trivial; but I should have to bear the whole rush of the law, because the magistrates were friends of this squire who had a bitter feeling against me. This is no imaginary instance, for such partial judgments and unfair punishments have been far too common, far too much a matter of course.

I have also witnessed the strong feeling of game-preserving landlords against small or large tenants who interfere with game. I have known farmers who have been boycotted by their landlords simply for destroying game; regularly sent to Coventry they have been, as if they had committed some crime or outrage against humanity. Farmers have been great sufferers; I know this, and I have seen it. During my travelling up and down the country I have seen fields all over rubbish. I have asked the reason, and the answer would be, "Oh, it's on account of the game." Some of these fields had not been cultivated for two and three years; there were several such fields in the neighbourhood of Wells, and also around Cromer. Not only there either; for in my own time, when going to work in different parts of the country, I have seen a great number of crops that have been eaten down by game, and fields where rubbish has grown up faster than the crops have. In my opinion, and it is a deliberate one, cultivation of crops throughout the country has been lowered considerably, and some land has been thrown out of cultivation altogether, by the plague of game.

I do not think the preservation of winged game is so detrimental to the interests of farmer and labourer as that of the ground game is. For instance, if a man takes and plants a twenty-acre field, and there is no ground game to play havoc with the crop, it would perhaps grow fifteen or sixteen bags of three bushels each per acre; but if there were a number of hares and rabbits eating off it continually, the man might not get above ten bags. Then of course he could not afford to pay his labourers so well, nor would he employ so many. The farmer has to pay the same rent for the field, and if he finds his crop so messed about and spoiled he loses spirit.

It is a general rule that game farms are badly cultivated. When harvesting is on, we labourers always had an eye to the rabbits. If one was started, you would hear a cry of, " Run him down, knock him over, run him in ! " and we always do, if we can, just as we should knock over any other wild thing which was good eating. The farmers are often very sore about this custom. They will perhaps bring three or four men, and shoot all the rabbits they can. I remember a certain field where the farmer and his friends would come; when we got down to a particular corner of it, they would stand there with their guns and shoot away wholesale, and not leave one rabbit for us. After I had been served that trick, when I began to work in the morning I used to look out for myself. If I started a rabbit and it ran among standing corn I would run it in if I could, but of course I would be careful of the corn, for I should have to cut it, and and as every one knows it's a miserable job to cut trampled corn. There are many who are not so careful, not out of malice or wanton carelessness, but because the rabbit goes so fast that they follow on as fast as *they* can without thinking, till it is too late. Then the man has to pay after his fashion as well as his master.

I have said more than once in public, that on account of the Game Laws many a farmer was obliged to take land at a disadvantage or he could not get it at all; and not only that, the right of shooting is often reserved, and men come on the farms, break the fences, destroy the crops, shoot the rabbits and hares the farmers have made fat, and go off with their spoil, grinning at the poor farmer, who has to bear it as best he may.

Labourers have suffered too in their humble way. Most of the villagers in my neighbourhood have allotments and gardens, which, to the poor man, are as important as the farm to the farmer, and they have found that hares and rabbits are very destructive to little crops. I told the Committee that I had just lately asked a policeman whether, if I wired a hare on my garden he could apprehend me, and he said he could report me, and if the Commissioners thought it a case that would be convicted they would empower him to summon me. I had the policeman's statement *verbatim* in my pocket. The Committee said the policeman was mistaken, that the law was not so. But that, unless I assign away my rights to do so, I may capture a hare or a rabbit on the land I occupy, and nobody can punish me for it where there is no preservation of game. If the policeman was wrong, how were *we* to know? The labourer has mostly to learn *his* law by bitter experience. There was nothing said about game on the allotments in our part of the world. I occupied twenty perches of land unfenced. Of course no man would go to the expense of putting up a wire fence against hares and rabbits which some one else might claim. Why, at that rate, he might be asked to put up a deer fence! I know only too well that our gardens are very much liked by the hares; and there is a feeling abroad among us, that if we meddled in any sort of way with the game, or it was known that we had killed any on our ground, we should soon hear of it, and have notice to quit. A labourer may have some nice young cabbages coming up, and they may be done for by the ground game, but he is afraid to move actively in the matter, for he feels as if " Notice to quit" is being shaken like a rod over his back all the time, when it's a question of game. Labourers looking at their little gardens will see their greens and broccoli eaten, and will say, " Just look here what a mischievous affair!" If some one says, " Why don't you catch them?" "Oh," they will say, "it would not do, we should lose our land." We feel that we must be very careful; that we must not commit ourselves.

I said to the Committee that we, on our part, had our allotments from year to year, paying twelve months in advance; mine I had had eight years. I had been careful never to knock over a hare on my allotment field, I should have been a marked man if I had; and if the police had come about it I could not have answered for the consequences. A man with any of the Englishman in him won't stand knocking about. I was extra particular after the start of the Union, both for my own sake and on account of the credit of the cause. In 1871, if I had been placed before the magistrates of the county of Warwick in a case of larceny or felony, I might have been leniently dealt with; but after the start of the Union it would have been another pair of shoes for me.

The Game Laws

They would have dealt out to me the utmost rigour of the law. So I had to be wary and look to my goings.

I told the Committee I did not want to see game exterminated. I want to see it reduced. A man may preserve game on his own ground if he wishes to—far be it from me to wish to interfere with the liberty of the subject—but he must keep it on his own ground and not let it go spoiling other people's, and making promiscuous meals at the poor labourer's expense. A man may breed twenty thousand hares if he so choose; but they should be bred for his own sport and not for our plague; they should be kept on his own grounds, and not be running and skipping about and doing injuries to the helpless tenants. Catching is having as far as game is concerned. It comes pretty much to this, it is partly a question of identification and partly of feeding. I should say to a preserver, "Have your stray game and welcome, whether it is the sort that flies through the air or runs on the ground, if you can identify it. If a partridge comes picking about in my garden or allotment, or a hare runs about nibbling, and you can point to a brand or a stamp on them and say, "There, that's my mark, and so is that," I should say, "Very good, remove them to your own land and the quicker the better; but as they have damaged my good stuff I must ask you to make compensation—just compensation and not a farthing more, for I don't want charity."

But, if the preserver could not identify them as

his beyond dispute, I should say: "Then they are wild and astray; they have been feeding at my expense; I am going to put them in my pot, and feed on them; they will make very good eating."

Or, suppose I am walking along the public road, which is everybody's property, and which I, with many others, help to keep in repair by contributing to the road rate, and I see a bird or a hare or a rabbit; it may belong to Brown or Jones or Jack Robinson for aught I can tell, and it is wild on the highway. I think I should be quite justified in catching that hare and killing it. That is my view, and it is the view of agricultural labourers generally, however much some of them, through fear, may pretend to the contrary; and that view will not be altered while the Game Laws remain in force. My remedy—I don't consider it perfect—is to abolish the Game Laws, which are an abomination in our eyes, and to make the law of trespass strict; but anyhow let the Game Laws be done away with. I should like to see game free, as free as it is in America; and that day of freedom will come yet, though I may not live to see it.

I was very glad to have my bit of a say to these gentlemen about the Game Laws, not that in my opinion special committees and commissions, Royal or otherwise, do much practical good. They ask questions, and draw up reports, and issue Blue Books. There is a lot of talk, and there is a sight of printer's ink and papers used up after the talking is over-past; then perhaps a little Bill gets dragged through the two Houses of Parliament. There is too much sitting and talking, and not enough pushing and acting. They are better than nothing; but they are lame kind of things when they are going at their fastest. The Ground Game Act of 1880 has done something for the farmer, but we do not want all this tinkering at a worn-out kettle; we do not want a little letting out here and there of this legal strait jacket, and a little granting of this and that right to shoot ground game, when we believe that ground game is wild and ought therefore to be free. Pheasants are on the increase, I hear, and they will go on increasing while there are rich men who can afford to preserve and breed them. Well and good; so much the better for the market in the end. They are dainty eating; and so they ought to be, for they are fed and guarded and kept close, better than many a poor man's children can ever be. I should like to see the day when a plump, well-fed pheasant would be within the reach of the labourer's purse, but that will not be in my time. The whole question was a sore and burning one with us in 1873, and it rankles still.

There was another thing I was glad of; I showed the farmers once more that I was their friend, and that when giving evidence before influential landlords seated together in a place of power, I was not afraid to speak up in the interests of the farmers as well as of the labourers.

At most of the meetings I addressed during this period, I spoke a great deal of the tenant farmers' condition, and I spoke to them also. I remember addressing some six hundred farmers at Dorchester fair and they listened most attentively. My interest in their affairs was growing stronger the more I looked into the whole question of land tenure and rent. I found, and on good authority, that a quarter of the whole class had no security whatever for the investment of any capital. A paper of their own had said that at that time there were some four hundred farmers nearly bankrupt, and another four hundred who only managed to hobble on at all by the good will of the landlords.

Of course, if this was a true statement, and I believe it was not an exaggeration, then the farming interest was the most depressed and most insecure of any great industrial branch of employment in the kingdom. Farmers had their vote, and now they had the ballot; political power was theirs, but for all that, instead of using it to advance their own rightful interests, they would crawl snail-like to the feet of the squire, and vote as they were bid. The ballot was getting safer, and there was less intimidation and spying, and fewer attempts were made to mark a man down in a note-book according to the way he voted. I know for a fact that, in those early days of the ballot, the Conservatives started what we christened the "Tory Ticket Dodge." When an election was on, there would be Tory agents stationed at the entrance to the polling place with note-books in their hands. Up would come a farmer to vote. "Your ticket, please," says the agent. If the farmer had one, and gave it up, it showed publicly that he was a Tory. If he had not a ticket telling him to vote for the Tory Candidate, the agent would put a black mark against his name in the notebook. If the farmer's name was not known to him he would take good care to find it out. It was a disgraceful attempt to make the ballot of no use; but these Tory agents and their note-books soon had to make themselves scarce. Since the Ballot Act had made voting safer, and so strengthened the independence of the voter, and since the Union had been started, the labourers—the more thoughtful men among them—were asking themselves why they should not have the vote also. A shorter working day and a little better food were giving some of them the time and the spirit to consider, and to resolve that they would not long be politically non-existent if they could help it.

CHAPTER VIII.

MY VISIT TO CANADA.

ABOUT this time I was contemplating a visit to Canada and the United States. Meanwhile I took a short run over to Ireland, and made myself acquainted at first hand with the condition of the people. From that day forth Home Rule was down strong on my programme. The lowered condition of the farmers, their attitude to us, and the question of emigration for the betterment of the labourer, were forcing themselves on our attention. At one big meeting —it was at Newbury, if I remember aright—I was moved to speak strongly on these subjects, more especially as I was shortly going to Canada with a view to putting labourers' emigration on a sound basis. I told them at the meeting that some three hundred thousand had emigrated from our shores during the last year, and this represented forty millions worth of bone, sinew, and muscle. I was going to Canada and the United States in August, but if I found there farmers who bought and sold, and had both sides of the bargain, I should say: "Stop where you are, chaps; the crows are as black there as in England." But if I found that country across the water the true home of the working man, where a labourer was free to make his own terms; if his boy could sit down on the same form with the boy whose father has got wealth, and could read out of the same book and write on the same slate, and where the poor man had the same political power as the classes above him; then, if farmers here would not treat their labourers like men, let the working men follow me, and I would lead them across the broad Atlantic to the fruitful fields of America, with its ninety millions of acres yet untilled.

It was a question I had neither shelved nor muzzled, but I had appealed to the farmers again and again. Though I had advocated the rights of the farmer as much as those of the labourer; I had met with insult and contempt in return. Farmers had locked out our men by scores and hundreds, till we had been compelled to raise two thousand pounds from the public to save the men and their families from starvation.

I considered the farmers guilty before God and man; and I said if they began to play that dodge again I would make them before that day twelvemonth know the worth of a man. I wished to treat them with the utmost courtesy and friendship; I had fought their battle before the Game Committee of the House of Commons, and they knew it. I had depicted the farmers' wrongs as vividly as ever I had those of my fellow-labourers. I had shown the great landlords of the country that they were doing an injustice to farmers as a class; and yet, in face of my humble advocacy and honest statements, they had tried to put their heel on the necks of my coadjutors and myself.

All this had only put me more on my mettle; it had not frightened me. Some of the foolish farmers in my part of the country had said the Union would only be a nine days' wonder; but one who had known me from a boy had said: "If Arch has got anything to do with it, before you can make him loose his hold, you will have to cut his head off." It was the truth, too. When I saw some six hundred thousand tillers of the soil in slavery and mocked, I would traverse America from end to end, if I lost my life for it, in trying to raise my fellow-labourers to better things. I was not afraid of walking, if there were no other means of transit open to me; for I had been a Methodist preacher twenty-five years, and had walked seven thousand miles on my own conveyances to preach, and had never had a sixpence from the State. And whether I preached to peasant, to peer, or to prince, I should preach alike to one and all the same grand old Bible doctrine:

> "Let Cæsar's due be ever paid
> To Cæsar and his throne;
> But consciences and souls were made
> To bow to God alone."

I had never in the course of my life bowed a single muscle in my neck to the monster of oppresion, and I was not willing that any man should. I would go cringing to the feet of no mayor, public officer, farmer, or landlord, while Almighty God stretched above our heads the broad canopy of the bright blue sky, and under our feet the green sward. Those of us who had been accustomed to what some people called ranting preaching, were prepared to take our stand where thin-skinned gentlemen would feel a delicacy in treading. We would tread firmly and we would march very far. We did not ask for miracles, we only asked for what was possible and right.

I said: "Place the labourer in a free market, in good surroundings, under happy conditions; invest him with his rights; give him a moderate stake in the soil of two or three acres to till for himself. Let landlord and labourer and farmer shake hands, the cordial handshake of good fellowship; let them pull in one boat and let them have an eye to each other's interests; let England be the land where this shall come to pass, and then, should a foreign foe rashly put foot on English soil, the stalwart labourers of England, well fed, independent, honest and industrious, would rise up in their thousands, and would march out to fight for country and for Queen, and the world would be made to know that on the face of God's broad earth there is no better soldier than the English labouring man.

"But much as I love my country—and no man could love her more—if I see within her men who are slaves; men allowed to pine, and sink to death and the grave; men denied the common necessaries of life, who yet spend their lives in unremitting toil for the millions above them ; I shall raise my voice and use my influence on both sides of the Atlantic till England, the rightful mother of men and not of slaves, shall be driven to consider her ways and be wise, and treat her industrial population as she ought. Let England be the fruitful mother of men, the nursing mother of heroes ; then may her banner be waved proudly aloft, and no man would more delight than I to see stamped on her insignia that which she should ever carry waving in the winds of the world :

"'England—the pride of the ocean, the first gem of the sea.'"

Emigration as a complement to migration was the next piece of work I had to tackle ; there was no getting away from it. Though thousands of acres here were lying uncultivated, and thousands more were only half tilled, yet we could not find work for hundreds of our men. Emigration agents were busy, and they hankered after the English labourer, who had the reputation of being the best of his sort. We had been discussing the matter at our meetings for some time past. The Canadian Government wanted men ; many had already gone, and hundreds of our people were now turning their faces towards the American continent ; but neither they nor the Executive of the Union wished their exodus to be a wild-goose chase.

They came to me and said : "We want you to go over first and look at the country, and then come back and report to us, so that we may know what prospects there are of our being able to better ourselves."

I said: "I'm very willing to go."

I was then given an official mandate from the Union to "proceed to Canada and to make myself acquainted with the condition and resources of the country as a field for emigrants of the farm-labourers' class." This direction and request expressed the wish of eighty thousand members of the National Agricultural Labourers' Union and not only of them, for there were thousands of labourers who had not yet joined the Union, but who—and I am proud to quote the words —"looked upon Joseph Arch as their natural and incorruptible representative in the eyes of the world." The Allan Line offered me a free first-class passage out, and the White Star Line offered to bring me back. I accepted both offers.

I started from home on August 27th, 1873, going from Leamington to Liverpool. At the latter town I met a deputation of the Trades Societies in the evening, and they gave me a cordial reception and expressed their full sympathy with the object of my journey. Arthur Clayden, a member of the Consultative Committee of the National Agricultural Labourers' Union, accompanied me. On Thursday, August 28th, we went on board the *Caspian*, Allan Line steamer, Captain J. Trocks being in command, and we loosed from Liverpool about 2.30 p.m.

I remember how kind and attentive Captain Trocks was. I was a bit upset for three days, for we had a tumbling sea and variable winds, so he let me have my meals on deck, and told off his cabin boy to wait on me. There were two or three distinguished Canadians among the passengers. After I found my sea-legs I enjoyed every knot of the voyage. I remember passing by the rocks of Newfoundland and New Brunswick on our left, and Labrador on our right; the scenery on both sides was splendid. When we left the rocks behind we steamed up the Straits of Belle Isle, with the Island of Anticosti in view; then through the Gulf of St. Lawrence to Father Point, where a pilot came on board to guide us safe into harbour. On the right from Father Point is the Island of New Orleans. For more than a hundred miles I noticed, as we steamed along, beautiful cottages, bright little homes standing in the midst of small farms. These holdings were mostly the property of the French settlers. I noticed that the farming was slovenly, and I heard that these settlers were much behind the times in their agricultural methods. As I looked at them I thought of what the English labourer could do, if he had such a chance of acquiring a bit of land. The scenery was a feast to the eye on both sides.

On Sunday, September 7th, we steamed into the harbour of Quebec beneath a bright sun and surrounded by some of the finest scenery I ever beheld. We landed safe and sound at St. Louis about 1 p.m. At about 3 p.m. we crossed the St. Lawrence by boat, and went to the St. Louis Hotel, where we were met by Mr. L. Stafford, the Emigration Agent, who paid us every kind attention. I can well remember how glad I was to get a quiet night's rest.

On the Monday morning, after a refreshing sleep, I felt a new man, and I set to work without loss of time. I met the editor of the *Quebec Mercury* and then I went to call on Mr. Lesage, Deputy Minister of Agriculture and Public Works for the Province of Quebec. The interview was a long and satisfactory one. Mr. Lesage listened with the closest attention to my plans, and we discussed a practical emigration scheme. The idea was to supplement free grants of land with some provision for immediate starting in life of the man without capital. A rough home would be built, seed would be supplied and a portion of land would be cleared. The cost of this to be repaid after the third year or so by annual instalments, extending over say ten years. This seemed a feasible and sensible scheme. I left Mr. Lesage feeling very cheerful, and I said to myself: "This is a promising start; cheer up, and go ahead!"

I also inspected the Emigrants' Home, an extensive pile of buildings, clean, airy, and commodious, erected by the Dominion Government for the temporary accommodation of emigrants, and placed under the capable direction of Mr. L. Stafford. As many as a thousand people could find shelter here. The women had a lofty wing set apart for their especial use, there were admirable lavatories, there was a capital laundry, and ample cooking accommodation. Upstairs the large rooms were fitted with sloping, sleeping benches. Altogether, I was surprised and delighted with the Home. It looked like business.

On Tuesday, September 9th, I visited the King's Bastion, which is some three hundred and seventeen feet above the level of the sea; also Wolff's monument, which is near the city gaol. In the afternoon I again waited on Mr. Lesage and got my railway papers.

On Wednesday, 10th, I received an invitation to dine with Lord Dufferin that evening. During the day I paid a visit to the Huron Indians, and was very much interested in what I saw. The men make snow-shoes and manufacture leather articles, and the women execute very fine work for ladies. In the evening, Lord Dufferin sent a carriage and pair with attendant servants to fetch me, and the guard fired a salute when I entered the citadel. The dinner was a splendid one, and I relished it very much. There was a brilliant assemblage to meet me, and I had the opportunity of conversing with several public men. I had to go rather early, and for that I was heartily sorry. No one could have been more kind and courteous than Lord Dufferin was, and I fully appreciated the honour he did me, and through me the working men of old England.

It is my opinion that, if all the Colonial Governors were like Lord Dufferin, we should have no difficulties and no 'strained relations' with our colonies. I do not say this because he treated me so well, though of course that counts in my judgment, but because he was the man I found him to be—a man of catholic tastes and sympathies, a scholar, and a gentleman. A more honest man, with views more simple and genuine,

I never conversed with in my life. He was a worthy representative of our Queen, and he treated us right royally. He was good enough to order the Colonel of his Life Guards, Colonel Denison, to take me and Clayden round the country, and show us the ropes. The Government paid all our expenses. It showed plainly that our mission was regarded as of high importance, and we were treated as persons travelling on business of public moment.

On Thursday, September 11th, Clayden and I, having been provided with the requisite passes and credentials, started by the Grand Trunk Railway for Sherbrooke and the eastern townships. We travelled the whole day through wonderful scenery, and I remember we were well shaken up in the train. I got a rapid view of the country as we shot through it. Often and often during the tour I wished for eyes in the back of my head, and at each side as well, for I was eager to see everything, and to pass nothing by either. On Friday, September 12th, we started for Stanstead, a village some forty miles from Sherbrooke. We passed through several villages and by a number of farms, and I did not much like what I saw. The farmers looked careworn and toil-worn, and this was partly owing to the rough life, but more to the scarcity of labour. As I looked at some of them I thought to myself: "A jolly-faced, beef-fed English farmer is a Merry Andrew by the side of his scarecrow of a Canadian brother. The burly Englishman can take life pretty easy when all's said and done; he can jog to market comfortably on his stout cob, or bowl along in his gig, and do his bit of business in the market, and have his dinner at the ordinary and his chat, and then jog comfortably home again to his wife and his supper. His farm isn't so big, but then he can have it well under his eye, if he wants to; and there are labourers and to spare, if he likes to employ them and pay them a fair wage. But out in these eastern townships it is a very different tale."

Labour was terribly scarce. A man owning some three or four hundred acres would have one hand, or at the most two; and miserable, haggard, lank specimens of humanity they would be, with the hopeless look you see on a man's face when he knows he has more work before him than he can hope to overtake. The farmers hereabouts seemed to have but one idea in their heads, and that was to see how much work they could squeeze out of the hired labourers. I had a little conversation with one of these owners of hundreds and hundreds of labour-starved acres. He said the labourers' hours were from sunrise to sunset during five months of the year, and from six to six during the remainder, and he said he did not think there ought to be any difficulty in getting more labourers over.

"Oh!" said I, "don't you just wish you may get them?"

"But," said he, "look what good pay we give; a dollar and a quarter a day, and board and lodging!"

"I can't help that," said I, "good pay or poor pay,

you want not a man, but a slave. Well, since the Union has been started the English labourer is more determined than ever he was to be a true Briton, and as you know, 'Britons never, never, *never* will be slaves.'"

That farmer dried up; he knew it was the truth. He looked surprised when he should have known better. They say the self-made men among them are the worst task-masters and the hardest drivers. No doubt the struggle they have undergone has hardened and embittered not a few of them. There seemed to be good openings for young farmers with moderate capital, however. One enterprising man, a farmer of the right sort, had shown what could be done. Within six months he had sold ten head of cattle, of his own raising, for some ten thousand guineas; and for one splendid animal, which had gone to England, he got three thousand guineas. This was something like business.

When at Stanstead I visited the Methodist chapel, a splendid building erected in 1856. I also saw the new College in course of building. I remember what a rough buggy ride of forty miles we had, through village and bush. I think we started at five in the morning, and when we reached home again about six o'clock in the evening I was all spattered with mud, and regularly tired out. A visit we paid to Scottstown was more cheering. Mr. Scott, a Glasgow man, was the moving spirit of this new and thriving settlement. He had bought some thousands of acres, and had erected a saw-mill on the Salmon river, which I thought a first-rate plan. There were over a hundred Highlanders hewing down timber, and the engine driving the timber-saw was a sixty horse-power one. Later on they meant to use water power.

Everywhere was a spirit of industry, common sense, and enterprise. Mr. Scott said he would build a cottage for each settler and family, and grant them an uncleared plot; also, he would buy the felled timber from the man, thus enabling the settler to clear his land and get ready money as he went along.

I had a long ride with Scott—a shrewd Scot if ever there was one—and I was much struck by the immense resources of this part of the country; the land was splendid and was crying out for cultivation. The owners are chiefly French Canadians, and they cannot hold a candle to a Scotch or English farmer of the better class. After visiting Lennoxville, we made our way to Sherbrooke again, and then took train to Montreal. As we rushed along we had a fine view of river, and mountain, and fertile valley; it was truly a magnificent country. We put up at the Donegana Hotel, and I remember we could not make head or tail of the French language, which was the one used. It was so much gibberish to me. We reached Montreal on September 16th, and we went to a Provincial Agricultural Show there, and the Committee received us very well. I saw some splendid specimens of short-horns; in fact I never set eyes on better. There were a few fine South Downs and some very good horses on view. The cereals and roots were remarkably fine, too.

They told me, and I soon saw it for myself, that the soil in this part is wonderfully prolific. One man had grown, he said, thirty tons of Indian corn, and nearly the same in root crops, to the acre, and he could get enough off one acre to keep a cow for a whole year. Here was a land of plenty! Why, it was a vast mine of agricultural wealth. There were farms of one and two thousand acres, well cleared, lying waiting for the farmer. All this made me realise how ignorant the average Englishman, more particularly the labourer, is of the immense natural wealth of Canada. Seeing is believing, they say; well, I saw, and could not but believe.

I had an interview of quite four hours with Mr. Pope, the Minister of Agriculture, a shrewd, intelligent, and practical man. While in Ottawa I had several important interviews with heads of departments. I had more than one with Mr. Lowe, Secretary of the Agricultural Department; and Sir J. A. Macdonald, then Prime Minister, gave me a most cordial reception. He very strongly urged the colonisation of Manitoba, where there were millions of acres waiting for the settler. It was plain enough that in this country there was lack of labour and loads of land. I took care to see something of the sights as we went from place to place; but, business came first and pleasure after. We got to Toronto on September 25th; a long, tedious journey of four hundred miles. I remember that Colonel Denison met us at the station and took us to the Queen's Hotel, and we were the honoured guests of the Provincial Governor during our stay in Ontario. Both the Premier and the Attorney General gave us a warm welcome, and we dined with some of the chief men of the City at Government House.

The practical result of our visit here was very satisfactory and promising. The Dominion Government and our Union would co-operate systematically, and so make certain of a regular and continuous supply of first-class English agricultural labourers. A registry was to be kept, and a list of wants and requirements was to be regularly sent over to our Union to be distributed.

That piece of business done, we had a bit of pleasure. We took a trip to Niagara Falls. It is a sight I can never forget; it was stupendous! it was sublime! As I gazed at that mighty mass of rushing, roaring, foaming water I could but exclaim, "O Lord, thou layest the beams of Thy chambers in *mighty* waters!" What waters they were! It was a most glorious, a most solemn, almost a terrifying spectacle. Never did I realise, till that day, how small a thing is man when brought face to face with the mighty forces of Nature. It was an overwhelming sight, and one which I would not have missed for worlds.

From Niagara we went to Pelham township, driving through a fruitful land of orchards and vineyards. We went to an Agricultural Show at Fenwick, and met a number of prosperous farmers. There were magnificent apples, pears, grapes, and melons ranged on tables in long rows, and there were some of the finest specimens of beets and swedes any man could wish to see. There were splendid teams of horses here, and also at an Agricultural Show at Hamilton, where we met the mayor and town council. Indeed, both these shows were a treat, and were a credit to all concerned. In this district of Pelham there were some thirty thousand acres of fertile land divided among three hundred owners. The average was one labourer to each farm, and so of course the land was labour starved. At least half-a-dozen labourers more on each farm were required. We noticed that the farmers in these parts drove very light traps, which could go at a great rate, and so cover long distances in a short space of time. As the distances from place to place are very long in a thinly settled country, I suppose it was another instance of old mother Necessity and her daughter, Invention.

At Hamilton I remember the Trades Unions gave us a capital supper and a very pleasant evening, during which they presented me with an endorsed address. We went over the Wanzer sewing-machine factories, and fine ones they were.

On October 2nd we returned to Toronto and lunched with the Lieutenant-Governor of Ontario and the provincial Cabinet. I remember we had a sharp debate. In the evening I had an interview with Mr. Lowe, of a satisfactory character, and the next day we started on a tour through the Muskako district. We travelled on the Northern Railway to Washago, through woods brilliant with the tints of autumn. I had never seen such colours on the trees at home. We went up the river Muskoka to Bracebridge, enjoying fine bracing weather.

Bracebridge consisted of a few streets which were nothing but hard mud tracks, the houses were built of wood, and the people were ragged, and poor-looking. There was no air of prosperity about this township. We drove to Huntsville next day, some twenty-five miles through a wild forest track. It was a rough, uncultivated country, and only fit for rough hardy men. As they said: "The land here pretty well takes the life of a man, and these great tracts are little better than white elephants." One farmer who had had to carry on a hand-to-hand struggle with the Indians, and had often gone in hourly fear of his life, said that, after years of constant hard labour, he had only managed to properly clear forty acres. Ordinary clearing meant cutting the trees down within about three feet of the ground, and clearing away the felled timber. When a man cleared his stumps away too it showed he was going ahead properly. I know we could not help saying: "Well, if our men at home would work as hard and live as hard and leave the drink alone, and *had the same chance of owning their land*, there would be no call for them to forsake their native country, as they are doing and wishing to do."

Why, some of the poor labourers of Wilts and Dorset were rich, by comparison, with these owners of hundreds and hundreds of acres, but—and it was a mighty big *but*—the labourers had no hope of rising, and these toil-worn men were working their *own land*, and what would be the land of their children after them. They were not pouring their labour away like water into a pail without a bottom. The hardships in Canada were the voluntary hardships of free men toiling for themselves and their children.

While in the Bracebridge and Huntsville districts I went into the woods, and the lumberers found I could swing an axe with the best of them, and they offered me high wages to stay.

"Oh, I've another axe to grind," I said, "and I must lumber along to other parts."

The Huntsville country was a fine one for fishing and shooting, and did not belie its name. I remember the church there was a log one. When I got back to Toronto, I again had an interview with the Premier, and laid my plans before him, and then I went to the Great Northern Railway Office to meet a deputation, and had I remember a very long and sharp debate on the emigration subject. I also saw some friends who had come out and who were doing well. On October 8th we visited Paris, and there I found an old schoolfellow, and several friends from the old country. This schoolfellow had done uncommonly well. He had been twenty-five years in Canada, and now he owned his house, and had some two thousand pounds out at interest. He was foreman of extensive flour-mills, the property of the mayor, with whom I lunched. I remember we met some of the leading men at the mayor's house, and we heard stories of the early struggles and trials of these pioneers. It did my heart good to see master and man flourishing and working away side by side, each respecting the other in good fellowship.

We saw the Agricultural Show, too, and drove over Mr. Brown's farm. We had a beautiful drive to Bowpark, through a country as different to Huntsville and Bracebridge as night is to day. The farms were in a high state of cultivation, and the land looked like a fruitful garden. It was a great temperance place; tea and coffee and iced water were our drinks. The air was as bracing and as good a pick-me-up as sparkling cider, so no wonder drunkards were a rarity. This Bowpark farm was a splendid one of some nine hundred acres. The soil was alluvial deposit, and it was nearly enclosed by the Grand River; it was a picked spot. The cattle were the pick of their kind too, and the Berkshire pigs beat any we had come across in the old country.

"Oh, yes," I said, "a man may be a king among farmers out here, if he only drops the fine gentleman, and puts mind and muscle and money into his business. Let some hundreds of Englishmen with a nice bit of capital, and go and grit, and youth as well, come out and serve for a year or so under a successful emigrant farmer, and then take up their own farms and employ good English labourers, who can have land of their own in turn, and then emigration will be as good as a tale come true."

We travelled to London next in a Pullman's car, and a deputation of the Town Council received us in the station, gave us tea, and showed us round the city. I went to see the oil works and sulphur springs in the neighbourhood, and here and all around I noticed the general prosperity. Poverty was not to be seen; only comfort and abundance in this western district. It was a bit like the Promised Land we thought, and I wanted to plump down and settle there myself. The old friends I met gave me some valuable advice and information, and they said: "Oh there's no doubt but it's a good land for good men. If a sober, honest, hard-working man comes hereabouts he can be a landowner. He can have a good farm of his own, a well-built house, money out at interest, his children well educated; and, what's more, they may, if they've got it in them, rise to good positions in the State. There's nothing to stop them. They may rise and rise if they have a mind to; if they've the will, the way's all open."

Aye, that was what the labourer at home wanted, an open way to rise up and up, if he had the wish and the brain and the grit to do so.

By the time I got back to Ottawa on Thursday, October 23rd, I was nearly used up; but though I was so tired and had travelled all night, I had breakfast, and went to see the Parliament opened. It was a grand display. I remember the place was so full we had hard work to get a bed. On Friday, October 24th, I went down to the Parliament offices and had a final four hours' interview with Mr. Pope and Mr. Lowe. It was as satisfactory as could be wished. The Government was fully prepared to co-operate with the National Agricultural Labourers' Union in an extensive emigration scheme. They wanted me to accept an appointment under the Dominion Government in England, and they offered me a much larger salary than I ever got from the Union; but, in the first place I never was an office-seeker, and in the second—though it came a long way first in my mind—I was bound heart and soul and body to our Union and our cause, so I said, "No, thank you."

It was agreed that a book of warrants for assisted emigrants should be forwarded to the Leamington office, so that in future adult members of the Union would be entitled, on the recommendation of their President or secretary, to a grant of about forty-five shillings towards the passage out. It was a great point gained when Mr. Pope said he would take my signature or the secretary's, instead of a clergyman's or a magistrate's, to the forms of application for assisted passages.

I had promised to bring out the following spring a hundred picked men and their families and see them safely through to their lots, if the Ontario Government would co-operate by clearing a portion of their free grants and helping them to build cottages, so that work would be found at once, together with enough capital to start and go along with.

I had also arranged with the Government Emigration Agent at Toronto that a registry of applications should be kept for such men as might prefer service for a time, and that a list of places with full particulars as to working hours, wages, and accommodation should be kept, and should be certified to as genuine by the reeve of the town whence the application came. We thought more men might go to Toronto, as there was a demand, and then they might settle themselves on the land later if they wished.

So, after having settled all this, I could leave the Dominion feeling that something had been done, and that our mission had not been in vain. We started for New York on Saturday, October 25th; but owing to the lateness of the season, and the unsettled state of affairs in New York, we made up our minds to investigate the United States of America more fully at some future day, and start to old England on November 8th, by the *Republic*, White Star Line.

When at Brooklyn I took the opportunity of hearing De Witt Talmage preach; and he gave us a most telling discourse on the text, "*He began to be in want.*" I preached myself in one of the Primitive Methodist Chapels there on Sunday, November 2nd. During my tour I was able to preach at a good many places, and to take part in prayer meetings.

There was a thing that made me very angry while I was in New York. I may say—and I do not say it from vanity; there was nothing to be vain about, for it is the way of the people over there, who like what is new and will make a noise over it—that I was regularly besieged by interviewers; papers heralded my coming, and the day after I got to the city nearly every New York paper had a description of me. What made me angry was a hoax played on me and the citizens by some sort of a Working-Man's Union. Some-one said to me: "Do you know that your coming was announced two months ago, and also that you would address a monster meeting of working men in the Coopers' Institute?" The papers spread it abroad, and at the appointed hour thousands were assembled; and I was told that an entrance fee was charged.

"Who," I said, "got up this infamous hoax?"

"Oh, the Central Working Men's Union, or some such organisation"

"Then," said I, "I'll have nothing whatever to do with them," and to that I stuck. When one man after another besought me to address them, I said, "No, you have acted dishonourably towards the public, and whatever may be your American customs, we in England know only two things, right and wrong. You had no authority for publishing my name as a speaker at your meeting. You did not even know where I was, and yet you deliberately advertised me all over the city, and so associated my name with an imposition. I wish you good morning, gentlemen; I'll have nothing whatever to do with you."

So I gave the New York Trades Unionists the cold shoulder—the coldest I had got—and I am of opinion they richly deserved it.

On Monday, November 3rd, we set off for Boston

at the urgent request of a deputation of citizens. I remember, on the Tuesday I went to Reedsferry to meet some old friends, and spent a very pleasant time with them. On the Wednesday they gave me a downright splendid reception in Faneuil Hall at Boston, when I spoke for more than an hour. Wendell Phillips was in the chair, and there was a number of prominent politicians present. The Hall was beautifully decorated for the occasion, and no man could have asked a more hospitable welcome. After the meeting, at which there were over four thousand present, I went to a banquet at the Adam's House Hotel, got up by the Trade Societies. It was a very nice affair indeed, and I enjoyed my dinner. I am not above saying that I am every inch a John Bull in the latter respect; I have said so before, and I will say it again. I do not care where the dinner is—it may be in Windsor Castle (though I have only taken light refreshments there at the Queen's Diamond Jubilee Garden Party to Members of Parliament), or in a labourer's humble cottage—but if it is a good one, I thank God for it and fall to. I am a good trencherman as they say, and so every healthy hearty working Englishman should be.

The Mayor of Boston drove us to see the chief places of note, and I visited, among several others, Senator Sumner, the poet Longfellow, and Jeanie Collins the philanthropist.

On Friday, November 7th, I was back in New York, said good-bye to friends, and went on board the *Republic*. The next morning at 8 a.m we started for home in pouring rain. We encountered some very rough weather, and I remember only too well the great waves rolling over the deck with terrific fury. One went over my head and smashed one of the boats in. The storm lasted about thirty-six hours.

On Tuesday, November 18th, I rose at 8 a.m. and went on deck. It was a beautiful morning, and calm. As we entered St. George's Channel I caught sight of Old England, and I had a good look at her, and as I looked, the poet's words came into my mind :—

> "Breathes there a man with soul so dead
> Who never to himself hath said,
> This is my own, my native land!
> Whose heart hath ne'er within him burned,
> As home his footsteps he hath turned
> From wandering on a foreign strand?"

Ah! the heart of Joseph Arch burned within him; and I am not ashamed to say that a tear came to his eye too, when he saw the old country once more over the tossing waves; "England, old England, the home of the brave and the true and the free," rose before me once more, and about 12 p.m., November 18th, 1873, I again set foot on her shores.

CHAPTER IX.

MY VIEWS ON EMIGRATION.

WHILE I was away in Canada I had left the Union in charge of a vice-president who had been a right hand to me all through. When I came back I took up my special work again, and made a report on my tour and its results. Clayden had been sending home some capital letters to the *Daily News*—our old and faithful friend among the big London Dailies—and they were afterwards reprinted in his little book, " The Revolt of the Field." Directly I landed I put myself in communication with the Union, and on December 1st we had a meeting of the Executive Committee at Leamington. In the evening we held a great meeting at the Circus, and I gave an account of my stewardship to an audience of about four thousand people. The Rev. F. S. Attenborough presided, and with him on the platform were the following :—Messrs J. Campbell, R. W. Collier, H. Taylor, A. Clayden, Ball, Edwards-Wood, J. E. M. Vincent, E. Russell, C. R. Burgis, E. Haynes, R. G. Sweeting, G. T. Haigh, and W. G. Ward.

I made a long speech, and I told them that, for a long time, I had been one of those who could not see that emigration was the right thing, and was strongly opposed to it. Now I had been brought to see things differently, although when I commenced the agitation in 1872 it was to better the condition of the farm labourer in the land of his birth. I said, "I love my country; but I love my countrymen better. The name of a country is nothing to me, if she leaves her countrymen out in the cold. The name of a nation is nothing to me, if she leaves her honest working-men to live upon starvation wages and die in the wards of the workhouse." Because I loved my country I was cut to the heart by the knowledge that the flower of her labouring men were being driven away from her, and I said to myself: "So be it; if they've got to go, let them go to an English colony, that they may be Englishmen still. Canada is calling for our men; let them then go to her, and she shall be their mother by adoption, for Canada is England's loyal daughter." I said to them: "I think I showed myself a true-born Englishman by going to Canada. I had many pressing invitations to go to the States before I went there, but as an Englishman I went first to that land where the British flag waves." There was a thing which Clayden and I noticed, and in one of his letters he says: "It is a somewhat significant fact that even the smallest village has its drill sheds for the use of volunteers. Canada is prepared, and can take care of herself. Any one who has seen the tens of thousands of lithe, active, intelligent, well-disciplined men of Canada, and has witnessed the innumerable proofs of their patriotism, loyalty, and respect for the parent institutions, will never again have one moment's uneasiness respecting its future." It was true then, and I believe it is just as true in this year of the Diamond Jubilee of Her Most Gracious Majesty Queen Victoria—God bless her!

It was a loyal and a prepared Canada in 1873: it is a loyal and a prepared Canada in 1897. I told them that night that I also was the same man as I was on February 7th, 1872. I said: "I fear no man's frown; I court no man's smiles; but I will have honesty, truth, and justice between man and man, whether it is between prince and prince, or beggar and beggar." I went over as an officer of the Union, as a representative agricultural labourer, and all the honour done to me was done to the Union and to the men I represented. I said: "His Excellency, the Governor-General, who is the Queen's representative there, gave me the right hand of fellowship, and listened as attentively to what the representative of the farm-labourers had to say as if I had been the Archbishop of Canterbury." I felt honoured, but I was not uplifted.

"I found a few old Tories in Canada," I told them; "but I must say, for the honour of the different public men of Canada whom I was introduced to, and with whom I had conversations, that a more business-like and a more honourable class of men, as business men and men of responsibility, I never met with. But my business was not to curry favour with officials; my mission was to do business with them; and when I laid my programme before them, they said they would consider the question, and let me know."

In two letters I had, one from Mr. Pope, and the other from the Hon. Mr. McKellar, chief of the Department of Public Works, Ontario, I received the fullest assurance that the Government of Canada, both Provincial and Dominion, would do their utmost to facilitate the emigration of the farm-labourers to that country, and would pledge themselves that the members of our Union emigrating there should be properly looked after and cared for.

The audience cheered, I remember, when I gave them that assurance. There had been, as there always is, and ever must be, men who had said, "Oh, be careful, be *very* careful about sending men to Canada. Look at the Brazilian fiasco; take warning by that." I told these cautioners that it was no good throwing the Brazilian scheme on my shoulders, for I had opposed the emigration of those poor men. Lord Carnarvon, too, rose in the House of Lords to ask a question concerning the poor emigrants who were "suffering in Brazil as the victims of that merely capricious man."

In the first place I was not a capricious man, and in the second, I had nothing to do with the Brazilian mess. I went on to tell the audience something about the plans we had made, and what they must expect if they went out. I said: "I will give you my plans with regard to the free grants of land offered by the Government. There may have been some misunderstanding and some misconception with regard to those free grants of land. I am satisfied of this: if any man goes out there thinking that, because he has got a thousand pounds or two in his pocket, he is going right out into the bush to make his way there, and have a lot of powdered-haired flunkeys to wait upon him, he will be terribly taken in. I visited, not only those towns that had been settled some thirty or forty years, but those districts which had been opened only about ten months. I was determined to see what bush-life was, and what a lumberer's shanty was. I have stripped to my shirt and chopped the trees, and I can tell you that, in sunny England—the land of the free, as they call it—I have suffered ten times more hardships in the rural woods than any Canadian suffers in his shanty in the pine forest. More than that; I have suffered these hardships for sixteen and seventeen shillings a week, for which a lumberer of Canada offered me forty-five shillings. The honest, industrious, hard-handed farm labourer is just the boy to do it; and any English farm-labourer—when the Government have carried out their plans which I am promised they will do directly, and for aught I know they may be already building shanties for Englishmen—who goes there will have a shanty, and a comfortable one; for I insisted that they should be built in a way by which chastity, virtue, and decency should be maintained. Perhaps you may say that is strong—what right had you to insist on that? But I say that the mission on which I was sent was not one of a frivolous nature or character.

"I wanted the prosperity of my fellow working-men to be enhanced. I wanted to see them on lands where their children could be well educated; I wanted to see the morals and virtues of these people cared for. Let me say, too, that, if anything has given me greater pleasure than another, it was that in the remotest district I visited—which I may say was twenty miles beyond the confines of civilisation—I found the log-hut built by the workmen themselves, in which they assembled every night in the week for their mental improvement and religious purposes, and where, on the Sabbath day, three times they assemble to bow before the Throne of our Creator. Then, during the week these places were used as schools for their children. As an Englishman, I value the morality, the virtue, and the chastity of my family; and where I could not take my dear boys and girls, I would not advise my fellow-labourer to go. But I say this to-night, that, if I had not upon my shoulders the responsibility that I have in this country with regard to this movement, and if the farm-labourers of England will release me from my responsibility, I will take with me my wife and family, and will go to Canada; for it is a better land than England. I am not come here to play the part of hypocrite. I did not go to Canada to play the part of hypocrite. Some of the papers have said I was 'sold,' that the Governor-General of Canada had bought me, and that I induced others to go where I would not go myself. But I say again, to-night, that, if the farm-labourers will now release me from my responsibility, Joseph Arch is the man that does not fear bush life, but can wield his axe as well as any man, and he will go to Canada to-day.

"Now, fellow working-men, these are plain facts; they are simple statements. Next Spring, the Government of Canada will send over to our office the number of cottages they have built, and the number of allotments they have cleared. Now, I wish to be clear on this point. The Government is prepared to build a comfortable and decent log-hut for a man and his wife and family, to shelter him the moment he arrives. They will also clear from five to six acres, and they will find you the seed to plant it. The moment you get there, you may begin to put your spade in the sod. I will not tell you that every stump will be out; but I will tell you that on some of these stump lands I have seen some of the finest crops of corn growing I ever saw in my life. The Government, I repeat, will find you seed; they will find you from five to six acres of land ready for the deposit of that seed; and as soon as you have got your land, and at any time find your strong arms idle, the Government will take up every day, every hour, of your spare time, and will pay you the equivalent of five shillings a day for working on the colonisation roads. More than what I have said—beyond that five or six acres of cleared land, you will have a hundred acres uncleared given to you free, and the sooner you can clear that the better. But here I would say, for the information of persons present, that if you think of going to settle upon these free-grant lands, and of cutting down every stick upon the land, it would be a mistake. I should like to see some of the timber left, and I will tell you why. I pointed out to the Government the imprudent conduct pursued with regard to cutting down timber. They had driven it so far away from the towns that it costs a large price to obtain it.

"Now, with regard to hired labour. I met with bodies of farmers who said they wanted English farm-labourers if they would come out. I wanted to know what would be about the price they would give for that labour. They said they could not talk about that; but I replied, 'You must tell me there or thereabouts.' Some farmers told me candidly that, if they could get good English farm-labourers, they would give them at the least twenty dollars a month, or £1 a week, besides their board, a good cottage to live in with their wives and families, rent free, all their fuel found for them, an acre of land attached to the cottage, and the run of a cow among the farmer's cows. I tell you, gentlemen, this is not mere theory. I went to a friend of mine, who sat beside me in Barford school, and he told me that every man had got his cow; and he took me round to show me what a splendid cow his man had got. With regard to food allowances, what did I say to the Government? I said, 'Gentlemen, I would rather you would pay these men in hard cash, and let them sit round their own tables at home.' I believe in family fraternity; and if there is anything that does my heart good, it is when I can sit at the table with my dear wife and family with a good joint of meat. For my part, though, I never saw a leg of mutton on my table since the day I was married.

"But I saw plenty of joints in Canada, plenty of great lumps of beef in working-men's houses; and I do say seriously, that it is the ambition and glory of every loving father, whether he works in a smock-frock or not, if he has a father's heart, to sit at his own table and cut the food for his own family. Nothing delights him more. As an Englishman then, it appeared to me that it would be better in Canada, if the farmers were to pay the wages in full, if they unanimously said they would rather pay good wages and let the men be in their own homes.

"Now for a few facts. I went into the city of Toronto and met one of our Union men, who left Hertfordshire, and who landed in the month of May last—he, his wife, and his wife's sister. They all went to work, and I found that, up to about October 2nd, the woman had sent her father—who was then on the parish at Hitchin—ten dollars to comfort him, and they had saved one hundred dollars into the bargain. I met also three of our poor Dorsetshire slaves. They are not slaves now. One of them, Charles Davies, because he had dared to join the Union, and had got his wages raised from ten to twelve shillings a week, was told that he would have his allotment taken from him. He said, 'I will go to Canada'; and to Canada he went. He went to Paris, where some of my old schoolmates live to-day. How did I find him? Not the poor poverty-stricken man he was in Dorsetshire. He was at work upon the Great Western Railway of Canada, at five shillings a day. He had got five cords of splendid firewood, all his own, to face the winter with. He had twenty bushels of prime potatoes that he had bought, and he had got them all in his cellar; for, mind you, they have got cellars in their log-huts. 'Now then,' says he, 'Joe, you come down to-night to our house, and spend an hour or two with me.' I went down to his house, where he had with him his two fellow-labourers from Dorsetshire, who only went out last April. Since then, one of them has paid the fare for his wife and family to come out. I went into the house, and what did I see? I saw on the table a lump of roast beef weighing about sixteen pounds. He said, 'This is not all, Joe.' 'Well,' I said, 'let us see the whole.' He took me into the pantry, and there hung a quarter of beef. Said he, 'I gave five cents a pound for it'; that was twopence-halfpenny. 'Now,' said he, 'come here'; and he showed me a couple of pigs that he had given a dollar and a quarter for (five shillings), which, I am satisfied, in the English market he must have given twenty-four or twenty-five shillings for. 'Now,' said he, 'that is all my own.' It was clear that neither men nor women in Canada need starve; and that is only one of the scores of cases that I witnessed.

"But now I must give you just a little about the dark side of what I saw. You will bear in mind that I am not going to speak disparagingly of any particular district. I speak of things just as I found them. In the Eastern townships there were three of our Union men who were not receiving the wages they expected to receive; but I must tell you that the men seemed in good spirits. I will tell you what they said, 'We are not paid as well here as up in the Western province, but we do not mean to despair. We are in the country, and it is big enough to move about in.' They never talked that way in England, because they never had anything to move about with. I happened to be with the man who engaged them, and I believe him to be a good man. 'Now,' said I, 'how is it these men are not getting the wages they anticipated getting?' Well, of course there were several excuses, but I would not admit of any excuse. They wanted to make me believe that the English farm-labourer in Canada had to work for a few months on rather low wages in order to learn his business. I said, 'Well, gentlemen, you are talking to one who was a farm-labourer from nine to forty-seven years of age, and you tell me I have got to come to Canada and pay a certain premium for my apprenticeship at forty-seven years! I will not believe it, and I will not have it.' I went up to one of the farm-labourers and asked, 'Is this man a good labourer?' The reply was, 'He is a very good labourer.' 'Then,' said I, 'pay him the full amount of his wages.' I did not leave it there. I went down to the Ottawa Parliament, and laid the case of these men before the Minister of Agriculture. He wrote down to that neighbourhood, and the last time I saw him, I was told that the men had got their rights. That was what I saw, and all I saw, of the dark side of the question, and that is not much to make a bother about.

"What is that compared to the dark side of the labourer's picture in England? What is to be said of poor Gooch, the victim of the spleen of the farmers of Bedfordshire? And yet we are told by the great Leviathan, the *Times*, that we can have justice if we like. There are some people perhaps who are anxious to settle this question, and to solve the problem of the English farm labourers. If the landlords of this country would do as Sir John Pakington suggested at a very early stage of this movement at the Worcestershire Chamber of Agriculture, they would solve the problem at once. But we are not content with Sir John Pakington making speeches to Chambers of Agriculture; we want him to put his sympathy into a practical form. He has the land, and we ask him to set the example. Now, I maintain this, that the problem to be solved is connected with the very strength of the farmer's position in this country; and I say that, if our programme is not very speedily carried out, many of the farmers of England will do what the chairman said they would, 'Weep for the crust they wasted in years gone by.'

"Now about our Union programme. We do not want to carry it out as it was carried out in my poor father's time—about 1838 and 1839—in the village of Barford. I can remember the circumstances which happened when I was a boy. The men wanted some land which they could plant with vegetables. They got the land; but how much was doled out? Half-a-quarter of an acre, and for this they had to pay at the rate of £3 8s. 6d. an acre, while the farmer on the other side of the hedge, paid only thirty shillings an acre. We must have some different process to that. I say, Let the farm-labourer have from three to four acres of land, to cultivate for himself and his family, at the same price as the farmer. But I say also, Give to the farmer, too, security for what he puts into his land. Members of Parliament have talked about what they believed would solve the problem, and the landlords talk about solving the problem. I say it would be a good thing. We want it done; and we want it done between this and next Spring. I do not want to see my fellow-labourers leave the country. I do not want to see the bone and sinew, which are to make this country rich and wealthy, leave us; but I say this, that if the farm-labourers of England are to be treated in the future as they have been in the past, I would say to all honest, industrious men, willing to work: 'Throw down your tools and go to the country which will give you wages, and give you land and opportunities of independence.' Now, is there anything unfair, is there anything dishonest or unjust, in my request? I ask, Would not the artizans in the towns be better off if the farm-labourers had got land to till? What is the reason why your vegetables come so scarce into the market? Because the land is held in large plots, and the farmers are too proud to cultivate vegetables on it. There is no class of the community which would not be the better by it, as well. There has been a dispute as to the increase in the yield; but we have the case of land at Long Itchington yielding only fifteen bushels, which now that a working man has got it yields sixteen bags. The landlords would be wise if they would do something to settle this question. They have done nothing yet; but we will agitate until they have done something—until by emigration the men have left the country, and the lands are left to till themselves.

"The Chairman wishes me to say a word or two about the emigrants' homes in Canada. I must tell you that I visited every emigrant's home in every town I went into, and I found everything that a humble working-man need wish while he is travelling through the country. I inquired very closely as to where they put the men, and where their wives and families. They said, 'We put them in that room; there, we put the single young men; there, we put the single young females.' And I say that in the Dominion of Canada, they have in their emigrants' homes displayed the greatest caution and respect for the virtue and chastity of our farm-labourers' wives and families, when they get there.

"Now, I just want to say a word or two upon another point, and that is with regard to my plan of the labourer having some land to cultivate for himself. There is a great deal said about the heavy taxation of the country. I see the Chambers of Agriculture are discussing as to what they shall do with their poor paupers. Well, if I was a member of a Chamber, I should make a proposition that the men should have some land to till for themselves. A gentleman said to me the other day, 'Why do you not teach these men to be provident?' 'Why,' I said, 'do you talk like that? How can a man be provident who has not enough to live upon?' What a monstrous thing to ask a man to save when he does not get enough to find his family bread! Why, it is mocking us. What I say is this, 'Put the men in the position to be provident; and, if they are not provident *then*, blame them.'

"Now, what I want to say in this country is that the farm-labourer, instead of being a forced burden upon the taxation of the country, and on the pockets of the people, should be allowed to make his way for himself by being put in a position to do it. When a man has three or four acres of land, I ask how many of such men, when they come to the downhill of life will become chargeable on the parish? How many will want to go to the parish doctor? Farm-labourers with three or four acres of land would scorn the action of becoming paupers. You would do the same as I did to the parish doctor when he came into my home and wanted to cut my children for the cowpox. I quickly showed him the door. Let the labourer have three or four acres of land, and he will not be a pauper. I appeal to every honest son here, whether he would under those circumstances be summoned before the Board of Guardians to pay a shilling a week for his poor father or mother in the Union Workhouse, if he had three or four acres of land to cultivate? If my plan were carried out, you would not have five per cent. of the poor agricultural labourers' parents in the Union that you now have. They would teach themselves to love them and take care of them."

I finished my speech by thanking the Trades Societies, and acknowledging the obligations our Union was under to them for their friendly aid and advice. Then I ended up by saying, "I tell my opponents that, while I can raise my voice and there is a single link of slavery left upon any single agricultural labourer in England, I will agitate this question until he is free."

During the discussion after, some questions were asked about the winters in Canada, so I said, "I tell you that I have seen men, my own schoolfellows, who have been eighteen, nineteen, and twenty years in Canada, and they tell me that they like the winters of Canada better than the winters of England; and I am sure that any man with the will to work has no need to feel the Canadian winters more than those of the old country. It's true I have not been in Canada during the winter, but I have been with truthful men, and have made the closest inquiries into the matter, and I am perfectly satisfied on the subject."

The following resolution was unanimously carried:—"This meeting desires to congratulate Mr. Arch on his mission to Canada; and, seeing that emigration has become a necessity to the labouring classes as a means of advancing their interest, this meeting is pleased to know that the Government of the Dominion of Canada is prepared to bring the matter to a practical issue by co-operating with the National Agricultural Labourers' Union."

"Thorough does it," was my motto whilst in Canada, and I soon convinced my audience that I had not been on a pleasure trip. They saw I was no work-scamper. The reception I met with that day, both at the Committee and at the evening meeting, was most gratifying to me. It was a good wind up to what had been a very anxious time; though I got all the enjoyment and benefit out of it that I could. I had, however, been on the strain and stretch from the moment I sailed for Canada in August till the close of that first of December; and I can tell you, I felt when it was well over that I had earned my night's repose; and I took it, too. Now in these later days, when my warfare is ended, I look back on that Canadian tour with great pleasure; I would not have missed going for a pot of money. I was living and learning every minute of every day, and I fulfilled my mission to the best of my ability. I remember I had some fine fun with the farmers over it, and I made several of the cantankerous ones wince. The mere fact of my being received so well was bitterness and gall to them, and I could not resist rubbing it in a bit when I saw how they took it. I told them that an English farm labourer was of some account in Canada, that he was reckoned a very valuable article, that the farmers there wanted more of such a good thing, and that if he was not exactly worth his weight in gold, it was because he was worth more, and that he could turn into a farmer himself if he had a mind to.

The farmers made wry faces at all this and some of them blustered away; but they dared not say much, because I had been to see for myself, and they had not. I proved once more the truth of the saying that knowledge is power, and the more of that sort of power I could get the better, for it was very useful to a labouring man fighting our Union battles. Then some would say to me, "Well I suppose as you were sent over on an emigration job, that was about all you did." "You are mistaken there," I would say; "I killed a good many birds with my stone, just as many as my stone would kill, in fact. And if I did most of my bird-killing in Canada, it was not because I had no chance of knocking over a turkey buzzard or two in the States—or a spread-eagle for the matter of that. Why I had not been in Canada five days before a deputation of wealthy men crossed the frontier from the States, and wanted me to go back with them at once. But it was Canada first, where the English flag waves; and the United States another day. "Oh," some would say, "but you can't have seen much of the country tearing through it at the rate you did, and on Union business too." "Oh, didn't I?" I would answer. "I got a firm grip of the country as I went along; the rivers, mountains, lakes, and forests I saw are fixed in my memory, and will remain there as long as memory lasts. And I took care to see something of its aboriginal inhabitants, too. I went into four or five Indian settlements, and slept in their wigwams; and I never took a revolver with me, nor was I ever in any way molested.

"What's more, I preached in the log huts of forest clearings, and in the stone-built chapels of town and city. I drove miles through country fertile as a garden of Eden, and tramped with lumberers to their daily toil in the vast and lonely primeval forests, where civilised man has never trod before. I dined with the great of the land and supped with the humble: I fared like a prince in gorgeous palaces, and I fed like a labourer in humble shanties. I met old friends, and I made new ones. And wherever I went in my journeyings to and fro in that great and prospering country—a country I was proud to call an English colony—I met with hearty welcomes and good cheer, and many an honest 'God speed you,' warm from the heart, sent me on my way rejoicing. I set more store on the friendliness and good will of my fellow-men in Canada than all the rest put together. We want more of it in England. When landlord and farmers and labourers, when employer and employed, can sit down together, and rise up together in a spirit of good fellowship, then the millennium will be at hand, when it is said the wolf and the lamb shall lie down together; but to my thinking the wolf has got to become lamb-like, or else, if we try it on too soon, the lamb will be there, but he'll be inside the wolf, and the beast of prey will be master of the field."

Then some men would say, "Well, Arch, what conclusions have you come to about Canada and emigration to there?" "Well," I would say, "the conclusions I have come to are, that the colony offers splendid opportunities to a man who is prepared to face a rough life. He has plenty to eat and plenty to drink. He rolls his bed down in a big shanty, and before he turns out to work in the morning there is always plenty of good meat, bread, and coffee for him; he has not, like his English brother-labourer, to commence work on an empty stomach. The lumberers supply their men with very good food. The standard of living is far higher than it is in England, the rate of wages much higher, and the cost of living much cheaper. Clothing, however, is rather dearer. In the winter the clothing is all lined with flannel and the trousers are stuffed into waterproof top-boots. It is a rough and ready life, but there is plenty, and above all there is *hope*. A man there may rise, and the knowledge puts life and spirit into him. He says to himself, 'I may get on if I've a mind to, and I *have* a mind to'; and on he goes, felling, and clearing, and planting, and reaping, and building, and flourishing, he and his family, like a patriarch of the olden days in a new land. Why I would go myself to-morrow, if I could."

At this they would say, "Oh well, if what you say is true, and you would go yourself to-morrow, there's something in this emigration after all."

My saying I would go myself influenced a number of men. "If you would go but can't, why, we can go and will," they would say; and they did, scores of them. For some time after this, the emigration went on steadily; but then, as now, I only looked upon emigration as a disagreeable necessity, not as a thing to be recommended. I could not bear to see our best men pouring out of the mother country when I knew we wanted them badly.

I consider that it is largely owing to this emigration movement that we have such great tracts of land in England out of cultivation now. The best men have been drained away steadily for years, and the result is, that to-day, in this year of 1897, it is becoming very difficult to find practical labourers from thirty to thirty-five years of age. We have only boys and old men left; the best have gone abroad, and as far as I can see they will continue to go whilst land and labour are divorced. Migration not emigration is the cure I cry for now, as I cried for it in 1873; but with migration must go partial redistribution of land and readjustment of land tenure. Free the land of the legal fetters that hamper its transfer, and you help to free the labourer and put him on his feet. If he finds he has a bit of English soil to stand on he will soon say: "I am going to stay in the old country; there's hope for a man here now. Life is worth living, so I won't emigrate. I will stay on the land when I have the chance to call a morsel of it mine; and I will prosper, and so help to make England prosperous too."

Yes, I say, let the labourers migrate if they will; but do not let them emigrate while there is English land for them to settle on, and to till, and to live by. Let the labourer live on the land and by the land; then England will keep and not lose him, and I say that a good English labourer is well worth the keeping. In the name of our country's prosperity then, let us keep him.

CHAPTER X.

MORE WORK FOR THE UNION.

I HAD been on my travels abroad, now I was on the stump at home again; and if there were stormy times for the Union in 1873, there were fighting days and desperate struggles in 1874. We had commenced the fight on February 7th, 1872, with five shillings, and we won it in April 1873, with a balance of £800 on deposit in Lloyd's Bank. That was very well and very good; but we had not only to stand our ground, we had to go ahead. Go ahead we did; and during 1874 the movement extended all over the country, and I was sent for from east, and from west, and from north and south. I pretty well boxed the compass, and I worked like a slave. In fact, all through these early years I spoke on an average at five or six meetings a week. We could not do much in the north; about Newcastle and those northern districts the men were much better paid, and they said, "The Union is a good thing, but we are well off and can get along without it." The Union was strongest, and kept so, in the Midland, Eastern, and Western counties. In 1874 we had the great Suffolk lock-out! there were some four thousand men thrown out of work. The farmers, naturally enough, were angry with the men because they asked for an advance of wages, so they locked them out as they had done elsewhere, their main object being to kill the organisation. We made a second appeal to the country and to the Trade Unions. I started off and travelled through the North of England, and in a month and four days—I worked desperately hard day and night, till I was about done up—we collected just over £3,000. Then we held a great demonstration in the Pomona Gardens, Manchester, and Manchester took the matter up splendidly; even the Bishop, Dr. Fraser, took sides with us, which in my opinion was a very brave thing for a prominent dignitary of the Church of England to do, but then he was a man as well as a bishop. A good many other towns backed us up as well, but none of them so enthusiastically as Manchester. Many wealthy merchants were present at this meeting, and at its close cheques to the value of £340 were placed in my hands for the relief of the distressed labourers of the Eastern counties. The outcome of it all was a triumph for us, because the National Agricultural Labourers' Union was established on a firmer, and a broader basis than before—on a truly national one.

I had a bit of a tussle with Bishop Fraser of Manchester, and it happened in this way: I had been addressing a public meeting in the Temperance Hall at Leicester. Just before that I had been reading the papers, and had found that a great number of men were deserting the army—it was estimated six hundred a week—and we could not get five per cent back again. The majority of them went off to America, and as soon as they landed there they were beyond the reach of English law altogether. We found also that the emigration agents were very busy—far too busy—taking our best men away from the villages; shiploads were going off every week. At this Leicester meeting I happened to say that I thought we were approaching a very serious crisis in this country, and that I had seen, in a cartoon, Disraeli standing on a landing-stage watching hundreds of labourers leaving our shores, and John Bull was represented asking him the question, "Is it wise to drive these men out of the country?" "Oh!" says Disraeli, "it does not matter, they have no votes." We had an old Unitarian Minister in the chair, and I turned to him and said: "Look here, Mr. Chairman, as an Englishman I must protest, and most solemnly protest, against this driving of the best of our men out of the country. Surely most of my audience have read history! If so, let them think seriously of the time when one of our Kings devastated the Isle of Wight and turned it into a deer forest. What happened? France sent her men over and sacked the Island, knocked Carisbrooke Castle into ruins, and laid waste the whole of the Island. What if our country is devastated in the same way! What if the cold and envious eagle eye of some foreign potentate were to be cast over our little sea-girt isle! What if he had a large army at his despotic command, and seeing our soldiers deserting us, our labourers leaving us—we know that the rank and file of the British Army is recruited from the ranks of the labourers—what if, seeing this, he fell upon us like a wolf on the fold! What if he invaded this country, sacked it, and cut off the heads of these hard-hearted landlords, who are responsible for so much of the mischief, until the streets ran with blood! I, for one, sir, should never weep a tear."

This had the same effect as a bolt from the blue, and the Bishop of Manchester got hold of a paper containing a report of my speech. Two nights after this Leicester meeting, I was due at Manchester for the first time; it was when the great lock-out was on. When I got into Market Street—that was where I had been directed to go—I found a committee of gentlemen there who had been to the bishop to ask him to take the chair for me that evening at the Town Hall; but he had just been reading my speech, and he said he could not do it for a man who talked like that. "I thought you said he was a local preacher," said the bishop. "I should like him to justify that statement." It was put in black and white that I was to justify my statement by the Word of God.

Well, at the meeting, after the preliminaries had been disposed of, I said: "Mr. Chairman, I have been called upon to justify the statement I made the night before last, by the Word of God. I will soon do it. I have been called the modern Moses: I do not lay claim to the piety nor the pathos of that ancient patriarch, but when he delivered the children of Israel from bondage, and they came to the Red Sea, what happened? The Egyptian Army was behind and the Red Sea in front. Moses smote the waters with his rod and, contrary to the laws which govern liquids, they parted, and the children of Israel passed through. The Egyptian army was mightily incensed at this, and dared to follow them into the chasm of the deep; but Moses saw them, and as soon as the last of the Israelites had passed safely over on to the other side, he waved his rod back and the waters rolled on and engulfed the Egyptians. Then, when he saw the Egyptians lying dead along the shore, what did Moses say? Did he tell his followers to go on their bended knees and weep? Did he tell them to put on weeds of mourning? No! He bade them take their harps and timbrels and sing unto the Lord, for He had saved them from the Egyptians."

That was my answer from the Bible to the Bishop of Manchester. He sent a special reporter to the meeting, and when he read the report he said, "Well, this is a marvellous reply; I should not have thought him capable of it. That man must read his Bible. Now I am perfectly satisfied that the labourers are in the right hands."

Then he wrote a letter to the *Times* entitled, "Are the farmers of England going mad?" I got complimented from all parts of the kingdom on that speech. They have not forgotten it in Manchester to this day. The last time I was down there several people said to me, "You have not forgotten the Bishop, have you?" Bishop Fraser was a fine man, and an honest and a well-meaning one. The operatives and the people knew he was their friend, and when he died he was deeply and sincerely mourned by the thousands of poor in his diocese. He was a wonderfully liberal man, considering his cloth and his lawn sleeves. I wish some of the parsons about had taken a leaf out of his book, and had tried to be a bit more after his pattern; for, as a rule, I found the cut of their clerical cloth was not on true Gospel lines, but very much to the contrary. I was continually having tussles with them; if they did not—the bulk of them —oppose me openly, they either did nothing one way or the other, or they stuck in my way like a rock, or stood, like a stone wall, blocking up the path to Union.

I can remember how the parson at a little place in Oxfordshire bitterly opposed me. He did not oppose me in a fair hand-to-hand fight; instead of debating the matter properly in public, he kept close at home and sent his curate to do his dirty work. Perhaps it was just as well for him that he did stay at home, for I verily believe the people would have tried to lynch him if he had come out, he was so unpopular in his parish. The curate, when he arrived at the meeting, began, as they always do in such cases, to riot a little bit; but I shut him up with, "Look here, young fellow, you just try and behave yourself till I have finished. You have been to college and ought to have learned good manners; I have not been to college, but I will give you a fair hearing." I can tell you he kept pretty quiet until I had finished; and then I asked him to come up on the platform and say what he had to say. After a little hesitation he got up and began in the usual affected clerical manner, "Labourers and friends, Mr. Arch, you know, has not been giving you the right doctrine. He must know that the law of supply and demand must rule the wages market. Now, if there are more labourers here than are required, you must work for low wages," and so he went on for some time.

When he had finished I said, "You are a curate, are you not?"

"Yes."

"Well," I said, "you ought to be the very last man to preach that doctrine. How does your class stand to-day?" I pulled a copy of the *Daily Telegraph* out of my pocket, and said, "I noticed here that a very large meeting has recently been held in London, to discuss the best means of obtaining money to buy clothes for the children of poor curates. There are some three thousand like you in England to-day, out of work. Bring your labour into the market on the same law of supply and demand, and see how you fare; we can get plenty like you at nine shillings a week,"

"I want to go," said he.

"Sit still a little longer," I said; "you are in good company. When you leave here, go and learn the first principles of Christianity and fair play. Your wives and children can go begging; the labourers' wives and children cannot. Would it not be a wonderful thing to see half-a-dozen curates going through this village, with their pulpits on their backs, asking for a job?" This was enough for him. He did not stop to say he wanted to go, he went; he cleared off just as hard as his legs could carry him.

I used to consider it a real treat to be able to make short work of a parson or a curate of this description. There was another parson I remember who worried me. Those fellows—that particular brand of parson—used to haunt me more than anybody else; they were ten times worse than the squires; they nagged so. I held a meeting one night at a village about two miles from Heyford in Oxfordshire. The next morning I went to Heyford Station to catch my train, and continue my journey. When I got there I found the station crowded with emigrants just off to America.

A little curate came up to me and said, "Is your name Arch?"

"Yes; and what's your name?"

"So-and-so. Have you seen the *Banbury Guardian*?"

"Yes."

"Did you see that they called you a 'tallyman'?"

"Yes."

"You are going to reply to it, I presume?"

"No. It takes me all my time to reply to wise men; I have no time to answer fools." That settled him—he soon cleared off the platform.

But I am bound to say that, if the parsons and their weakling curates nagged and worried, and tried a little word-scratching when they could, it was the farmers who were the most abusive. Not all, be it understood, any more than all the parsons—there were enlightened exceptions in both classes. I used to catch it very hot from the farmers when in railway carriages. Very often when travelling they would recognise me, and would get into the same carriage, and go for me. I used to be frightfully abused, and more than once I have been threatened with assault. I remember an instance: It was Smithfield Cattle Show week, and I got in at Leamington with some farmers. They had come from a considerable distance to Warwick and then changed, and were going on to London. There were four of them in the carriage, but they did not know me. By the way, it was just when the emigration agents were working their hardest, and were taking our men away by the shipload, and a great deal was being said on the subject. Well, these farmers began to talk about "that fellow, Arch"; so I sat still as a mouse and listened. One said, "Look here, he's making a thousand a year out of these poor emigrants; poor fools, he's selling them like cattle to the foreigners." So they carried on for some time capping one lie with another. At last, when we got to Ealing, I turned to the farmer next to me—he was an old man, between sixty and seventy years of age, but he was the worst of the lot for abuse—and I said to him:

"Do you mean to say, old gentleman, that Arch makes a thousand a year out of selling emigrants?"

"Yes," was the gruff reply.

"Can you prove it?"

"Yes, I can."

"Do you know Arch?"

"No."

"Well, I am the man; and I am going to make you prove what you say."

At that he looked as mad as an aged March hare.

"Now look here, old fellow," said I; "as soon as we get to Paddington I am going to have you locked up, and" (turning to the others) "I insist on you gentlemen bearing witness against him."

When I said this the old chap got properly frightened.

"Oh, don't make a fuss, don't try to lock me up," he said. "I want to go to Smithfield."

I tormented him for some time, but at last out of pity I said, "Poor old fool, for that's what you are, it seems, I will let you go this time; but I will tell you what I'll do; I will come to your place and hold a public meeting, and I will tell the men how I frightened you."

"Oh Lord! Oh Lord!" he cried. "Don't tell the men, for it's more than I can do to manage them already."

But I affected to be stern and unbending, and I

left him. I do not think the old fellow had a very pleasant trip to the Cattle Show!

He and his like were spreading lies broadcast about me, and the emigration, and the Union; and the worst of it was, like all lies, a few of them stuck pretty fast, as such mud will, and I was a good deal worried and bothered by them later on, too.

I well remember another encounter I had with some farmers. I was going to Cambridge from Bletchley Cattle Sale, and four or five of them got into the carriage where I was. They did not know me. The Union and Arch were the topics of the day, and the conversation naturally turned on them. They were a particularly fine selection of bullies—a choice lot—and they started slating me for all they were worth. One said I was a worthless humbug; another said that I was a cadger; another said that I made two thousand a year at the game, and so on. They credited me with all the vices and none of the virtues of this world. Hanging was too good for me by half. Well, after a time, and without making myself known, I joined in this beautiful conversation, and I asked one of the farmers how he knew Arch made two thousand a year. He seemed to resent the question, and started bullying, and was going to knock my head through the carriage. On my informing him that, as I had only one head I meant to take care of it, and I should not allow myself to be treated in that way; also, that if he started that game, I should in self-defence have to start punching his head, which

I did not want to do, he got very wild, and mad as a bull of Bashan. He rampaged like a lunatic and fairly lost his head. At the next station he got out, and I asked him if he would give me his card as I should like very much to correspond with him.

"Card! I ain't got no card," he growled, with a face as red as a beet root.

"That's a pity," said I, "but perhaps you would be so good as to take mine. Here it is."

I handed him one, and he took it. When he saw the name on it he rapped out an oath and made a dash at me. The train, however, was moving, so he was held back, and the last I saw of him was a picture—he was stamping up and down the platform like one possessed, and regularly foaming at the mouth with rage. He was in a pretty taking! There were three commercial travellers in the carriage with me, and they said they did not know how I managed to keep my temper, considering the bullying I had had. I told them that it did not trouble me, as I did not think it any good to lose my temper and fall out with people, who were at the least half-lunatic.

This was the sort of way the farmers went on, and hardly a week passed at this time without some such ruction. The sound of my name would set their tongues clacking; and if the lies they passed on had turned into stones, all I can say is there would have been enough for road-mending, and heaps to spare. The sight of me would start them off puffing, and prancing, and snorting, and crying, "Ha, ha!" like the war-horse in Job; they would gnash their teeth and butt at me like rampaging unicorns. And they were not the only ones I had to contend with, besides the parsons and the squires—though as regards the squires, I seldom, if ever, fell foul of them personally, as they generally sent their flunkeys to say their nasty things for them—but I have also had plenty of scrimmages with village shopkeepers. I remember one I had at Pillinghurst, in Sussex. I went down there to address a public meeting, or rather to test the right of public meeting, and when I got to the village I found four or five hundred labourers wandering about and forty-two policemen, if you please, in charge of a sergeant, to keep order. I had just come back from Canada and had a Canadian suit on, so nobody recognised me. I, however, made myself known to two or three and the secret was soon gone.

Well, we proceeded to the village green—a fine open space—and a gentleman from Brighton wanted to take the chair, and he did so. He said he had heard there was going to be war so he had come down to see the fun. Up I got on to a stool, and I started the meeting. Up came the sergeant of the police and said, "Move on; you can't stand there."

"Are you aware," I said, "that any Englishman can stand on any public ground, and deliver a speech in favour of a petition to the House of Commons? I have a petition here for the House of Commons, and you must not touch me." I knew my law on that point, after our previous experiences.

The farmers who were present stood dumbfounded and made no further opposition. We proceeded with our meeting, and while I was speaking a butcher, whose shop was within twenty yards of the green, came up and bullied me. But while he was trying the bullying game on with me, some one else was playing a different sort of game with him; some one just slipped up and stole a leg of pork from his shop. This too, within twenty yards of two-and-forty policemen! The butcher did not hear the last of that leg of pork for some time.

They say that threatened men live long; if that is so, then I ought to be a second Methuselah. And talking of threats reminds me that, once when I was going to address a meeting at a small country place, I was told on arriving, "You had better look out; the squire, I've heard, is going to turn the fire-hose on you and make you dry up your spouting."

"Oh," said I, "is he indeed! It'll take more than the play of his fire-hose to dry me up. Let him come, and I and my mates will give him a fiery welcome."

But that was all the squire did—nothing came of it. I expect when he got wind of the determined attitude of the labourers he thought discretion was the better part of valour. Those who meditated a watery welcome decamped, taking their hose with them. The men would stand no nonsense, and no tampering with me either. You see it was not merely because I was Joseph Arch, it was because I represented the Union to them, and they knew I was toiling almost night and day to further their interests.

But I met with ingratitude and insult and opposition inside the Union. In 1874 rather grave accusations were brought against me by certain persons. They charged me with malversation of funds, among other things. One member of our Consultative Committee was very bitter against me, and some of the others also. He was made to pay for the unfounded charges he made, because his name was expunged from the Consultative Committee, and the Committee passed this resolution:—" The attention of the Consultative Committee of the National Agricultural Labourers' Union, having been directed to certain charges made by Mr. ——— in the public press against the Executive and its officers, is of opinion that such charges are groundless, and cannot for a moment be sustained; and expresses its unabated confidence in both Mr. Arch and the other officers."

I suffered a great deal at the time from these misstatements; they hurt me far more than anything outsiders could say, or did say. I shall quote here from a letter which J. C. Cox wrote to the *Labourers' Union Chronicle* of September 19th, 1874. " The character of Joseph Arch is too pure and true to suffer in the long run. I have seen, and learnt, and heard more of that man than, probably, any one else out of his own rank of life; and I fearlessly say that, if I was to be asked to point out the man of all others on God's earth at the present moment, whom I believed to be absolutely incorruptible and true as steel to the work before him, I should unhesitatingly lay my hand upon the shoulder of honest Joseph Arch. Many is the cheque and banknote which that man has received from admirers, intended for his own private use, and which he has, to my knowledge, in his own quiet way, handed over to the general funds; and if self-aggrandisement was his object, as Mr. —— implies, he might have retired from the business of an agitator long ago on a comfortable competence. Did Mr. —— never hear of him refusing the handsome salary of the Canadian Government, on Sir Edward Watkin's farm? And I know of several other like opportunities that have never been made public."

What vexed me so much was that I knew the Union was certain to suffer for this disunion; a house divided against itself is bound to come to grief, and I felt very sore at the thought of outsiders scoffing and pointing the finger of scorn at us and saying, "Look, for all their talk about Union they can't keep united among themselves!" Instead of brethren working together in unity, it looked as if we were going to split in pieces; and at that thought my heart, stout as it was, would sink within me. Only those who have studied the subject, or have done such work as I put my hand to, can understand what difficulties I had to contend with from those very men I wished to help. It was not merely the prejudices of landlords and farmers and parsons I had to overcome; there were prejudices as blind, backs as stiff, and ears as deaf, within our own borders. There was a man who showed that he understood my difficulties in this respect; that was Thorold Rogers. He was a fine fellow, a genuine and a sincere man. He took an active part in the Union work soon after it began, and he followed it through to the end. This is what he says in Vol. II. of that valuable book of his, "Six Centuries of Work and Wages":

"Some years later, Joseph Arch, a Warwickshire peasant, undertook the heroic task of rousing the agricultural labourer from his apathy, of bearding the farmers and the landowners, and of striving to create an Agricultural Labourers' Union. I believe that I was the first person in some position who recognised his labours, by taking the chair at one of his meetings; and I have been able to see how good his judgment has been, how consistent his conduct, and how prodigious are his difficulties. I believe he has done no little service to his own order, but I conclude he has done more for the general interests of labour, if only by showing how universal is the instinct that workmen can better their condition only by joint and united action. And it should be said, that other workmen, trained for a longer period in the experience of labour partnerships, have aided, and that not obscurely, the undertaking in which Arch is engaged.

"The difficulties in creating and maintaining a labour partnership of agricultural hands, are very great. In the darkest period of their history, artizans, even when their action was proscribed by the law, still clung together, had common purposes, took counsel, though secretly and in peril, and struck against oppressively low wages.

"But for three centuries at least, agricultural labourers have had no organisation whatever on behalf of their class interests. I shall have written in vain if I have not pointed out how effectively the employers of rural labour contrived to enslave and subdue them. It is hard to see how any one could have hoped to move them. But even when they were moved, it was still more difficult to make the units cohere. I remember that an eminent clergyman of my acquaintance, now deceased, told me that when he first took a country living—some of Arch's kindred were among his domestic servants, and he was entirely friendly to Arch's policy—nothing struck him more painfully than the evident suspicion with which the labourers in his parish met kindness. He said that he very early despaired of their confidence, for he noticed that invariably any trust he showed in them was distrusted, was supposed to be tendered with the object of overreaching them. I do not comment on the experiences which must have induced this habit of mind in them, but simply say that this was the material with which Arch had to deal.

"I am willing enough to admit that my clerical friend's position was more awkward than that of other persons. But though, being one of their order, the advocate of an agricultural union occupies a more independent and more confidential position than the intelligent parish clergyman. The temper of the peasants must be, even to an enthusiast, no easy instrument to play upon. He has to combat with the persistent apathy of despair. He has to contend with the sluggishness of ignorance. He has to interpret the habitual mendacity of distrust. He has to rebuke the low cunning with which the oppressed shirk duty, for only those who are worthy can take a good part in the emancipation of the English serf. I well remember that a friend of mine, earnestly anxious to better his labourers on his model farm, gave them high wages, regular work, and showed them infinite consideration. At last he despaired and sold his property, because they thought him, in their poor puzzled way, a fool; and he found that he had made them worse knaves than he found them.

"Again, such a man, constrained to be a leader of men, is obliged to assert an authority, and exercise a decision which others, inevitably less informed, cannot understand, and are loath to submit to. This difficulty is universal. The most awkward persons to deal with when debate is needed, are two mobs, one of uneducated, and the other of fairly educated persons; for the former are generally suspicious, the latter generally conceited. Neither will concede to the expert unless there is danger, or till patience wearies conceit. The greatest difficulty we are told, even with the comparatively well-trained artizan, is willing obedience to necessary discipline. It is said that the ill-success which has attended various schemes of co-operation, has been due to the disinclination of operatives to obey the necessary orders of one who is of their own order, whom they have invested with authority. They will obey an overlooker whom their employer selects, even though his rule be harsh and severe; but it is not so easy to induce them to acquiesce in the directions of those whom they could depose at their pleasure. But the difficulty is greater the less instructed persons are, and the less familiar they are with the process by which the reality of liberty is achieved,—by the sacrifice of a portion of liberty itself. I have heard that in Mr. Arch's efforts he has been constantly baffled for a time, by revolts from the necessary authority with which the manager of a labour organisation must be invested.

"Again, the scattered character of the agricultural population must needs be a great difficulty in the way of adequately organising them. The heads of a trade union in towns can summon their men speedily; and take action, if action seems desirable, promptly. But it is far more difficult to manipulate the scattered elements of an agricultural union, especially when the hostility to it is so marked, as has been generally shown, and the opportunities of giving effect to that hostility are so numerous. I do not believe that the mass of peasants could have been moved at all, had it not been for the organisation of the Primitive Methodists, a religious system which, as far as I have seen its working, has done more good with scanty means, and perhaps, in some persons' eyes, with grotesque appliances for devotion, than any other religious agency.—The poverty of the agricultural labourer is a serious bar to the organisation of the order.—The economies of the Agricultural Labourers' Union are rigid, the expenditure is cut down to the narrowest limits. I am persuaded that the jealousy which the farmers feel and the resentment which they express against Arch and his Union are a mistake. The first condition under which a workman can be expected to be honest and intelligent, efficient and effective, is that he should have a sense of self-respect. Half a man's worth, says the Greek poet, is taken away on the day that he becomes a slave. The increase in the labourer's pay, if it be obtained, will be much more than compensated by the moral education which he has got by submitting to discipline and by understanding the principles of a labour partnership. When working men make a free contract,—and they can never make such a contract as individuals,—I am persuaded that they will make more intelligent and more beneficial bargains for the use of their labour, than they ever will if they are hindered from corporate and collective action, or remain under the impression that their wages are fixed without any discretion on their part, or are constantly called upon to defend or apologise for what they believe is their undoubted right —a right which no consistent economist would dispute.

"The public is profoundly interested in the efficiency and the independence of the working man. By the former the industrial success of the country is guaranteed and secured. In the latter, there lies the only hope that we shall ever be able to realise in our day what the trade guilds of the Middle Ages aimed at, and in some directions unquestionably secured—the character of the workman, as contained in his moral and professional reputation, and the excellence of the work which he turned out, to say nothing of the practical refutation of social fallacies. Among the members of the Agricultural Labourers' Union, sobriety, independence of public charity, and education are conditions. The Trade Unions of London and other large towns do not perhaps exercise the moral discipline over their members which they might do if their fellows more generally enlisted in the system, and which they will do, as they get stronger and better informed. But I am abundantly convinced that the English trade unionists include in their numbers the most intelligent, conscientious, and valuable of the working men."

I have quoted all this, because I endorse it and know it to be the truth, and because I consider the opinion of such a man as Thorold Rogers very valuable; it is the opinion of a man who has given much time and thought and trouble to the labour question—he is no ignorant hotheaded tattler; and if he did take a side it was after he had thought the matter well out and considered it in all bearings. What he says about sobriety, independence of public charity, and education being conditions of our Union, is the truth. We went strong on all three points. I do not object to a glass of beer, or something hot of a cold night; but

I do say, let there be moderation in the enjoyment of the drinks of the earth. Use them and enjoy them as we would and should any other good thing, but do not let them get the mastery over us. Often and often have I spoken on this subject at our meetings. I would say, "You know as well as I do that there is one great evil to be removed from among the labourers of this country, namely intemperance. No one could be more disgusted than I am when I see a drunken working-man. I do not wish to criticise you as to how you should spend your money, but I do ask you to keep in your pockets the pence, and shillings too, you are only too ready to waste in beer. I do not place all the blame on the labourer," I would tell them, "far from it; it is with the Government the chief blame rests. A system has been introduced into this country, by the selling of intoxicating liquors, which victimises, paralyses and pauperises mankind. Of course it bears hardest on the poor; if a poor man is found by the roadside drunk, there is no remedy but to take him to the station house; but if the squire's son is found in such a position, or gracefully reclining in the ditch, it would be readily attributed to the fact that he was suffering from dipsomania, and he would be gently conducted to the ancestral home." I knew—none better—what dire temptations the poor agricultural labourer had, to drink more than was good for him.

There was one very general temptation which came round regularly with each harvest season, and was the cause of much mischief and misery and riot. This was the harvest frolic, as it was called; and it took place at harvest-home time when the corn was gathered in. After a harvest supper, which the men had either at the farmer's own house, or if he could not manage it, at the public-house, and where any amount of eating and drinking went on—not the hearty eating and drinking of hungry but self-respecting men; but a regular gorging of victuals and swilling of beer, and something stronger too—after all this, the men, half-drunk, and stupid or riotous from the feast, would start off the next day and go round begging for tips and nips. They would stop at the publics on their way and have another drop to carry them on; and what with "drops" here and there and all along the road, nine out of ten of them would be in a disgraceful condition long before the day was out. Then they would quarrel among themselves, and they would go home too, and give the wife a black eye or a beating, and turn the place upside down. This harvest frolic was a bad old custom, and was the cause of many going astray and getting into trouble. The worst of it was, too, that the more respectable men were pretty well forced to get drunk then—it was the custom, so they had to. A frolic like that would just be the last straw to a man trying hard to keep a sober head on his poor shoulders; and it would push some weak-headed youngster, trembling on the verge, right over the precipice of habitual drunkenness, right over for bad and all; for he would get into some mess, lose his self-respect, and go the whole hog after, with a worthless wife like a millstone round his weak neck to help drag him down to the bottomless pit of perdition. Many such cruel cases have there been.

Many an honest, right-down, good fellow I have also seen overcome by drink, because he was suffering from the pangs and the gripes of an empty stomach; many a poor, half-starved, overworked man have I seen sink into a drunken sot and a hoggish beer-swiller, because he could get no sort of comfort in his wretched home, and had no hope of ever being anything but a slave and a pauper. The law, of course, could not consider and stay to inquire into all the causes which had brought him to such a state; the law has only time to be just, it cannot spare time to be merciful; and if a man was brought up charged with being drunk and disorderly, it would say, "Fine him," or "Put him in prison," or both. I do not say the law is wrong. What I do say is, that the law should be applied to rich and poor alike; that the liquor laws should be altered and amended, and that the poor labourer should have his conditions, his surroundings bettered. Change a man's conditions and you change your man. Give a man the chance of rising as far as it is in him to rise; but you must begin early with him just as you would with a young sapling or any growing plant. Take a man while he is young and tender, and train him; put the best into him and draw the best out of him just as you would do to a valuable plant or any growing thing with life in it.

It was because I and others felt so strongly upon this

point that we made education such a plank in the Union platform. I knew from bitter, cruel experience how hard it was to get even a working-day sort of an education, and it was strongly borne in on me that if the labouring man did not get himself educated somehow there was no hope of his rising to manly independence. Now we had the Elementary Education Act of 1870 in operation, I felt that we were in duty bound to take every advantage of it we could—that we should be false to our trust if we did not, that we should be shortsighted fools and no wiser than madmen if we did not make full use of such a priceless blessing. Over and over again I used to say, "If you want your dear children to have a fair chance of rising, of bettering themselves and enabling them to better their surroundings in time, you must see that they are educated—not only stuffed up with a little or a lot of useless knowledge and facts, but taught what is likely to prove useful to them, so that they are put in a fair way to start well, and on the right lines of their life journey. Yes, start them fair on the right lines, and if they have the go in them they'll go; some will go like a parliamentary train, and some will go like an express, each according to his way, but they'll *go*." There were too many of us who had stuck in the mud, and stuck fast for life. The children were not going to stick in the mud of ignorance if I could help it. Ignorance is the blockhead mother of misery to my thinking. Half, aye, and more than half, the difficulties I had to contend with in my Union work were due to the dreadful ignorance I had to encounter among my fellow labourers. They were obstinate, suspicious, and stupid, because they were so ignorant; their brains were ill-nourished and so they were dull; their uncultivated minds were like dark lanterns with a rushlight inside; they did not know how to think a thing out, and they did not even know how to try. Hundreds of these brothers of mine in the country districts were sunk in brutish ignorance, and time and again I used to feel after I had been speaking to them and trying to reason with them till my voice was hoarse and I was nearly worn out, that I had been as good as knocking my poor head against a thick stone wall.

Headaches and heartaches and throataches, many a one, they gave me. I could not blame them as I should blame the present generation if they behaved in the same way, because the old folk had not the privileges the young folk have had since 1870. Children were employed till the law compelled them to be sent to school, and when the father was able to earn so little who can wonder at it? Boys, as soon as they were big enough, would be sent out into the fields, just as I was. Some would say, "Oh, it is a good thing for the boy; he will get into working ways early and learn to be a good farm hand." But there were others, and those were the most respectable and the best men who would say, "There is no need to set a boy to work on a farm till he is twelve or thirteen, if only his parents are able to keep him at school and get along without his earnings."

A boy was supposed to spend five years at school, but generally he would spend about three, and then not attend regularly. There were night schools it is true, but at their best they were mostly makeshift sort of affairs. The boys would often attend them in the slack winter months from November to March, or they would put in their day schooling then, but the irregularity and the poor teaching did not give the ordinary lad a fair chance of getting even a decent elementary education. Then, many of them were at work all Sunday as well, and the farmers who employed them did not trouble themselves about the education of their labourers, young or old. Work was all they troubled about, and the consequence was the boys were often nothing but young heathens, and were made stupid with toil before they had a chance of getting what wits they had sharpened up a bit.

I remember that the ordinary payment for school was twopence a week, sometimes it would be only a penny, sometimes it would be as much as fourpence, and for a better school it would be sixpence; there was no system worth speaking of. Of course, if a lad could earn money—and some managed to earn a pretty fair amount, as much as eightpence and tenpence a day—the parents were only too thankful. But the worst of it was, not only was the boy missing his small chance of being a fair scholar, but he would be almost his own master when he was not at all fit to be. He earned money enough to be independent of his mother, and ten chances to one he would get into all sorts of mischief, and there was no one to control him. His master did not care, as a rule, what he did out of work time. Oh, it was a very bad state of affairs!

Then the gang system was in full force when I was a young man, and indeed right on into the sixties, though it was then beginning to die out. I have always been opposed to this form of labour organisation. There were private gangs and public ones; small ones and large ones; fixed ones and wandering ones. Sometimes the gang would consist of one man and three or four children working under him; they would go turnip-singling and bean-dropping. Sometimes there would be a mixed gang of men and women weeding and picking "twitch"; some would consist of women only. The potato gangs would be among the largest. You would see a line of women and children of all ages placed along a furrow at irregular distances; the piece allotted to each would vary a little and was called a "stint," and all the potatoes in that furrow would have to be picked up before the plough came down the next one. Behind the line would be two or three carts, and the men with them would empty the baskets in. Such a gang would frequently number as many as seventy, and there would be a man walking up and down behind them superintending. Generally he was a rough bullying fellow, who could bluster and swear and threaten and knock the youngsters about and browbeat the women, but who was nothing of a workman himself. Pea-picking gangs were generally very large, consisting of four and five hundred women and children. The language the women, and the children too, would use was beyond belief. Women who could get no decent indoor work, or who were rough and coarse and bold, would take to gang work, and instead of considering the poor little children by the side of them, these unnatural women have been known to teach the children vile language, and to encourage them in wickedness. There was no limit as to age, and I have seen little mites of things in potato fields who were hardly old enough to walk; and I have seen poor little toddlers set to turnip-singling when they should have been indoors with their mother.

There were regular ganging villages near and about Leicester and Nottingham, and, as was to be expected, the ignorance among them was very great, was a disgrace to a civilised country. It was a cruel and a thoroughly bad system; it was all wrong. The children should have been at home or at school, and the women should have been minding their houses, or should have been in domestic service, or working at some trade suited to women. I am glad to think it more or less a thing of the past. Of course it was not all bad; some of the private gangs working for a respectable farmer would be made up of men and women and children in his regular employ, and would only form into gangs at certain seasons when combination of labour was an advantage. But, generally speaking, the system was a bad and an injurious one. Directly, and indirectly, our Union put a spoke in its wheel. We advocated the regular attendance of the children at school, and we tried to raise the moral standard in the home. "Give your children a good education and a decent home, and make them members of the Union later on," we used to say. Sometimes I used to feel as if I was on a bank I had climbed up, and was pulling other labourers and their wives and children out of a Slough of Despond, till my arms ached fit to drop off, and my head was swimming, and my legs were shaking under me. But I, and my mates standing by me, kept on pulling and tugging with might and main; we did not stop longer than to fetch our breath, and then we set to work pulling and tugging again. And I may say, and do say without bitterness now, that the "thank-yous" we got for our pains were not as plentiful as blackberries.

CHAPTER XI.

THE DAWNING OF THE FRANCHISE.

ALL through the seventies the Ark of Union was storm-tossed; now it would sail along on the waves of fair weather, now it would be rolling in deep and troubled waters; but through storm and shine, in fair weather and in foul, it still sailed on, and I still stuck to my post. It had to suffer attacks from foes without and from traitors within. I had to bear what I may call the slings and arrows of outrageous slander, assassin stabs in the back of my reputation were dealt me, my character was defamed, and the purity of my motives was called in question by those who should have known me better. Self-seekers and place-hunters strove to knock me down, trample upon me, and cast me overboard—but the fate of the fallen angels was theirs, and it was they who fell and were cast down and thrown over, while I stood firm, and true friends stood by me and struck many a doughty blow in my defence. Cast down in spirit I often was, and sore at heart, but never—no not when the storm was at its highest, or the fight waxed hottest and fiercest—did I lose heart altogether, and fall a prey to ugly old Giant Despair. I never saw the inside of Doubting Castle, though I won't say that I have not peeped in at the door. There were days, too, when I have said to myself, " Why, the poor Union Ark is a worse vessel to sail in than the venerable old patriarch Noah's—his was choke full of wild beasts of all sorts as well as human beings, but they all lived in peace together, they had a little millennium all to themselves, in fact —and yet here were we in these nineteenth-century days of civilisation fighting like cats, and dogs, and tigers." In my opinion these traitors to the cause were no better than heathen savages and cannibals, for what were they doing when all is said and done, but trying to swallow each other? It was a cruel shame and a bitter disgrace, and I felt it to the marrow of my bones when outsiders twitted us and pointed the finger of scorn at us, and hooted. And you may depend they did that, for there were malignants about in plenty, just as there were in olden days. All the same I went right on and I made myself as blind as I could to the scorn-pointing finger, pointed it ever so scornfully, and as deaf as I could to the voice of the hooter, hooted he ever so loudly.

The numbers in Union and the cash in hand fluctuated of course, but, speaking roughly, there was on the whole an increase through the seventies. Up to the end of April 1875 the members numbered

58,650—this was the total returned for 38 districts with 1,368 branches. In 1874 the total income was £21,000, and in 1875 it was £23,130. The expenditure for relief in cases of lock-outs and strikes during 1874 was £7,500, and in 1875 £21,400; this increase was owing to the great lock-out in the Eastern Counties. Over £6,000 was spent for migration and emigration purposes; nearly 2,000 men had been assisted to emigrate to Australia and New Zealand, 500 to Queensland, and nearly 4,000 were sent to Canada. Over £26,000 was received from the various Trades Unions and the general public. Law expenses and other liabilities came to £690. The cash in hand in 1875 was £4,150. By the end of 1875 we had about 60,000 men in Union, and over £7,000 in the bank. Of the thousands who went to Canada and our other colonies I can only say that the bulk of them were picked men; the drones of course would not go—not they—so they were left more or less on our hands, and there is not a doubt of it but that they proved a drag on us.

A parallel case is, I hear, going on in Wales; the Canadian Government is going to take out about a thousand of Lord Penrhyn's miners, the very flower of Welsh working men. It is a lamentable thing that such men should be forced to leave the native land they love so well, because they dared to maintain their right to combine. What is worse is that, while our best workmen are being driven out of the country, we are letting the riff-raff and the refuse of other lands pour into England. I am very strongly opposed to the immigration of alien paupers; as a man who has the best interests of his country at heart I am bound to be. Owing to bad treatment at home, several thousands of our best men emigrate every year—this is bad enough in itself—but instead of this relieving the congested state of the population, we get in about three times as many worthless pauper aliens, foreign Jews, vagrant Italians, etc., the scum of their own countries, three of whom cannot do the work of one honest Englishman. Brassey always said he could not find in any nationality three men who would answer to one good English navvy. With regard to emigration generally, I think, if people in this country find it a hard task to get along, and if they have friends in the Colonies who are willing to look after them until they can make a fair start for themselves, by all means let them go. I do not blame them for going, but I blame the system which permits of their being starved out of the country, and which lets in the rubbish, so to speak, of other countries. I know how I felt it when, at about the time the Union was started, a great number of tradesmen, carpenters, glass-blowers from Lancashire—especially the latter, and in fact the majority of the best skilled labourers—took advantage of the cheap rates and emigrated.

Still, in spite of drones, and strikes and lock-outs and other difficulties, we went on progressing through 1876. A number joined us that year, when they found that by so doing they had a better chance of getting good wages. All through 1877, 1878, and 1879 we managed to keep the wages well up, and so were doing one of the chief bits of work we were organised to do. If there were drawbacks in one direction, there was a steady keeping up to the mark in another; we were all alive—our very quarrels and dissensions showed that, and the thought used to bring me a little cold comfort at times—and we were growing. We were making our power felt, and a Union man who wanted legal or other help, if his cause was good, had not to ask in vain.

For instance, we took up and agitated the case of Luke Hills, who was carter to a certain farmer and landowner at Cuckfield, in Sussex. Hills had been convicted under the "Master and Servant Act" for breach of contract. He had hired himself for one year, but leaving before the expiration of that time, his master had him arrested and taken before the Petty Justices, who convicted him and fined him £5. His employer had claimed £9 damages. Of course Hills could not find the money in the fortnight allowed him for payment, and he was committed to Lewes gaol for three months. It was proved afterwards that Hills had never made any such contract, and that when his master engaged him he had merely made an entry of the transaction in his note book. There was no definite contract, and Hills never understood that there was. This way of dispensing Justices' justice raised a great deal of indignation throughout the country, and well it might. The question was raised in the House of Commons, and Sir Richard Assheton Cross, the Home Secretary, ordered Hills to be released after he had suffered a month's imprisonment. The conviction was both unjust and illegal—no agreement was proved, and Hills never knew there had been any; there must be more than one party to an agreement, which should be duly signed by both parties, and duly witnessed and stamped.

There was another case of imprisonment which roused a great deal of feeling, for it was a very cruel one. Samuel Dawson, a farm labourer aged fifty-seven, whose wages averaged twelve shillings a week, was sent to Bedford gaol for two months with hard labour by the Sharnbrook Justices, because he could not pay one shilling a week towards the maintenance of his parents. Dawson served his time and came out of prison on August 10th, 1875.

It was a cruel business, and it touched scores and scores of labourers on the raw, for this question of maintaining parents was a burning one. It touched me, because I knew from personal experience how hard put to it a man can be to make both ends meet, if he has a wife and a young family and even one aged parent dependent on him. My father was a ratepayer for thirty-two years and never troubled the parish for a farthing. When the poor old man was taken ill, of course my wife had to attend on him. She was pleased enough to do it, and she did her duty by him as a good daughter-in-law should; but she had her little family to see to, and she had been accustomed to bring in about two shillings a week by going out charing, and so help to keep the pot boiling. The growing children were hearty and wanted a lot of food. It was a serious thing for us just then to lose that two shillings a week, and to have to provide little extras for my father into the bargain. All the money he had by him now was just a few shillings, and that though he had toiled hard, and lived hard, and kept himself respectable all his life. So I said to my wife, "There's nothing for it but going to the guardians and asking them to give me a little help." I did not like it, but I went. The overseer had said he thought the parish ought to assist me a little as long as I had my father ill on my hands, considering I had a pretty large family to support, and he advised me to go before the board. I went and I said: "Gentlemen, I don't want you to support my aged father, but I should be glad if you would give my wife one-shilling-and-sixpence a week towards nursing him, as she is cut off from her charing. What I ask is less than my wife's earnings, and it is nothing to the expense of my father's illness." Well, they refused me that, and said that my father could go into the workhouse, and I could pay one-and-sixpence a week towards his expenses.

My blood boiled up at that. What! my honest, respectable old father turned into the workhouse to end his days—never! I up and said to these gentlemen,

"I'd sooner rot under a hedge than he should go there!"

And he did not go—he died under the old Arch roof-tree, and he breathed his last breath in my arms. We managed to make his last years comfortable somehow; but I know this, that after all was over, and my father was decently and respectably buried, I was in debt £10, and I had extremely hard work for twelve months to get out of it again. I felt it bitterly at the time, and I should have been something less than a man and a dutiful and affectionate son, if I had not. Of course, when the strain was off I could say to myself, "Joe Arch, I am glad you had no parish help, not a stiver,"—but I shall never forget the day I went before the guardians to ask for it, and they refused it. It was a day of humiliation and anger for me. And mine was but a test case. I can honestly say now that I am not sorry I had to bear that bit of trouble, because, not only was I sharing the common lot of my fellow-labourers, but I could, therefore, truly sympathise with those in a like case. There were numbers then and later, up and down the country, in just the position I was in, and who were treated in the same way. It was short-sighted policy on the guardians' part. There were scores of hard-working married sons and daughters who, for the sake of two shillings a week, and a loaf outside the house, would have been enabled to take care of their aged parents at home, and see them decently buried. If they were put into the house they would cost the rates at least another shilling a week; more, if, as has been calculated, it costs the ratepayers from three shillings and ten pence to four shillings a week per adult. Then, if a man with his wife, and say six children, went into the House, they would be better off there than they would be outside; if the man could only earn eleven or twelve shillings a week in wages. When this could be the state of affairs it was in my opinion, as good as offering a man a premium to become a pauper.

I never have advocated indiscriminate outdoor relief; very far from it. I wish I might live to see the day when every working man in England will be beyond the need of asking for such degrading help, because he is able to earn fair wages and be a self-supporting member of this great community. Still, in such cases as mine, the Poor Law administrators should have tempered judgment with mercy, and granted me a little discreet and temporary help. I happened to be a strong man, so I pulled through—it was a hard job, though—but for one who could, there were hundreds who could not, and for want of that little, and in my opinion deserved help, they broke down. A respectable man broken down, who has, as it were, the back of his self-respect and independence snapped in the middle, is a sight to make angels weep, and what is more, he becomes a drag on the community in the end and a burden on the ratepayers. A man with natural affection would put up with a great deal before he would let his old father die in a pauper's bed in the workhouse.

The Dawning of the Franchise

There was a little poem written by John Harris, entitled, "The Dying Labour-Lord," from which I shall quote a few verses, because it shows what the feelings of the labouring man was on the subject, and will be always, I hope:

> High over the whispering pines
> The rooks in flocks were flying,
> As in the cell of a lone poorhouse
> A labour-lord lay dying.
>
> His frame was of a giant mould,
> Which time had partly broke;
> His breast, his shoulders, back and sides
> And limbs were like limbs of oak.
>
> Now the mighty man was low,
> His life was feebly flying;
> Old age had bound the village hind
> And the labour-lord lay dying.
>
> Men passed along outside;
> The rich, the great, swept by,
> But none enquired for the labour-lord
> Who was so soon to die.
>
> He oft had tilled their fields;
> He oft had reaped their grain;
> The profits swelled their shining hoards,
> But his the crushing pain.
>
> He gave to them his youth,
> His manhood's golden prime;
> And now they leave the labour-lord,
> Wrecked on the strand of time.
>
> None could compete with him
> To cut the granite rock,
> To guide the plough, or wield the scythe,
> Or shear the fleecy flock.

> He was an honest man
> As ever delved the sod;
> Misfortunes came and turned him here
> To die alone with God.

Yes, it was the unfortunate pauper, not the drone pauper, our hearts bled for. I firmly believe in the apostolic injunction, that if a man will not work, neither shall he eat. The drone, high or low, whether robed in lordly purple or clothed in labouring fustian, should be forced to work, or left to feel the pangs of deserved hunger. The born drone and the willing drone should have a taste of the spare rod of starvation and a spell of hard labour; but the honest man who wants to work, and who cannot get employment try he ever so, or who through misfortune is reduced to the condition of a drone, that man should have a helping hand held out to him, so that he may rise to his position as a worthy worker in the industrial hive, and feel once more a manly, independent spirit rise high within him. The Union had done, and was doing, much to make this possible. We were keeping up wages, we were protecting labour against the oppression of capital, we were educating our people by means of speeches and papers, we were awakening their intellectual life and making them reason and think. We were working hand-in-hand with the Act of 1870, and now we were making another step forward: we were beginning to agitate for the extension of the borough franchise to the counties. That was a long and a persistent agitation, extending from about 1875 up to our triumph in 1884.

We sent up petition after petition to the House of Commons, and those kept our men busy and also helped to keep them united. They would pick out a man in the village, give him a few pence, and send him tramping round the county for signatures to the different petitions. I myself took one up to the House of Commons which was about seventeen yards long. Mr. Dixon presented to the House the petition from eighty thousand farm-labourers in favour of household suffrage in the counties. I was in the House when Trevelyan introduced the Bill, and Lord Hartington walked out.

On the motion for the second reading of this Household Franchise Counties Bill, Trevelyan proceeded to move it in a very able speech. In it he said: " We draw a distinction almost unknown in any constitutional country or in our own colonies, and which did not exist even here in its present invidious and aggravated form before 1867, between the inhabitants of towns and those of rural England. We brand our village population as if they were political pagans, because four hundred years ago, one of the worst Parliaments that ever sat in this country robbed the county inhabitants of their votes on the ground that (to use the very words of the Act) ' being people of small substance and no value, they pretended a voice equivalent with the most worthy knights and esquires ' —so we keep up a difference between the town and county franchise because in 1429 a parliament of Henry VI. was afraid of our rural population."

I was bitterly disappointed when the Bill was defeated in 1875 by a majority of, I think, one hundred and two. But of course we only kept agitating more and more, and the franchise was a front plank in the Union platform from this time onwards.

We met with the usual opposition from farmer and parson, aye and from dissenting minister too; for it is a true word with reference to any cause that, "he who is not for us is against us." And those who openly befriended us, or even were known to have listened to us, had to suffer. I heard that Mr. Easton, for instance, who stood in the Liberal interests, largely owed his defeat in the West Suffolk election of 1875 to his having subscribed to the Union, and also to his known sympathy with our cause. The farmers were mad with him for that, and said, "Oh, if Easton is the labourers' friend he can't be, and he shan't be, ours." The Conservatives made the most of it of course, and there was a rumour spread about that I was going round with him as a sort of right-hand man and backer up. Well, he lost the election. I do not say it was wholly owing to his known sympathy with us; but that had a great deal to do with his defeat. As to the dissenting ministers who turned the cold shoulder of indifference and distrust on us—well, I said my say on that matter on more than one occasion. I remember speaking out at a meeting in 1875, and I said:

"I am just going to say a word or two with reference to the class of men who really could not have been ignorant of the grand result of this movement—I refer now to the ministers of the gospel. I don't ask, Are they of the Church or are they of Dissent? I am myself a dissenter, and I have asked ministers of the denomination to which I belong,—'Why do you give us the cold shoulder as you do? Has the Union made us less reverential towards God than we were before it began?' 'No!' 'Has it made us more drunken, dissipated, and wretched than we were before it began?' 'No!' 'Has it made us less loyal to our country, less true to our trusts, and less honest to our employers?' 'No!' 'Has it made us less intelligent than what we might have been?' 'No!'

"It is a fact, an undeniable fact, that before 1872 there were thousands of our honest, hard-working farm-labourers, who didn't know a letter in the alphabet; who attended our churches and chapels, and to whom the Bible was a sealed book; and why? because they could not read it. But now there are thousands of these men, who, by virtue of this agitation, and by virtue of themselves, have begun to read; and now, instead of finding hundreds of them wandering about the lanes on the Sabbath day, you will find them in the bosom of their families reading the Word of God —that Book they never knew a syllable of before. And I say, if I know anything of my Bible and the teachings of Christ, of His Spirit and Character, at the great day of account these ministers will stand condemned for leaving the agricultural labourer to find his own way to heaven, when they ought to have tended him and taught him that themselves. I have had conversations with a great number of Dissenting ministers, and Church ministers too, upon this matter, and I don't say that we have not found them in many places really and truly sympathising with us—I mean especially the dissenters—but then they daren't speak out their minds. Let a Dissenting minister come into your town; let him settle down in one of your chapels—I don't know how many you have got—and let him dare to say a word in favour of the movement, and on the side of the poor man who is down in the ditch, then you will find the little capitalist and deacon down upon him like vultures—and yet they do it in the name of godliness and Christianity and love to mankind.

"If there is a minister here—I don't care what your creed or denomination may be—but, if you can show me a single instance where your Master, whom you profess to teach, turned the force of His influence to go with the strong and to crush the weak, then I will say you are right in what you do. But while I cannot find a single instance where He would turn his attention to such dastardly, and mean, and unchristian conduct, and you are mean enough to do it, I shall certainly enter my protest against you; and I will make England ring with the hypocrisy which is blinding the eyes of men, and leading thousands down to hell. I know there are a great many who want to frame hosts of excuses for their neglect on these great points I have alluded to. True religion fears the frown of no man—no, never. True religion shirk its duty, and pander to the crotchets of the money-monger? No, never! I tell you, my brethren here to-night, that this agricultural labourers' movement has shown the dark deeds of a corrupt and so-called Christianity more than anything that has been started could do.

"Now I will just give you one instance out of the many that have come under my notice, with regard to the great sympathy and honesty of clerical men. I was travelling in a railway carriage, and a minister was in the same carriage with me; but, of course, he didn't know who I was. We got into conversation about one thing and another, and at last I introduced the labour movement. He was very pleased indeed to find it had been done so remarkably well—to find it had been conducted so peaceably; and his firm conviction was that it was in a very great measure attributable to the very good and sound advice that their leader, Joseph Arch, had given them.

"I said, 'Sir, you express yourself as pleasantly surprised at the conduct of the labourers, but I confess I am disappointingly surprised with you as ministers for having treated them in the way you have.'

"'Well, but you know,' he said, 'as ministers we have got to be very watchful.'

"They have—for their money! Well, in reply to his views on the question, I said, 'Now, sir, look here. You say you have got to be very careful and watchful; you didn't know which way the movement would turn; you didn't know what shape it would take; you thought perhaps it would result in breaking machinery, and setting fire to ricks, and everything that was wrong and violent and bad. But sir, do you mean to tell me that if you had fear of anything of that sort, it was not your duty, when you knew the labourers were going to assemble on their village green, to have been there first on the spot and have advised them to go right. Do you mean to tell me that you have done your duty in keeping at home, and letting these men go on, and then say, ' Aha, that's just what I expected you would do' ?

"Well, having hit him rather plain and straight, he said that now, as long as it had assumed the shape it had, ministers generally were beginning to be favourable to the movement, and he had no doubt for a moment, that they would as a rule come round, and give it their best assistance and advice, and guide it properly.

"I said: "Sir, I beg your pardon ; if in the hour of our ignorance, when you dreaded us, we had common sense to do right and have done it, I tell you now—you and the rest of the ministers of all denominations—as we have done without you in the past, we will do without you in the future.'"

So much for ministers in this matter—there were too many Laodiceans among them, and they got from us the treatment they richly deserved. On another occasion, when speaking in Lincolnshire with reference to a franchise petition, which was going to be sent to the House of Commons, I said I considered that to keep somewhere about a million of hard-working and honest Englishmen out of their rights as citizens was dangerous to the interests of this country; and that while these agricultural labourers and rural artizans were void of the rights of citizenship there was something radically wrong which needed immediate reform, if the country was to be made and kept secure. Why I wanted the farm-labourers and other workmen to have their rights was this: it was all very well for a tyrant minority to hold a lot of poor dupes in ignorance and slavery, and treat them as a tyrant and despot like the Shah of Persia would; but when the subjects of that tyrannised country became intelligent and thoughtful, then I did not care who the tyrant was, nor where he lived, nor what his power—the arm of that tyrant must be broken down by the force of the intelligence of the people over whom he had tyrannised. What then for the agricultural labourers?

In 1871 the farmers could meet these men with a terrible threat, if they dared to stand erect. I myself had been the subject of some of these threats; I had seen my brother labourers stand and tremble like an aspen leaf shaken by the smallest breeze of wind, at the dark look of the employer. And what was the cause of all this? Was it that they had not within them the hearts of men? Was it because they had not the brains of men? No; it was simply because they had not the pluck of men, or if they had, they dared not develop it. These things, however, were changed; and to any of the middle or wealthier classes who were present I would say, that upon the success of this Union movement would depend the success of our country. Let the movement be blighted; let majorities or minorities, or farmers, or landlords, try to blast it, and at the same moment that they had blasted the hopes of the men who were the bone and sinew of the nation—that very moment, I did not care what their army and navy might be, they might write up on the chalk rocks of their nation, "Ichabod," "Ichabod," for their glory, of a truth, would have departed from them.

This agitation which had caused so much uneasiness in the midst of certain parties, was an agitation which I considered every right-minded man ought to have welcomed with some degree of satisfaction, even though he might not approve of its every principle. There was a time when men talked under the hedges as to what means they should adopt to elevate themselves from the thraldom and slavery in which they had been plunged. I ventured to say this: that, if the tenant farmers in this country had not in the end met them in 1872—thousands of my brother labourers, honest, law-abiding citizens—they would in time have been met by the fire of the incendiary, and the knife, and the barricade. It was utterly impossible to keep these men in slavery. God had designed the freedom of mankind, and if it had been in the arrangement of His Providence to have tamed the pride of Belshazzar by the destruction of his empire, He could have done it in His might. Never, too, until the farmers exerted themselves to secure for the labourers the franchise would the labourers assist them in passing a respectable

Tenants' Rights measure. Nay more, failing the help of the farmer, the labourers would turn upon him and would concentrate their attention on the Land Question, demanding the cultivation of the soil where it was now waste, and increasing the productiveness of it where it was now comparatively barren. I considered it an important hour in our national history. When the history of the nineteenth century was written, as with a pen of iron in letters of eternal brass, it would be seen before the great judgment bar of God that this great movement was holy in its purpose, righteous in its design, and honest at its core; and God who had blessed it thus far would bless it in the future, if we acted like honourable men; and thus would be seen the hand of a gracious Providence, in wiping away from our so-called Christian country one of the foulest, and blackest, and direst spots that ever stained it—the poverty, and suffering, and slavery, of the agricultural labourer.

I spoke all over the country for the Franchise, at our Union meetings principally. I saw, too, that the day might come, when the next bit of work my hand would find to do would be to speak for my fellows in the Parliament House of the nation. I had never seriously considered the question of my entering the House of Commons until in 1874, Mr. W. E. Forster, in his speech on the Franchise Bill said, "I should very much like to see Mr. Arch in the House of Commons now."

In 1877 I was asked to contest two seats, Southwark

and Woodstock, but I refused them both. In the first place, I felt the time was not ripe; and in the second, I was sure that I could do better work outside; also, I thought if I was sent to Parliament then, somebody would be sure to spoil the work already done. The Cause came first with me from first to last, whatever malicious enemies might say to the contrary. The very idea of my entering Parliament roused the anger and jealousy of several Union officials; of course, they gave various reasons and some plausible excuses, but the real reason was plain enough,—they were jealous, and they could not bear the thought of my going so far up the ladder and leaving them behind. There were ticklish times for the Union just then, owing more to inside dissensions than anything else, and I knew without any telling that my place for a while longer must be, not on the floor of the House of Commons, but on the platforms of district and branch Union meetings, at sittings of Committees and at Union Council Boards. But all the while I kept the franchise ball rolling, and the franchise petitions going round and up to " The Honourable the House of Commons of Great Britain and Ireland in Parliament assembled." A sure sign that the franchise agitation was a genuine and deep-rooted one was the fact that the men sang franchise songs at their meetings; sometimes they would start with a well-known Union one, but just as often in the later years they would sing some political verses as well. Here is one that was a favourite:

THE FRANCHISE.

There's a man who represents our shire
    In the Parliament House, they say,
Returned by the votes of farmer and squire
    And others who bear the sway;
And farmer and squire, when laws are made,
    Are pretty well cared for thus;
But the County Member, I'm much afraid,
    Has but little care for us.
So we ought to vote, deny it who can,
'Tis the right of an honest Englishman.

Whenever a tyrant country beak
    Has got us beneath his thumb,
For Justice then he ought sure to speak
    But the County Member is dumb.
Whenever the rights of labour need
    A vote on a certain day,
The County Member is sure to plead
    And vote the contrary way.
So we ought to vote, deny it who can,
'Tis the right of an honest Englishman.

We ask for the vote, and we have good cause
    To make it our firm demand;
For ages the rich have made all the laws,
    And have robbed the poor of their land.
The Parliament men false weights have made,
    So that Justice often fails;
And to make it worse, "The Great Unpaid
    Must always fiddle the scales.
So we ought to vote, deny it who can,
'Tis the right of an honest Englishman.

CHAPTER XII.

FOES FROM WITHIN.

BUT if we were singing Union and franchise songs at our meetings we were singing tunes of a different sort as well, and they were not songs to be proud of. Why, some of our conferences and meetings might just have come out of the Tower of Babel, there was such a confusion of tongues; officials trying to cry one another down, and trying to push one another out, and struggling to get the upper hand, beset us on every side and gave the enemy cause to rejoice. However, when the confusion was "worse confounded," as one of our poets says, I used to say to myself, " Never you mind, Joe, just you keep going ahead. The cause won't be the worse for it in the end. If the Union is founded on the bottom rock of Truth, the Union will stand. It's no impious Tower of Babel, but one of Freedom's Forts, and we've got to hold it. A free tongue and a free press are the rights of all. Let's have free discussion and fair play out in the open. Truth's but a poor candle if daylight puts it out." But discussion is one thing; abuse is another. Discussion is one of Freedom's children; abuse is the offspring of tyranny and hate, and should be stamped out as you would stamp out a viper.

We had the press for and against us, of course. In 1872 *The Labourers' Union Chronicle* was started, and was conducted by J. E. Matthew Vincent. It was entitled, "*The Labourers' Union Chronicle*: an Independent Advocate of the British Toilers' Rights to Free Land, Freedom from Priestcraft, and from the Tyranny of Capital"; and it had a great influence on the movement in its early stage. The next paper we had was entitled, *The English Labourers' Chronicle*. The Property and Organ of the National Agricultural Labourers' Union, combining *The English Labourer*, and *The Labourers' Chronicle*.

This paper was started by a gentleman, because a few gentlemen of means said the labourers wanted a paper to ventilate their grievances. They invested in the paper and the Union also contributed part of its funds to give it a good start. The labourers took it in and it went well for a considerable time. It stopped through lack of funds caused by the outside subsidies being withdrawn. This was the only paper subsidised by the Union. Others, however, were started in Lincolnshire and Kent, but they were purely local. Both of these papers have long been defunct. They all played a useful part and dropped when their day was done. I know, though, that the editors had no beds of roses—

I do not suppose any editor has that, but some of the labour paper editors had beds that were no softer than harrows. I did not envy them their worrying work, for they sometimes did not know which way to turn. One would say, "Oh, you publish too many of So-and-So's speeches," or, "You do not publish enough of them," and so on. I remember when the Rev. F. S. Attenborough was editing *The English Labourers' Chronicle*, for years he was nearly driven distracted, what with this person and that trying to make him edit the paper as *they* wished. At our Annual Meeting in May 1878, held in the Lecture Hall, Weigh House Chapel, Fish Street, London, when he read his report he said:

"Without solicitation on my part, you asked me twelve months ago to edit your newspaper. I undertook the duty in the determination to discharge it to the best of my power. The duty has proved to be the most difficult and anxious with which I have ever been concerned. In discharging it I have had to deal with many persons, and with more opinions. The conflict between these opinions has been my greatest trouble. Some friends have asked me to publish fewer of Mr. Arch's speeches. Others have blamed me because I did not publish more. Some have urged me to give prominence to teetotal matters; others have said that if I did they should give up the paper. Some have complained of the presence of district news, others of the absence of it. Some have asked me to blame given persons, others have asked me to praise them. Some have thanked me for the paper as embodying every excellence, others have assured me that it has been scarcely worth reading."

This statement was well within the mark, and is only a sample of what labour paper editors, at any rate, have to put up with. I wrote an article every week for the *English Labourers' Chronicle* for two years, giving a history of the first four years of the Union movement.

Among the various matters that came up for discussion, was the Castle Bytham Farm business. To put it straight, and I should like it to go straight, there were four men in that part of England who had nearly spent themselves as public speakers; I may say that three of them had absolutely done so. Then this farm was to let; the Union at that time had some funds on hand and the Executive Committee met and decided to take it. I was attending a series of meetings down in Surrey then, and therefore was not present, and knew nothing about the matter until I came back. The whole thing was carried through by the vice-president, who took my place when I was away. He was one of the four men I have referred to, and they wanted to get this farm. They got it, and the Union had to find the funds wherewith to cultivate it. This I strongly objected to, as I did not see why a few men should get a good living out of a farm run by the money of the labourers who had no land of their own. This was the ground on which I based my objection. Besides, we were not entitled by Act of Parliament to buy more than one acre of land out of the funds of the Union, and they had taken fourteen acres, and hoped, if you please, to add another fourteen to it in a few years' time. Well, under the Trades Union Act this was illegal. No doubt the object of this Act was to enable trades' unions to hold land for office purposes, but not for the purpose of tilling land. As our solicitor said, "When the Union comes to take plots of land and to enter upon co-operative farming it is undertaking business entirely different from that set forth in your rules, and under the Trades Union Act it cannot be done." It was suggested that the Executive Council should take steps for the formation of a society under the Industrial Societies Act, an Act which, said the solicitor, "enables societies like yours to engage in any kind of trade whatever, including of course the acquisition of land, and there is consequently no limit to which such a society may not carry its operations." I took no part whatever in the proposal to start such a society, though there were others who did. We got out of this Castle Bytham transaction, but it cost us a good round sum to do it. We had to deal with a person who, as may be imagined, wanted his pound of flesh—however, we did get out of it. The fact was, a lot of the men were craving for the land; as some one said, they were properly "land mad," and in 1875 there was a regular split on the question. A number of the hasty and too eager ones, thought the Union was going to do everything for them all at a stroke; they were just like a crowd of greedy, impatient children, and they either would not, or could not, get it knocked into their stupid heads that we had to go steady and go sure before we tried to go fast. We were not a set of conjurers.

It is always the case in any movement of this kind, but that reflection comes later; at the time I was very much troubled and annoyed, because I knew I was doing everything in my power to help them on to the land. What was such a handful as we Union officials against so many of the high and mighty? When there was a question raised in 1878 about the Charity Lands, I came forward. A deputation of our members, in which I was included, waited on the Home Secretary, the day before our Annual Council meeting. Mr. Shaw Lefevre, M.P. introduced me. I said then, that the education question was one great reason why the wishes of the labourers with respect to the Charity Lands should receive careful consideration. The labourers were now very properly compelled to send their children to school, but it so happened that in many instances this provision diminished the weekly earnings of the labourer and his family, as some of his children were earning a few shillings a week. Any decrease in the family income where the labourers earned but eleven or twelve shillings a week—and, in spite of all the Union had done, there were many such cases still—proved a serious drawback; and it was therefore highly desirable that any advantage, which the labourer was entitled to receive in respect of land, should be augmented rather than diminished. The agricultural labourers were eminently qualified for using a little bit of land to the best advantage, and, if such plots could be handed over to them, they might increase their incomes some three or four shillings a week, which would enable them all the better to comply with the provisions of the Educational Act, and send their children to school.

There was another point I brought forward: I said that the agricultural labourers strongly objected to the present provision in the Education Act by which Boards of Guardians were authorised to pay the school fees of the children of indigent parents. They believed that it brought them into contact with the Union in a most undesirable manner, and tended to pauperise them, by breaking down the feelings of self-respect and dislike to the Union Workhouse, which it was desirable to foster in the minds of the working classes. Also another advantage likely to arise from providing a bit of land for the labourer was, that it enabled him to make a little provision for sickness, bad times, and old age, on which occasions he was not so likely to apply to the parish, and in that way there would be a considerable saving to the poor rates. These were points we felt strongly about, and as spokesman for my fellows I made the most of the chance. These Charity Lands were nearly all let as farms until we got the vote. The vote broke the back of that; I knew it would, and I always told the men so. But they found waiting a hard job, as who does not? And my experience is, that the more uneducated a man is the worse hand he is at waiting, because he is as unreasonable as a baby.

For a while the numbers fell off, but then again more would join. During 1877 there was some decline in numbers, largely owing to the great depression of trade and commerce, and those districts which stood nearest the commercial centres felt the effect of it most. For instance, Hereford and Worcester had declined more than other places, because they were on the borders of South Wales where the coal and iron trade had been so bad. Men had gone into these districts, and then when slackness set in they came back again to their own districts, and in some instances, they actually went through the various districts proclaiming that the Union was a failure. Then, again, many fell into arrears and were thus lost to us; often, poor fellows, through no fault of their own.

This matter of arrears depended a very great deal on the activity of the branch secretary. If he kept looking the men up, and kept in touch with them, he would generally get his money. In hay and in harvest time the men would often be away from their homes for five, six, and seven weeks, coming back late on the Saturday night, and leaving again either late on Sunday night or early on Monday morning. The secretary had to catch them when he could. It was not that in most cases the men were unwilling to pay up; it was that they would forget, or spend the money in other ways, without considering. A district secretary's post was no sinecure, and a man who undertook it was bound to have his whole heart in the business and put self last. He had to be strong, too—a regular willing horse. It was a post that tested a man all through, and many and many a district secretary came out nobly—they tramped and talked and worked like heroes. But, as was sure to happen, there was dross among the gold; there were self-seekers, and there were the unstable and weak-kneed. The discontented made their voices heard, and like the daughter of the horse-leech they kept crying for more salary, more power, more consideration. "More, more!" was their cry.

When there was a question of cutting down their salaries in 1878 I stood up and said I had no sympathy whatever with such a thing as that. Nor had I—not a jot. There were grumblers, who said office and management expenses were far too heavy. Well, I was only too willing to have the organisation worked on the most strictly economical lines; for not only was I always opposed to waste of my own substance, but I was still more opposed to the waste of other people's. "Waste not, want not," was an excellent Union motto, but it wanted supplementing. An organisation was like a living machine, and it had to be kept going, and if the oil of money was lacking it would come to a stop and fall to bits, for in its motion was its life. That was where an organisation of human beings differed from a mere machine—what was rust in a machine was breaking up in an organisation. The fact was that a desperate attempt was being made by malcontents—and also by some of the short-sighted, well-meaning members, in hopes of bettering things—to federalise the Union. I said to them then, "What do we find in federalism in such cases as ours? Why, we find that the federalists are like so many Kilkenny cats, scratching each other to pieces to see who shall have the most power." I said, too, "If you wish to have your organisation complete, do not let it degenerate by means of bickerings and misunderstandings from its present high position. You are proposing to reduce the salaries of your officers; but why on earth did you not give me notice to reduce my wages?"

I told them, too, that every hour spent in wrangling cost upwards of £5 to the funds of the Union, and that sensible men would never behave in such "penny wise, pound foolish" fashion. There were those who wanted to knock me over, who wanted to cripple and paralyse the central body, and get the districts to federate.

"Oh," they said, "centralisation means despotism."

I, if you please, was the Napoleon of the despotism, a man of iron and brass who would crush them into nothingness. I kept on telling them that they could vote me out if they chose. I was kept there by their votes and I said:

"If the right man is not at the head, put him there; and if you send me about my business I shall always trust and pray that the National Agricultural Labourers'

Union may be truly national, and not a collection of local Federal Unions."

There was another thing I told them too, I said: "I know as I travel the country through—and I think my experience on the work of unions and unionism is as wide, and my information as great, as that of any man in the room—I have met with not a few of the leaders of the great organisations throughout the length and breadth of England, but I do not find that while they deplore, as we all deplore, the fact of stagnation—I say I do not find them coming forth in their Councils and saying, that their Unions are going to the dogs in two or three years. They have their organisations, and to a great extent those organisations are similar to our own."

The Chairman of this Council (Mr. Macdonald, M.P. for Stafford) who had a much greater experience than any of us, cautioned us against splitting our Union into sections, and he advised us, as a man who had forty-five years' experience in connection with Trades' Unions against our six years' experience, not to divide ourselves. "We have heard a great deal," he said, "about centralisation being despotism, but let me refer you to the great lock-out in 1874, and allow me to say that if it had not been for the National Union, you would not have had a Union to-day." I said also, "With regard to your executive committee, which is charged as being the embodiment of centralised despotism, I can tell you that I have never seen a question of a grant brought before them, but that they have always been anxious, as far as lay in their power, to grant a cheque, no matter whether it was for a strike or a lock-out or for working expenses."

"Let me tell you this," I said; "I have not a very high opinion of one district having plenty of money and another district being in poverty." I told them, too, that if our Union had suffered somewhat during the past twelve months, it had not suffered a tithe of what other unions had suffered. "We have got to pull a long and a strong pull altogether, and put our shoulders to the Union wheel, for we have a great deal of organisation work to do yet. If we are to reform our Union, it must be by perfecting the details of our machinery." I was enraged at the self-seeking, and squabbling, and back-biting, and that far more for the sake of the Union than for my own.

And then, as my custom as ever been, I spoke straight. If I have to hit, I hit as straight from the shoulder as I can, a good, honest, English, knockdown blow. "Face the foe, and don't fear the fall," was my motto. I did not mince my words fine with the labourers either. I told them at the different meetings, and whenever I got the chance, that if they did not care for better wages, if they did not want redemption from bondage, beer, ignorance, and tyranny, they might stay as they were, and be degraded serfs all their days, and die in the workhouse; we had done what we could, and would go on till we dropped trying to make men of them, but drop we too, soon should, if they did not join in and lend a willing hand. "One and all it must be, so one and all let it be," I said over, and over, and over.

The malcontents were at it harder than ever in 1879. They wanted to form the Federal Unions into districts; each district to have a president, and so forth, and each district was to send up so much for my support. I refused it, because the moment they stopped the supplies I was done. I told them so. I saw that my enemies had waxed so bitter against me that they intended to kick me out, their toes were tingling to do it; but I was not going to be kicked out—my work was not done, nothing like done. I was determined that if I was to go, I should be dismissed in an open, above-board manner; but that was just what my enemies did not want. They tried to hustle me off the Union platform, they tried to push me out of the president's chair. All I can say is, they did not know Joseph Arch when they tried that game on. I had desperate hard times in 1878 and 1879, but there was comfort brought to me, too, when I found so many members staunch to the Union and to me.

I remember a great meeting we had on the seventh anniversary of the Union. We held it under the old chestnut-tree at Wellesbourne. It was a pouring wet day and the roads were in a fearful state, but notwithstanding that, between two and three thousand assembled, many walking seven and eight miles through mud and slush. An open waggon was our platform; was drawn up against the trunk of the old chestnut and lit up with tallow dips. As some one remarked,

"There's little light from those dips, Joe, but there's plenty of grease."

"Enough light to see by, and more than enough to hear by," said I. From the top of the chestnut tree a Union flag proudly floated like the banner in the poem "Excelsior." George Mitchell was voted to the chair. I was a bit fagged out when I stood up, but once started I went ahead like a house afire. I know this: I carried the men with me, for they stood like one man during my speech which lasted a good hour and a half. I was greatly moved; I can remember now how all strung up I felt.

I began by saying: "Seven years ago to-night I responded to the call of a deputation of Warwickshire agricultural labourers to come here and speak to you on the question of Union. I felt the importance of my position at that time, and I see the face of a labourer in this gathering, who said to me after the first meeting had been held, 'You have lighted a torch which I have no doubt will light the whole country up before long.' When he made that remark to me I felt I had undertaken a work, which, if that prophecy were fulfilled, would require the most indomitable determination, the strictest integrity, the most sterling character and perseverance to carry it out; but to-night I feel I have a responsibility which I had not at that time. I felt it to be a great responsibility to start the Union, but I feel it to-night to be a greater responsibility to defend it against its internal enemies."

I went into the history of the Union and into details

of the internal struggles, and into the personal insults I had had put upon me. "But," I said, "when fourteen thousand and more of my countrymen rally round the standard of the Union, which, seven years ago, we raised on this memorable spot, I can well afford to stand against the calumny of the calumniator; I can well afford to smile at the opprobrium and contumely cast upon me."

I reminded them of our triumphs as well as our struggles. "When 1874 set in," I said, "you then fought one of the greatest battles—and when I say greatest, I mean in proportion to our genius for fighting, and I also mean in proportion to our skill in carrying on a battle—therefore, on that score I say we fought, as agricultural labourers, the greatest battle that ever was fought by working men in England. The country at that time rushed to your rescue with about £25,000; but you fought for the right to combine, and you won a grand and a glorious victory.

"In 1875 you are well aware that it was said Joseph Arch tried to wreck the Union; but when mistakes of a serious character are made, I am determined to ferret them out. I feel the dignity of my character, though a farm-labourer born and bred, as much as the Prince of Wales does. Though it might sever me from my nearest and dearest friends, I will never allow the highest power a man has, and that is his character, to be foundered in the mire of treachery. If to bring mistakes to broad daylight; if to unearth a mistake for the satisfaction of tens of thousands of men; if to speak the truth, and dare to stand single-handed, as I did in the Birmingham Council—if all this be the cause of wrecking your Union, I would far sooner see it wrecked on the sands of truth and justice, than that it should be buried in the mire of selfishness and trickery.

"As you know," I went on to say, "my character was libelled in the vilest manner week after week for something like eighteen months. I was advised to take counsel's opinion upon one of the very worst of these libels, and counsel returned his opinion that it was a very good case, and that I should make my opponents suffer; but he said it would cost a sum of money to start the action. I then said, 'Very well, let it drop; for, if the character of Joseph Arch cannot defend itself without taking hundreds of pounds of the labourers' funds, then let him die in ignominy and disgrace.'

"The last May Council (1878) came, and a committee was then formed to inquire into a cheaper method of working your Union. That committee drew up their report, and I was instructed to call a general meeting of representatives from every district, to consider their report. The committee decided upon nine out of the ten recommendations submitted to you. Some of the very men who voted for the acceptance of nine of these resolutions, went back into their districts and told their members that if these resolutions were carried, it would do the Union more harm than good. I ask, Was that constitutional? I think not.

That committee was formed from every district, and it authorised me to call a council in London. I felt certain there would be a little bit of antagonism, but what was at the bottom of this antagonism? I unhesitatingly say it was because it was the wish of your president and your committee, that these resolutions should be placed in your hands, and not in the hands of the district representatives. I said, 'Let every member of the Union have a chance to speak upon them.' Was not that constitutional? Then you are told that I want to form a Union of my own, and that I am a despot. Now, let us look where the despotism lies.

"In these resolutions it was said that you members should have the entire power of fixing the salaries of your officers, which power you have a right to. I voted heartily for that. It was also proposed that you should fix the salary of your president, and that you should have the power to elect him or send him away. Was not that true constitutionalism? But what about the men who, at the London Council would not let the votes of their members be known; who said they came there to represent their districts? Why, out of fifty branches in one of those districts I hold forty-five to-day. Those men went there to represent themselves. Who, I ask, is the despot? The country at large shall read what I am saying to-night, and let the country give the verdict."

I went into the question of the circulars which had roused a great deal of feeling. I had issued one, and my action had been stigmatised as unconstitutional. I said, "Well, with regard to this circular—it has gone, and why did I issue it? I should have returned from the London Council on the Thursday, but your chairman who is always so generous as to find me a home for nothing in London, knows that I was too ill to return from London on Thursday in consequence of the abuse I had received. On the Friday I got home and I found there was a circular which had been issued by the Oxford district secretary, from 'The Strand, London.' It was concerning a meeting on Federation or separation. I regard the Oxfordshire men with as much respect and sincerity as I do you men of Warwickshire. I looked at it and I said, 'If that is your game, to split the Union, I will take the bull by the horns.'

"On the Saturday night, after I had finished my correspondence which, as you may imagine, was rather large, I wrote out my circular, forwarded it to Leamington to get it printed, which was done; and it was forwarded to the Oxford district before the district secretary had an opportunity of carrying out his designs. What! Am I, at the head of your movement, to bow to every dog that barks; to tamely submit to every word of insult? Never!"

I went into the different points, but I came round again to the main point, which was centralisation *versus* federation. I said: "Centralise your funds. I should like you to send your funds to the central office. Let your district secretary be your agent, and let him be looking after your interests; let him audit your accounts, and let your general secretary receive the moneys at the central office. You may depend upon it that your Union will never be sound at the core till you have these reforms. Let the district committees be all unpaid men. Let your Executive be unpaid men. Let no outsider have any voice in your Council; it is your cause, and manage it yourselves. Have some good *bonâ fide* labourers on your Executive Committee. Send unpaid men to the Council I beg of you. If you send the same men, to a great degree my mouth will be gagged again; my hands will be tied."

"These are some of the measures of reform we propose; they may startle some of my friends, but I am not a weak man myself. It will require the most determined perseverance on your part, and the closest unity of action, and the widest possible discussion, if these things are to be brought about. I will be plain and honest with you. If you do not think me the right man in the right place, if you think I am not worthy of your confidence —I tell you sincerely and honestly, if it should be your will and pleasure to vote me out of office I will take off my hat and will say, 'Gentlemen, you had a perfect right to do it.' If you think that my salary is too high, it is in your own hands; but if the salary you offer me is a starving wage, it is not a question with me, 'Can I get more?' for I could have done that before to-day; nor is it a question with me how much I can get; but the question is, 'Can I live and maintain my family, and travel through the country, and expose my constitution and health for the wage?' If it is a wage that I cannot do so upon, I will deal truly with you, and say it is so low that I must get something else. You be honest with me and I will be honest with you. I tell you candidly that, whether I am a despot or Napoleonic, I will not stand humbug from either officers or men."

I think by the time I finished every man and woman assembled under the old chestnut tree saw plainly just how things were, and it was brought home to them that they must centralise, or the Union would split in pieces. I remember there was a cry for the old Union song, beginning "When Arch beneath the Wellesbourne Tree." It did me good to hear how heartily they sang it. There was such a hand-shaking after, that I thought to myself, "Seven years of hard labour, Joe, brings a reward with it; hearten up and make ready for seven years more."

I had need to, for there was plenty of fighting yet to be got through. I know there were times when it used to seem to me something like mockery at this period, if we opened a meeting with such a song as the following:

> Welcome to our Union meeting,
>   Friends and strangers, old and young:
> Farmers, tradesmen, labourers greeting,
>   Every hand, and eye and tongue,
> Every name to-day is "Brother";
> All our creed is—love each other.

All the same it *was* our creed and we were striving to keep true to it.

My theme now was—Unite and centralise; economise and popularise. In fact, I wanted the maximum of reform on a popular basis. When I was presiding over the Warwickshire District Annual Meeting at Leamington in April 1879, not long before we held our Annual Council, I told them that I (and others with me) was going straight for reform. I said I had hoped that the Committee which was appointed last May, and the resolutions which they sent out to the branches, would have been the means of stopping the expenses which they were obliged to incur in calling such meetings as those throughout the country. There might be, I said, some men who differed from me in opinion, but I had given the question very careful consideration; and, having submitted it to figures, I found that our officers, from first to last, could be elected with considerably less expense, by adopting the circular plan and allowing every member in the Union to have his vote.

I was a great advocate for a man, let him belong to what organisation he might, having his direct and individual vote for or against any great question affecting that organisation of which he was a member. I said: "During the past seven years I have presided over a considerable number of representative meetings like the present, and questions of great importance have been brought up from different branches, which the representatives of other districts knew nothing whatever about. I have sometimes wondered how these men could really vote upon questions which neither they nor their members had ever for one moment considered, and I therefore have come to the conclusion that the most democratic and the most thoroughly English way of doing business—especially in a great organisation like this—is not to place the responsibility upon the shoulders of one man, whom they may send to record his vote for them, but for every member to give his vote from the first to the last."

That was the way I wanted the Union to be governed. "Of course," I said, "we have been compelled to call this meeting, and we shall be obliged to call another General Council, but I very much grudge the expense. The necessity of calling the meeting has been brought about, not by the desire of the members throughout the Union, for I may say that their first vote on the question of lessening the expenses of holding large representative meetings was overwhelming in majority, but because their wishes, and desires, and votes were set at nought on the 21st of January last in London." The federals had been the peace-breakers, they had been wilful wasters in more ways than one—that was the opinion of a great number of our men. Numbers wanted the popular vote in the branches when they understood that by it they would be able to elect whom they liked to do their business, from the president down to the least official among them.

At our Annual Council, held in London in May 1879, we calculated that those assembled represented some twenty-three thousand labourers in Union, and in spite of appearances, there was reason for congratulation. To begin with we numbered in our Union some of the most intelligent labourers—the pick of the men; then those who had fallen out had done so because of the general depression; they were, the bulk of them, with us in spirit and fellow-feeling, and were only waiting for better times when work would enable them to be Union men once more. It was an undeniable fact, too, that in many parts of England, where wages had been kept up to twelve and thirteen shillings a week, they would have run down to nine and ten if it had not been for the Union. It was true that a number—a large number—of our men had been obliged to submit to a reduction of one shilling a week; but they were only sharing in the general depression, and it was not as much as other organisations had been obliged to submit to. Things were hopeful, there was no gainsaying it, and things I knew would look more hopeful still, if wisdom and discretion ruled our counsels. We had to aim at making and keeping the Union national as we had aimed at first; to have a good centralising fund; to encourage the placing of the management in the hands of unpaid men; and to give every member a direct vote. And we ultimately did decide to try for simplicity in arrangement, economy in management, and representation in government. I said again and again that the members must never forget that what they had to do was to represent an organisation; to support it if weak, and to eliminate, if possible, anything in its constitution which operated against the prosperity and good of their republic. What affected the left hand affected the right; what affected the head affected the whole frame. It was necessary, therefore, to look earnestly and diligently to the parts, since it was the correct adjustment of the parts that constituted the perfection of the whole.

It had been widely reported that the Union was going down; nevertheless it was alive and vigorous still, and I had never seen good men so energetic as they were now. Where false friends lived branches had been broken up, and in some places societies of fifty or sixty had been formed. It was obvious, however, that these must die out, from the impossibility of making local what could only succeed as a national and universal scheme. I told them that the history of trades associations taught us something in 1851. They were split up into little factions; consequently there was no unity of force or action, and the result was the masters easily beat the men. Whilst we stand at one another's backs we are strong; if we separate we ensure defeat. The central organisation of the Union had twenty-three thousand odd members, in connection with which a Sick Benefit Society had been appended with a fund now approximating to £4,000. Other advantages would be developed in due course, if the Union remained true to itself.

But there were malcontents crying out for concessions never contemplated by the Union. Some were asking for land. It was amusing what got into the labourers' heads sometimes. One official told me he had been asked for money to buy an old thrashing machine! Why, if such calls were recognised the Union might close its books at any time. I had been denounced as obstructive to the interests of the Union and its members. My obstruction was that I had objected to the spending of funds contrary to the object for which they were designed. An application had been made to me for £500, for the purpose of obtaining a farm. A gentleman would have advanced the money on my security but not on that of the Union. I could not clearly see the justice of being made responsible as a private security, simply because I belonged to the Union. Conditionally those who wanted the farm might have had it; but their own action deprived them of the chance, and for this I had been put down as an obstructionist. Well, all these misunderstandings would work themselves out in time. I could say from experience—travelling as I did in all parts of the kingdom—that the feelings of Unionism, and the principles of Unionism, were growing in the minds of the farm-labourers of the country. I knew only too well that there had been enough to check the warmest desires, and to blight the brightest hopes, but I was glad—thankful—to say that all the efforts to damp our desires and blight our hopes had failed. They might have succeeded with a few, but very soon, like the repentant turncoat, they would be singing " The Backslider's Lament." I was confident that the labourers, taking county for county, were more determined than ever to stand by their grand old Union.

Foes from Within

I spoke in this strain at meeting after meeting; warning, exhorting, encouraging, as far as in me lay. I remember there was a song which was rather popular at this period; and I will quote it as illustrative of the prevailing spirit of the men:

> All hands to the rescue, our Union's in danger,
> By sham friends in our ranks, which we plainly can see;
> So swelled with ambition, their togs it won't fit 'em,
> They vainly would climb to the top of the tree.
>
> There is this one and that one, a third, and yet more,
> Who legislate for themselves, regardless of we;
> But we, their paymasters, now fearlessly tell them
> That, though once we were blind, we can now very well see.
>
> They have grossly insulted our leader and pleader,
> A man of far greater fame and renown,
> Whose slippers they all are unworthy to carry,
> Or even his stockings or garters to town.
>
> Away with all tailors and president-railers,
> "Peace and retrenchment" our motto shall be;
> With Arch, for our leader we never can mend him,
> Let all that would spurn him from us ever flee.

"Peace, retrenchment, and reform," was our motto that year; and in spite of foes from within and without, I was ready to lead the van of our Union army on to victory.

CHAPTER XIII.

THE LAND AND THE LABOURERS.

THE land question, as well as the franchise, was just at this period pressing itself on our attention, and it was no wonder, for the agricultural depression had been, and was, so great, that a Commission was being held to inquire into the terrible state of affairs. Of course the Union was affected; though I may truly say it was solid, more solid than ever, but here and there men were dropping out. They had got into their heads the idea that once their wages were up, they would not only keep up, but would never go down any more. The farmers had been telling them so; of course it paid them to make the men believe that, and the men, like silly sheep, believed them. Well, they had to pay sharp and dear for their credulity. What was the first thing we heard?—this was during 1879 and 1880—why, that the farmers of Worcestershire had decided to drop the wages of their labourers two shillings a week! This was a big, a terrible, drop for a man earning only eleven or twelve shillings. When I heard the bad news I said, "Oh, now they will perhaps value their Union at its true worth. Big drop or little drop, it's all one; the men will just have to submit. They would not join the Union, or have fallen away from it, and so they have nothing to help them. They refused to pay twopence a week into the Union, which would have cost them nine shillings a year, so now they have to submit to a drop which will cost them £5 4s. a year. We have heard before of people being penny wise and pound foolish, but in this case the labourers have been penny wise and five pound foolish, and I say, 'Serve them right.'" The Staffordshire labourers, who behaved in the same foolish way, had to put up with a similar drop.

Farmers were down on the men whenever they got the chance, and a great deal of petty meanness they showed. I remember a case which occurred in 1876 as an instance of what I mean. There was a certain farmer at Shanklin. He had a dispute with a labourer named Coombs, who thereupon left his master's service. The farmer summoned Coombs to Newport for leaving his employment, and the case was dismissed. A second time the farmer summoned him for £1 damages for leaving the horses in the stable, and a second time the case broke down. So, to spite the labourer, the farmer goes and ploughs up his potatoes! However, at the Newport County Court he made the discovery that he could not do as he liked with a labourer's property; at any rate, if the labourer was a Union man, and could so procure proper legal assistance. The judge denounced the farmer's conduct, and declared he had been guilty of as gross an act of trespass as was ever committed. The farmer was condemned to pay at the rate of three-shillings-and-sixpence per rod for twenty-four and three-quarter rods of potatoes, £4 3s. 2d., and costs, including plaintiff's counsel's fee. It was rather a heavy bill for the gratification of such spiteful meanness.

Again and again men would be discharged for being Union men. There is one case which occurs to me; it took place when the Union was in its early days, but it was typical of what went on all through the seventies. This case was a good deal quoted. A farmer discharged one of his men for joining the Union—a man he could easily replace he thought—but he had a shepherd whom he could not so easily spare. He went to the shepherd and said, " John, have you joined the Union?"

"Yes, Master, that have I."

"Ah, well now I've got a sheep's head at home that I was going to give you, but now it'll go to a better man."

"Very well, master."

"And John, my wife bought a frock for your little girl, but that'll go to some one else."

"Very well, master," said the shepherd once more, and then off stumped master tyrant.

This sort of tyranny was still going on; but the farmers were suffering themselves, some of them as much as their bitterest enemies could wish. Things had been going down hill with them for a long time past. I remember in the autumn of 1878 how bad things were in Norfolk; the farms there were quite thirty per cent. worse, productively, than they had been in 1872, and many of the farmers' crops were mortgaged to the bank.

In Dorsetshire, again, many of the farms were in a state of scandalous neglect. On one farm three brothers, all farmers, were seen in a field of theirs, cutting down the thistles and docks with scythes. Another farmer in the same county sent his men into a field to plough, but as he had not provided them with gloves and gaiters they had to come out again. Mowers were sent to cut down docks and thistles in some of the fields. When they had cut them and carted them away, they were sent in to plough the land; but the roots proved too strong for them, so men and plough had to retire. Fields choke full of thistles was no uncommon sight. In county after county there was this terrible, this lamentable, blot of neglected, weed-covered land.

At a meeting in the spring of 1878, I said, "At the present time there are 897,000 acres less growing crops in England than in 1870, and 2,606,000 fewer sheep than in 1874." I also said, "The present average of money spent on the land is £5 10s. an acre, and this, it has been shown, is insufficient to nourish the land. If, instead of investing in Turkish bonds, men had spent their money on the land, they might now have saved the farmers from a state of bankruptcy. Mr. Mechi, a well-known authority, said that £10 an acre at least ought to be spent on the land. At the present time £225,000,000 is invested in land, but according to Mr. Mechi, £211,000,000 more ought to be spent on it. If this were to be done, the soil of England would take 50,000,000 more labourers to cultivate it."

"Is the farmer," I asked, "doing all he can for the land, or instead, is not the farmer who, a few years ago, kept twenty-five or thirty milch cows, now content with four, and are not seven fat beasts now sold off a farm where there used to be sold twenty? At the present time we send out for eighty-five million pounds' worth of food for the people of this country, for there is only enough produced in it to feed forty out of every hundred. The farmers have sixty more customers than they can find food for, and yet they say trade is bad!"

I remember saying as far back as 1875 that, if the farmers did not get a good Tenants' Rights Bill within the next five years, four out of five of them would be cracked up, and I was not so far out. If the farmers had their weepers on in 1875, they have kept them on pretty well ever since, and they have had enough to make them mourn. Why, in my own county it was reported in the spring of 1879 that there were over a hundred farms to let, amounting to a twelfth part of the entire county. It was the same sad story in other counties. Landlords were offering reductions of rent amounting to ten, twenty, and even thirty per cent.; but the farmers in many instances refused even this. Bad seasons, coupled with want of proper security for their outlay, proved too much for dozens of poor tenant farmers. In a long speech I made on the subject at a labourers' meeting at Abbot's Salford in October 1879, I said:

"I have always been a firm believer in the dignity of labour. Whatever that labour may be, if it tends to benefit the country and increase its happiness and welfare, the men thus employed are England's greatest noblemen. But, unhappily, labour in this country has never met with its proper share of honour, or been rewarded with the remuneration, which in my judgment it ought to have had. Although you have been told that labour is something inferior to capital, I maintain on the other hand that capital is inferior to labour. What is capital? As John Stuart Mill put it, it is the accumulation of labour, and if labour has thus begotten capital, labour ought to take the first position in the country. Surely the child should acknowledge its parent with respect! I say capital is the child of labour and it is a dangerous thing for the interests of any community when the child begins to strangle the parent.

"You have heard a great deal about the organisations of working men, and it may be that they have not always acted so wisely as they should have done; but what class of Her Majesty's subjects do you find perfect? Why, it is a certain fact that even by the highest Trade Union in the country, the House of Lords, great mistakes have been made; and if labouring men in the past have happened to be sometimes in the wrong, why should their organisation be decried by capitalists whom their labour had made rich!

"Whilst in Edinburgh a few weeks ago, I was surprised to hear a statement, more reliable than the information the Government gives the country on its foreign policy, that during the last year the various Trades Unions in Great Britain have, in relief for sickness, benefits at death or accident, payment to members out of employment, and some outlay on strikes, spent no less than a quarter of a million sterling. Not a penny of this vast sum has ever passed through the Mansion House, nor has any member of a Trades Union ever asked Her Majesty to patronise the fund. It has been raised by the horny-handed working men, without any aid, and such a result is an honour to you. I am happy to tell you that the Labourers' Union is growing, that its funds are in a prosperous state and increasing; every month shows our enemies, who asserted we were dead, that they have been telling falsehoods, for here we are still alive. I shall now move the adoption of the following petition to Parliament, from the inhabitants of Abbot's Salford and the neighbourhood:

> 'That your petitioners, seeing the large amount of uncultivated land in this country, and the conditions under which millions of acres more are held, are compelled to come to the conclusion that there can

be no permanent improvement in trade or in the condition of the people until we have a sweeping reform in the land laws, and this meeting therefore urges upon the people of this country the necessity of vigorous agitation upon the land question until such measures are passed in Parliament as may meet the requirements of the people.'

"I believe when Parliament meets, hundreds of such petitions will be presented. The landlords and farmers of England probably never dreamt, six or seven years ago, that the labourers would take this important question in hand. For centuries we have, as a class, been immensely docile, and if a labourer grumbled at all it was like the Irishman, 'as loud as possible to himself.' It was not because there was no need for complaint, it was not because there were not justifiable grounds for grumbling; but such was the hard lot of the farm labourer, that if he dared to speak out he very soon had to skedaddle somewhere else, and not unfrequently he was driven out of his native parish. In addressing you to-night I shall endeavour to give you what in my judgment, as a farm-labourer, is one of the main causes of the present agricultural depression. But what have we got to do with it?

"Well, we had the impudence to want to be represented upon the Royal Commission. Oh, for shame on these Billycocks! Do you not know that you are represented in the House of Commons as fairly as any other class? You have the landed proprietors, who understand all your wants; and when in that august assembly any question crops up affecting your interests as labourers, they will give it 'their calm and serious consideration.' I have closely watched the course of political events ever since I was a boy, and for the life of me, I cannot see that any single question affecting the agricultural labourers has received the 'calm and serious consideration' of the county representatives, except the poor laws; and their main object in considering them seems to be how nearly they can starve the poor without quite killing them. In all legislative movements we have, as a class, been totally ignored. At the present time there is a depression in agriculture, and yet the most important class, the labourers, are not allowed a representative upon the Royal Commission to inquire into the causes of depression. I say we are the most important class; because, if all the landowners in the county emigrated next week, it would be nothing like the loss to the country that it would be if the labourers left its shores.

"I do not, I can tell you, intend to be shut out on this question. But I will ask you, if there had been no Union, would the labourers ever have dreamt of making an inquiry, or even expressing their opinion on the present depression? Without our organisation would the press have recognised us as it does now, and record our meetings? We shall also make the Tory Government recognise us. We will show them that they cannot have it all their own way. You have heard that the cause of agricultural depression is the bad seasons we have had. There is no doubt a great deal of truth in that, but what has made the bad seasons tell upon the farmers is the fact that their land has not been properly cultivated. You may go from Dan to Beersheba, and the Royal Commission can sit till they are as old as Methuselah, and when they have searched the whole creation they must come to the conclusion that the tenant farmers, to a large extent, have to thank themselves for the present agricultural depression. What has been the policy of the tenant farmers throughout the kingdom for the last twenty years? I know, and you as labourers know, and we don't want a Commission to tell us. Their policy has been to do with as little labour as possible, and the labour they did employ was never paid for sufficiently to enable the men to do a good day's work. They have half-paid labour, and the result is half-fed labour. If a farmer's team of horses is not more than half-fed, he cannot expect them to do full work, and it is just the same with the labourers. Year after year, the men who have sowed and reaped the corn have known that, independently of the seasons, the crops have not been so fruitful as if proper labour had been put into the land. This is the very root of the evil from the labourers' standpoint.

"But there is a disadvantage under which the farmers labour, and that is the short and uncertain tenure of the land. If a farmer lays out £1,000, or £2,000 on his farm, he does not know that he may not be called upon to pay an increased rent; and if he does not think proper to pay interest on his own capital, he has notice to quit, and some one else is ready to give the landlord the advantage of the tenant's money. What power has the farmer to compel the landlord to pay for unexhausted improvements? I do not blame the farmers so much for being sparse with labour under such circumstances; but I do blame them for being such noodles as to take land upon such conditions as will allow the landlords to step in at any time and filch their capital. I dare say I shall be called an agitator, and be charged with setting class against class; but I am here to tell the truth, and if there is any tenant farmer here, let him deny anything I have said.

"When this movement was started, noblemen and landed proprietors used to invite me to discuss the question with them in London. It was amusing to hear them talk. They said that all these matters were regulated by the law of supply and demand; that with the present patent machinery and mechanical appliances, farmers could do with far less labour than they used to do; and that it was of no use my thinking of labourers getting high wages so long as they were so thick on the ground. My experience as a labourer is that, for the past twenty years, not half enough labour has been employed on the land. Just to show you that these wise men know nothing of the question, let us judge of their opinions by results. Take their patent machinery and mechanical appliances, that were to enable them to do without the strong arm of the labourers, and to send them to Jericho if they had nowhere else to go to, where have they landed the farmer to-day? They have landed him on his knees at the foot of Queen Victoria, as a humble suppliant, and saying, through the mouth of Lord Yarmouth: 'If it please your Majesty, will you please give me authority to go down to the House of Commons and tell that august assembly that you have consented to a Royal Commission to inquire into the miserable state of the tenant farmer, and to tell him how he is to pay £100 with £75 cash?' If the farmers had not listened to the twaddle that the earth could be tilled by machinery alone, and that the Almighty had not made living beings to till it, they would not have been in their present position. If some complicated machinery is invented, and the landlords applaud it, the farmer buys it at once.

"There is another matter which has much aggravated farmers' difficulties, and that is foreign competition. I was much struck by reading a speech of Lord Beaconsfield in which he said reciprocity is dead; and if he had told the truth, he might have added that it is buried, and that although he has educated his party in a great many matters, it is more than he or all English Toryism can do to raise it to life again. Reciprocity is buried, not with 'a sure and certain hope of resurrection,' but never to rise again: and all the Tories in Christendom will never dare to tax again the poor man's loaf. The farmers want a cure for foreign competition: well then, they should grow more food for the people at home. If people could buy bread and beef and cheese from our own farmers, they would of course do so; and if they grew a sufficient quantity of food for the people, they would not go to other countries for it. We send a hundred millions of British capital every year to the various colonies and the States of America, to produce food which might be grown at home, and yet farmers allow the Americans to have our labourers and to take the steam out of our markets.

"It does not need a man two months, let alone two years, to get at the root of the mischief. This foreign competition has been an awful bugbear to the farmers, but it was a great blessing to the workmen during the past winter. Let us thank God for Cobden and Bright. The fruit of their labours has been seen in thousands of homes which have been blessed with the cheap loaf. It may be said that the farmer is not responsible for foreign competition; but we must remember that they have foolishly sent thousands of men across the Atlantic, to grow beef and corn to send here to compete with English produce. When the movement started there was a terrible hullabaloo, and many farmers said they would sack their men and not employ a single Unionist. They have carried out their promise, and now they are reaping the reward of their foolish policy. I believe they have not yet got to a tenth part of what they will have to suffer. No less than seven hundred and fifty thousand men, women, and children have, during the past seven years, left this country for other lands.

"You have a right to ask who were the men who went? They were those with the most courage, and those whom the farmers could least do without; those who could and would turn their hand to anything. The very men that the farmers said seven years ago they would starve into submission, are those who are now helping foreign growers to compete with the farmers at home. These men would never have had the means to emigrate unless the Union had helped them. I have heard that, in various parts of the country, the farmers have threatened to pinch their labourers this winter, and to reduce their wages to ten shillings a week. Will that help the farmer out of his difficulties? Will that enable him to grow larger crops? Will that stop foreign competition? No! and God will avenge the oppressor. I believe that the succession of bad harvests are a visitation of the Almighty upon the farmers for their treatment of their labourers, and upon a luxurious and dissipated aristocracy. I believe in a God of Providence, and as sure as the sun rises and sets, He will avenge Himself on the oppressor. The farmer must not be too confident. There are broad fields in our colonies, with thousands of acres of virgin soil, only awaiting the labourer to till them, and large companies are being formed to induce the best men to emigrate. Only lately a telegram was received in Ireland from New York, stating that in America they are prepared to find £50,000 to send out Irish tenants to a country where they will have brighter prospects, better laws, and freedom for all. They were invited, in fact, to go to the grand States of America, the home of justice and liberty. All the English farmers who have any pluck at all are going out, and when they get to their destination, they will want farm labourers to till their fields.

"An intelligent tenant-farmer recently told me that it would be a sorry thing for England if this tide of emigration once set in in earnest to the States. The men who travel know the real state of the case; but, unhappily, too many farmers only know the price of pigs, and what was paid for beef and wheat at Evesham market, and if they go from this district to Birmingham market, they think they have been all over the world. Twenty years ago and now are widely different. The labourer then was a dull, docile being; but to-day he stands up and demands to be recognised as an Englishman. He claims his political rights; and I may say, for the comfort of the farmers, that their land reforms and their prosperity will never be consummated till they and their labourers go together to the ballot-box to send the proper men to represent them in Parliament.

"It is a very remarkable thing that, if the landlords in Parliament have any new tax, they put it on the shoulders of the poor farmers. I am inclined to think that when the tax-collector comes round for money to pay the horrible butchers' bills in Afghanistan and Zululand, Sir Stafford Northcote, if he wants the full tax, will in many places in this country have to take it out in thistles. Between this place and Warwick station, and especially along the line from Alcester, there are not five fields in sight of the railway fit to put autumn seed in. If there are, let any farmer point them out to me. If justice were only done to the land the people would have their food forty per cent. cheaper than it now is. If the farmers really carry out their threat to sink the wages, there will be no alternative for the labourers but to go to the workhouse, where they will cost the ratepayers four shillings and tenpence a head, whilst at home they would be satisfied with three shillings to keep their children. By making a man, his wife, and four children paupers, the farmers would have to pay about twenty-four shillings a week, whilst fourteen shillings was all they would give the labourer for his work. Will a state of things like this make the farmer wealthy and the poor man contented? We have in the United Kingdom, according to the Board of Trade returns, twenty-seven millions of acres of waste land that will amply repay cultivation.

"Who is to find the £25,000,000, which has been expended by the Government in blood and murder? What will England benefit by the Afghan war? And what will we get from the Zulu campaign except a large elephant's tusk? Just in the same way, we got a tremendous booty from Ashantee in the shape of an old umbrella. I care not what position you occupy, whether you are farmers, shopkeepers, publicans, or artizans, I call upon you to rise in the majesty of your manhood and say that, whilst agriculture is declining, and the full produce is not got out of the land, and whilst there are twenty-seven millions of acres of uncultivated land, you will not allow the bone and the sinew of the country to leave our shores, nor £25,000,000 to be wasted in useless wars; that you will hunt to the ground the authors of a blood and thunder policy, and place in their stead men of intelligence and wisdom, who will see the greatness of the nation, not in a blustering and wicked foreign policy, but in the happiness and prosperity of the people."

It was a long and an important speech this, and one I had carefully prepared. I remember that at the end of it I gave a mock Tory address, mimicking a certain Conservative parliamentary big-wig. I did it on the spur of the moment, and I finished up with the following adaptation of a well-known hymn:

>From Chatham's pleasant mountains,
> From Aldershot's bare plain,
>Where the British flag floats proudly,
> And the lion shakes his mane;
>From barracks and from mess-room
> Resound the bugle's notes,
>Calling to arms to cross the sea
> And cut some heathen throats.

>What though from every pulpit
> We daily Christ proclaim,
>And bend before the Prince of Peace,
> And worship in His name
>In vain, in adoration
> We bow before the Throne;
>Those heathen are possessed of lands
> Which we must make our own.

What though our souls are lighted
  With wisdom from on high!
Shall we to men benighted
  The Gatling gun deny?
Proclaim it, oh! proclaim it
  To Afghan and Zulu!
This is the way we Christianise
  And teach them who is who.

Blow gently, blow, ye breezes,
  Let the war smoke upward curl,
While bathed in blood and glory
  Stands forth our Premier Earl!
But weep, oh! weep for England,
  And bow the head in shame;
For sullied is her honour,
  And tarnished is her name.

I felt very strongly about these wars, and the awful expenditure of blood and men and money. It was a waste of God-given gifts I could not stand silent and contemplate. As I said elsewhere, " The Government has been kicking up a row abroad on purpose to stop legislation at home; we will therefore kick up a row with the Government by putting in a Liberal and a Peace one when the next election comes." I said too, " Agriculture is depressed, and will be so long as there is a landlord Parliament. Hundreds, I may say thousands, of honest working men are wanting to get a respectable living by the labour of their hands, but that privilege is denied them. The result of this lack of labour is that we have hundreds and thousands of mothers almost starved to death, and I have no hesitation in saying that the pinchings of hunger which tens of thousands of poor, dear children suffered this last winter will have sown the seeds of decay in their youthful systems, which will bring thousands of them to a premature grave before this day twelvemonths. We are not only murdering Zulus, but the innocents at home, and yet Englishmen can stand by, quiet as lambs, and see millions of their hard-earned money wasted in bloody murder, while at home tens of thousands are having their constitutions sapped to the core through it."

I also said, "I say to you labourers, join our noble Union. Stick to it like men when you have joined it; and if people in better positions turn up their noses in contempt never mind. Our numbers are great enough, our intelligence is powerful enough, and when we get the vote, we shall show them that our votes are numerous enough, to cast aside this war policy, and to bring back to England her peace, her commerce, and her prosperity."

I could not help feeling that this agricultural depression was a natural judgment on the farmers for their treatment of the labourers. They had, in their criminal folly, recklessly cast from them the best men—and a good farm-hand is a very good thing. This is what Thorold Rogers said at a meeting we held at Oxford in 1878; and he knew what he was talking about. He said: "Let me say a word or two about the functions of a first-class farm hand, and I am quite certain that there are many in this room who will agree with me. Suppose I ask a man whether he thinks it is an easy thing to drive a straight furrow over a ten-acre field, and to carry his furrow from one end of the field to the other, and from this side to that without any 'wobbling' in his work. What would he say? Why it is as hard work as painting pictures, and a man that has not had a good education in this direction is as incapable of learning it, except after a long and painful course of training, as is a man who paints pictures. Let me ask you about shearing a sheep. It is a much easier task to clip a boy's head at a barber's shop than to shear a sheep, and nothing is more artistic than a clean, well-sheared sheep. Then how about rick-building. You may depend on it that it is, on the whole, harder to build a rick well than a house well. My impression is, too, that the art of making a rick is peculiar to that part of England which lies between the Trent and the British Channel. I have spoken of three high arts possessed by a good farm hand. Now, how about making a ditch and a hedge! This is no easy matter; and it requires a considerable amount of skill to be able to make a line straight across a fifty-acre field, and do it to the particular point, having laid the drain-pipes in such a way as not to allow a break in the outfall of the water.

"Well, if you set to work, to compare the work of the agricultural labourer who possesses the five or six qualifications I have mentioned—and I am perfectly certain I could make them up to a dozen—with the work of an ordinary artizan who receives thirty-five shillings a week, the agricultural labourer, as far as regards the varied nature of his accomplishments, is conceivably superior to the artizan. Every one knows in manufacturing places it is constantly the business to get those hands who can do one particular thing with the greatest exactness and rapidity, but in agricultural work the best man is he who does the largest number of things with the greatest rapidity. I do not grudge the artizan his thirty-five shillings; but I want to know why the agricultural labourer should not get as much, too."

He went on to say that for five hundred years the legislature had been striving to reduce by force of law the wages of the agricultural labourer. In the beginning of the reign of Queen Elizabeth, who was a clever and an able woman, but who was obliged to consult some people about her, the legislature of the time contrived to pass a law which really did more to degrade the labourer than anything that could be imagined. In the fifth year of her reign it was decided that the Chairman of Quarter Sessions in every county should fix the wages which the agricultural labourer should receive, and mighty low they fixed them. They had the power, not only of doing this, but of punishing anybody who gave more or asked more than was fixed, and the consequence was the agricultural labourer was left entirely to the mercy of the employers.

There was another thing he said, which I had often said myself. "I suppose a labourer, among other accomplishments, knows a little about sheep and pigs, and is pretty well aware that if a sheep or an ox is starved, his carcass is not improved. Well, on the whole, the healthiest condition for the human being also is when he has enough to eat. But there is a higher consideration than his physical health, and that is his moral growth; and it is quite certain that a man who has no prospect, no hope, nothing to get but what is absolutely necessary for his daily maintenance and those depending on him, cannot develop those virtues which a man should possess. Along with a good physical strength and a good moral growth there comes a conscience; and one of the first directions which the conscience of a man takes in the work he is set is that of giving true value for the wages he receives. You may depend upon it an underpaid farm-labourer will no more have the inclination to do a good day's work than he has the power to do it, and when you have raised his condition by giving him the power you will also bestow upon him the inclination."

I remember he also said that a great squire who lived near Oxford had told him he was extremely thankful that the Labourers' Union had come into the parish, where he owned every inch of land. It had raised the men to a higher level, and in some districts this Union, led and guided by Joseph Arch, had been the cause of the diminution of pauperism; and the great service he had done was not denied by persons of intelligence, and only repudiated by persons who were fools. Of course I thought that was nothing but the truth; not because

I was Joseph Arch, but because I was leading our Union. If the farmers had had the sense to lend us a helping hand, when their hour of trial came, we would have stood side by side with them, and helped them—aye with might and main, and instead of cursing the Union they would have blessed it; but the turnip-headed farmer turned his back on us, and he has lived to rue the day when he did it.

CHAPTER XIV.

THE CAUSES OF AGRICULTURAL DEPRESSION.

IN the spring of 1880 I contested Wilton as a supporter of Gladstone, my opponent being the Hon. Sidney Herbert. Wilton was a pocket borough under the control of the Earl of Pembroke, who owned the estate, and whose nominee alone it was supposed could win the seat. The borough had for over twenty-four years sent a Liberal to Parliament, so it was looked upon as a Liberal borough; but in 1877 the nominee and warming pan gave up the seat, having accepted the "Chiltern Hundreds." Then Mr. Sidney Herbert, the earl's brother, a young man of twenty-two, was run out as an Independent candidate, promising to follow in the steps of his father, the late Lord Herbert of Lea. As there was a good deal of uncertainty as to Mr. Herbert's politics, and as the earl, the nominee, was a Conservative, the Liberal party consulted, and the result was a contest. Mr. Norris of Bristol was the Liberal candidate, but he was defeated, and so the "Independent" took his seat in

Parliament, and upon every important division voted with the Government, including the "cat."

The Liberals were very angry at this, and as the borough was an agricultural one, the Wilton Liberal Society invited me to stand; and I said I was willing, but that I could not pay my expenses. If they could be guaranted I would come down and fight my best against Tory landlordism, war, bad trade, starvation, and the "cat." A gentleman hearing of the money difficulty said, "Let Mr. Arch come; I'll willingly pay all his expenses;" so down I went, and an exciting time of it I had. We held our first meeting in the Temperance Hall, Monday, March 22nd, 1880, and things were lively—a bit too lively. Considering the behaviour outside, I wonder I got through this, my first, address as a political candidate without bodily harm. While I was speaking there would be crash! bang! and stones, great big ones, would fly through the smashed windows into the Hall. So bad was it that they had to put up window-boards inside, and in spite of precautions several of the audience were badly hit. The roughs outside hooted and howled in a most disgraceful manner; but for all the howls and the stones I finished my speech to the end as I set out to do.

There was a great deal of feeling in the country, largely among the agricultural labourers and artizans and small shopkeepers, about the Zulu War, and I alluded to it in my speech.

I said: "In the *Daily News*, some few months ago, I read a statement which made my blood almost boil in my veins. It was a letter from their special correspondent, and had reference to the unhappy affair at Isandula, a spot visited four months after the unfortunate affray. He says: 'A strange dead calm reigned in this solitude of nature; grain had grown luxuriantly around the waggons, sprouting from the seed that had dropped from the loads and had fallen in soil fertilised by the life-blood of gallant men. So long the grass in most places had grown that it mercifully shrouded the dead, whom for four long months we had left unburied.' And who were the unfortunate men whose bones were left there bleaching in the intense heat of an African sun? They were chiefly the sons of agricultural labourers. And what a thought for the mother whose son had been engaged in that sad conflict—the thought that the child whom she in pain bore and in anguish brought forth, whom she nourished in his boyhood, and hoped to have seen grown up to have formed and to have played some significant and useful part in the body politic, had lain weltering in his own life-blood on an alien shore, and his body had been open to the penetrating sun four months."

I also referred to the "cat-o'-nine tails," and I said: "I cannot forget that large and enthusiastic meeting which I attended in Hyde Park last summer to protest against the use of that monstrous instrument of torture. It is all very well for the people who reside in rural villages or in large towns to say that the soldiers themselves do not require its abrogation! Let us converse with the soldier, and what do we find? I have embraced every opportunity of ascertaining their opinion upon the matter, and I have never found a single soldier of the rank and file yet who ever attempted to bolster up the system; except to this extent, that, if you give it to the rank and file, give it to the officers too, when they disgrace themselves."

The feeling among the labourers about the abuse of the "cat" in the army was very strong. There were all sorts of stories going about; one was, I remember, that a young man, the leader of the Rifle Band and who was popularly known as the "Pride of Winchester," had been flogged to death with this instrument of torture in Zululand, within three months of his leaving home. There were all sorts of terrible tales, exaggerated no doubt, and sometimes untrue; but many of them beyond a doubt had too much brutal truth at the back of them.

There was another thing I alluded to in that speech—the question of the ballot and of secret voting. I said: "With regard to the ballot, I will not say a word deriding the powers that be, but if any gentleman tells you working-men that the ballot is not secret, he knows he is telling you a falsehood. I understand that, at the last election at this borough, which was in 1877, farmers were seen at the polling-booth with books professing to take the electors' names and telling them, 'Oh, we shall know how you vote.'"

Now just let me give you my experience with regard to the ballot. At the election of 1874—the General

Election—I went to record my vote. There were three gentlemen standing in the schoolroom when we went to poll, who had been telling working-men who happened to have votes, "We shall know how you vote. Mind what you are doing; you will lose your place; be careful."

They had been carrying on that little game nearly the whole day, so after recording my vote for the man I believed would go to Parliament to do the most good, I turned round to them, and as respectfully as I knew how, said, "Gentlemen, can you tell me how I voted?"

They looked very sheepish at me. I repeated:

"Gentlemen, can you tell me how I voted?

"Now," I added, "I am surprised at three gentlemen like you standing here and telling falsehood after falsehood for the purpose of intimidating the working-men. Why didn't you tell me when I came into the schoolroom you should know how I voted?"

"Oh," said they, "you are too old."

Well, I would simply say to the working-men here, "Be too old for 'em."

I finished up my saying: "Now, before I sit down, allow me to exhort every elector here—don't use intimidation, and don't be intimidated. Let us, if we are Liberals, fight the battle honestly and nobly as men. The Liberal cause of England requires no falsehoods to bolster it up. Men like Mr. Gladstone, Lord Hartington, and Earl Granville, want no secret intriguing to give them a standing in this country.

They have won it, not by trickery, not by 'scientific frontiers,' not by a series of Oriental surprises, not by depressing its trade, but they have won it by dint of indomitable perseverance for their country's honour, and by their strict integrity. And they will win again with a grand and triumphant majority, and we shall yet see this old England of ours what she deserves to be—noble, happy, and free. If it be the will and pleasure of you electors of Wilton to record your votes in my favour, don't for a moment think I am absolute perfection. I am liable to make mistakes, as are other men. Don't for a moment conceive I am an angel. If you do you will have a wrong conception of me. But meet me on the ground of a man and an Englishman. Meet me in the political area as a thorough Liberal, and, if by your votes I have the honour to represent Wilton in Parliament, believe that the name of Joseph Arch will never be disgraced, either on the floor of St. Stephen's or throughout his native land; but he will live and die an honest, true, and earnest Liberal and Englishman."

I remember we held another meeting under a great tree at Netton; and a most successful one at Coombe Bisset, when I spoke to a listening throng in the light of the full moon. The farmers tried to annoy me at one or two meetings; but we kept them down. There was some intimidation too, we heard; farmers putting on the screw with a view to preventing their labourers voting for me, and one labourer was actually threatened. The legal adviser to the Liberal Committee told the men plainly that any farmer who discharged a man for not voting as he wished, or who threatened to deal with a labourer in an unpleasant way for the same cause, was liable to six months with hard labour, and perpetual disfranchisement. Lots of the men were frightened here, and in other places, by the farmers, and of course they did not know how the law protected them.

There was one point on which I took my stand from the start, and that was, "No canvassing." I said: "I do not wish it. I regard the vote as a sacred trust, and I disdain to extract, by means of a canvass, that which the law directs is to be done in secret. Canvassing is, in my opinion, a mean subterfuge. Its object is to get at a man's vote in an indirect way, and I shall keep clear of it."

I shall quote here what the *English Labourers' Chronicle* said, because it expressed my own feelings, and also those of the labourers at my back. "Whatever may be the result of the election at Wilton," it said, "one thing we shall always be able to point to with feelings of justifiable pride. Mr. Joseph Arch is the first candidate who has had the moral courage to contest a constituency without resorting to the questionable practice of canvassing the electors, with the view of ascertaining the way in which they intend to dispose of their votes. That is something of which Mr. Arch will ever have reason to be proud." I do not know about pride, but I felt I was doing right, and as I would have others do to me in a like case.

I lost the election, but I was far from being disheartened. On the contrary, I was astonished to find how politically wide awake the labourers were becoming. I said to myself, "Never mind, Joe; better luck next time. You'll tread the floor of St. Stephen's yet, as the representative and the mouthpiece of your fellow-labourers. The time is not ripe yet; but it's ripening fast. Look alive, then, and don't waste a minute. Stir up the men; for once they get the franchise, they will send some one to speak for them in the Assembly of the Nation." And I went around stirring them up.

Here is a specimen of a petition of ours about the county and borough franchise:—

> "To the House of Commons of Great Britain and Ireland in Parliament, assembled:—The humble petition of the undersigned delegates of the National Agricultural Labourers' Union sheweth, That your petitioners, representing the opinion of the unfranchised farm labourers of the kingdom, feel it to be a monstrous grievance that they, who are the producers of so large a portion of the national wealth, and who are heavily taxed in proportion to their means, should have no voice in the imposition of those taxes, and that they should be called upon to obey laws in the making of which they have no share, laws which have been made for them by other classes unacquainted with their wants, laws which in many an instance press most unevenly and unfairly on those who are the

poorest paid subjects of the realm. That your petitioners are of opinion that the vote is of the greatest value to those who are the poorest and therefore the most defenceless, and they earnestly implore your House to grant them this right; for they feel that they are at present treated as aliens in the country of their birth, and are compelled to seek in other climes for those constitutional rights denied to them at home. Your petitioners hear that a Bill has been introduced into your House by Mr. Trevelyan for the assimilation of the county and borough franchise, and they therefore pray that this Bill may be passed into law during the present session."

At our Annual Council that year I said: "We now have a Government in office which will listen to our requests. It is a Government, I am pleased to say, that the National Agricultural Labourers' Union has helped to place in power. This has not been done by the votes which our men possess, but by the circulation of the paper amongst the £12 voters in the counties, and which has had an immense influence in winning them over from Conservatism to Liberalism. The day is not far distant when we shall have our political rights as householders in the counties." We had to wait four years longer for it though? But it took the working-man in franchised boroughs twenty-five years to get his vote.

After all I was called before the Royal Commission

to give evidence, and I came up twice. The first time was on August 4th, 1881; the second time in December of the same year. The Duke of Richmond and Gordon was president, and I remember I made him rather wild. When he asked me the question as to what was the cause of the depression, I told him that I thought the reason of the present depressed state of agriculture arose from three causes—*i.e.*, not sufficient labour employed, rents too high, and not enough money put in the land. He then asked me whether I knew the tenant farmers had no money. I told him I did not think they would ever be likely to have any. I had been reading a book on the subject, and from it I learned that the landlords had raised the agricultural rents of England twenty per cent. in eighteen years on the tenant farmers' profits. Something like ten and a quarter millions had to be paid away to the parsons in the shape of tithes. How then were the farmers to have any money, with the parsons on one hand and the landlords on the other? Why, they were topped and tailed like turnips!

I remember, too, one of the Commissioners said to me, "I am paying fully sixty per cent. more for my labour since you began this Union."

"I am very glad to hear it," I said, "but it proves one of two things. If you are paying sixty per cent. more for your labour than when the Union was started, you were either paying miserably low wages before it began, or you are paying very high wages now. Which is it?" He would not tell me.

Of course they wanted to know all about the Union, and I told them that though it was not perfection, it supplied a want, and was in my opinion a necessity. I gave them some details. I said: "Our headquarters are at Leamington, and we have a general meeting every year. The officers are now elected by a popular vote, and rules are made by the representative assembly—that is, so many branches are formed into a district; each district has the power of sending so many representatives in proportion to the number of its members, and these representatives make the rules. The rules are then submitted to every branch for the consideration of every member, and as they pass them so the representative gathering accept them. Rules are drawn up by a special committee. Representatives of the local unions are voted for, either by ballot or openly. Each branch has a paper sent it, 'Whom will you nominate as your president, your general secretary, or your district officers? or whom will you appoint to sit on the executive committee?'"

I could not help thinking of our early efforts at organisation and our little beginnings, and contrasting them with the organisation of 1881. Our numbers were on the increase now; there were some twenty-five thousand, spread over twenty-two counties, in Union. Though the farmers had scoffed at us, they had found it expedient to start a sort of a union of their own. We never feared it, for it was not a real thing—it was a rope of sand. I knew very little about it, as regards rules and management, etc. But I do know something about the farmer's inconsistency, and the following is a case in point. When a labourer, one of our members, wanted the recognised wage of—at that particular time—thirteen shillings a week, the farmer, if he was a member of the Farmers' Union, was compelled by the laws of his union to refuse to pay him this wage. The farmer had to advertise for a non-Union man to whom he often had to pay eighteen shillings a week, in addition to which he had to lodge him. So that, in order to spite our Union, farmers often had to pay eighteen shillings a week to, and lodge, a bad workman, instead of paying thirteen shillings a week to one of our men.

But this silly state of things did not last long. The farmers subscribed to this precious Association for a time, but as they got rather sharply twitted about it, they soon dropped it. Like a bubble it quickly burst. I believe the chairman of the farmer's sort of Trades Union, which they called a "Chamber of Agriculture," was generally, if not always, some great local landowner. Well, of course the chairman was considered. I need say no more. He practically gagged the meeting over which he presided.

I told the Commissioners that I did not agree with the Farmers' Alliance, which much resembled our Union. I said: "The time has come when labourers will not be mocked. We have heard a great deal of the identity of the labourers' and farmers' interests. I have always believed in it, but the identity has not been properly realised. The Chairman of the Alliance wrote to me that he was thoroughly satisfied that the interests of the labourers were bound up in the Farmers' Alliance, and that they were going to send a deputation to Mr. Gladstone. I immediately wrote back as courteously as I knew how, and I offered to get up a deputation of labourers, and let farmers and labourers go to the Premier together, and show that we had this identity of interest. Of course that was not allowed. Well, is that not mocking us?"

There was too much humbug and shilly-shallying and blundering about these Farmers' Unions and Alliances, or whatever they called them. I had no kind of patience with them. I told the farmers they must not look to the landlords to redress their grievances. In 1873 and 1874, when the labourers were trying to push their worthless selves into notice, the landlords said that landlords and tenants must row in one boat; well, they rowed in one boat till the bottom was out and it was water-logged. I said again and again to the farmers: "You must strike out into a new line of politics. You have been ploughing in the same furrow until your plough has not only got never a share, but you have never a share to put on it. Your political power is not more than two thirds of what it was in 1874, because so many of you have had to give up your farms. Well, you must bestir yourselves, and join hands with us and find a remedy—you will never do it alone, and the landlords will not lift a little finger to help you. Don't count on them. Join in with us, and the sooner the better."

Then as to the tithe, I used to tell them that I thought the law on the subject should be altered, but that if they took a farm, and agreed with their eyes wide open to pay so much in tithe, they ought to do so. I do not think now that tithes should be abolished altogether as a charge on the land, but they should be applied to relieving the parish and road rates. They should not, however, go to the parsons. Let those who want parsons pay for them. I pay for mine. Should tithes be abolished, the landlords would very likely raise the rents. In fact, the farmers will never be really safe till they get an Act passed fixing the scale of rents.

Then there was the question of security. I said to the Commissioners that the very fact of the tenant farmers holding their land on the present conditions is to my thinking a proof that they have no commercial brains in their heads. "Custom," I said, "has bound the farmer's mind, and he has not gone with the times. A large quantity of land is let to-day on the condition that the tenant farmer may put whatever capital he likes into the soil, and when the landlord thinks well to notice him quietly out of it, there is no clause in the agreement that will allow him to claim compensation for the money he has put in. For the last twenty-five years farmers have farmed to leave instead of to stay. I have heard them remark, 'Well, you know we farm to leave, and that's all about it.' The present system gives the farmer no guarantee that justice will be done him. His position is only safe paternally and not legally. And I for one do not believe in living under any one's patronage."

Of course agricultural depression did not spring up like a mushroom. From 1857 to 1875 the value of land in England went up enormously. Caird said that in 1875 the farmers were paying £9,000,000 more for land than in 1857. Who had made it valuable? Not the landed proprietors but the extension of capital brought in by the hand of industry. It seemed to me that the landed aristocracy owed a great debt to the tenant farmers and the agricultural labourers. But when the value of the land increased, their gratitude showed itself in a singular fashion— they raised the rents. The Agricultural Holdings Act was not favoured by the farmers—they called it a sham, because it was permissive where it ought to have been compulsory. I used to tell the farmers at this period, "Oh well, if you will be children you must take the chastisement of children." They let themselves be bested, and only grumbled or acted in a left-handed sort of a fashion.

Then again I advocated very strongly and persistently the abolition of entail and primogeniture. It had undoubtedly helped greatly to starve the land. I said, "I do not think people should have the power to tie up the land for more than one life." Entailed estates in my pretty wide experience were less well cultivated; and on such estates I have known many farmers pining for material to repair their fences, and they could not get it. These estates were dilapidated because the life owners were frequently crippled for want of ready money, and they had to provide dowries and sisters' settlements off the land which they could not do as they liked with. Land could not be sold freely, for, in a manner of saying, the dead bodies of centuries lay upon it, dead hands gripped it and held it as in a vice.

In my opinion, and in the opinion of hundreds, it was high time these feudal laws were abolished, and land transfer made as easy and quick as the buying and selling of an ox or a sheep. "Free the land from the dead hand," I used to say, in speech after speech. "Let the land circulate; let more share in it; give the labourers a chance. The farmer ought to be in such a position that, if at some future time he wants to make the land he has tilled his own, he may do so by fair purchase. I do not preach confiscation, I do not encourage thieving; but let the farmer have a chance of paying for the land if he wishes to do so." "You farmers," I used to say, "have grandchildren and great-grandchildren occupying land tilled by their ancestors; they have been paying rent for generations; and yet you are no nearer making a single yard of it your own than were your ancestors."

The land system is rotten, and the farmers are foolish. The land was labour-starved, and they held the threat of machinery over the ignorant labourer's head. I said to the Commissioners: "The farmers have used machinery as a sort of weapon over the backs of their labourers. I heard of a certain farmer who boasted for years at a market ordinary that he bought a reaping machine but he never used it, and he said, 'It has paid me a good percentage, keeping it in my coach-house to frighten the labourers with.'" He was one of many, too. As to machinery, I never had any objection to it as supplementing the labourer, but I consider it requires a strong complement of men, and must have them, if farming is to succeed. I always said I never wished any sort of legislative interference with machinery, unless the farmer makes a machine to eat the bread when it is baked! I said: "I think so far machinery has been at least a partial failure; it has been made too much of. I can take you across clay hills in my own neighbourhood to-day where I have cut crops of sixty-two, fifty-five, and fifty bushels of wheat upon an acre, harvest by harvest; and some six or seven years before these bad seasons set in, even the last four or five years, I cut over the same ground—though they were good seasons—not more than twenty, twenty-five, and in some cases not more than fifteen bushels. This was where they had been applying scientific machinery and leaving the labourer out of it. Mr. Giffen's figures will tell you that on the large farms the crops and the stock have not been so productive as on the smaller farms, where there is scarcely any machinery used."

Then as to labour-starving the land. Why, there were farms of five and six hundred acres with only two men and a boy to work them; there were such farms in Warwickshire, Dorsetshire, and Worcestershire—some of eight and nine hundred acres on which for a considerable time no horse's foot had been put to plough, nor a man's foot to hoe and clean, nor a single grain of corn grown. Many farms were thrown up, or were scarcely touched, and like the sluggard's garden, the thistles and weeds, the docks and the briar, grew apace and no man checked them. The farmers were much to blame for not using more labour, and also for not paying their men according to their worth.

I said to the Commissioners: "It has been a great mistake farmers have made ever since I can remember, that they have not given the best men the best price. Twenty-seven years ago I was putting in a large drain for a farmer; it was six feet deep, and he was paying me one shilling and sixpence a day, and was paying another man forking 'twitch' on the same land just the same price. I asked the farmer for two shillings and sixpence—I judged my work was worth it—but he refused to give it, so I just struck then and there.

"Then, again, an employer of mine told me years ago that I was worth twenty-four shillings a week on any farm. I said, 'Why don't you give it me?' 'If I were to give you twenty-four shillings, Arch, my labourers would be dissatisfied, and I should also incur the displeasure of my brother farmers.'

"Now why should I not have had that twenty-four shillings? I should have earned it to the full, because I could make gates, and hurdles, and hedges, and stack and thatch buildings and ricks, and shear, and drain, and mow. I say that, if the other men had seen me get that twenty-four shillings, they would have said, 'Oh, it's some use learning things and buying tools.' Tools are very expensive things for us to invest in. I have spent as much as £20 in tools in my lifetime. If I was a farmer, and had a superior workman at work, and he was getting twenty-four to twenty-five shillings a week, and another man said, 'I think I can do as well,' I should say, 'Then I will set you a job, and you shall have a try'; and if he could do the work, he should have the same money. Give the men a chance of doing better if they can."

I said, too, that I strongly advocated piecework where practicable; it was much fairer to both man and master. Then again, for years and years the farmers had said they were to fix the price of labour—"We fix the wages, my men, and you have got to take what we choose to offer you." However, the Union knocked that little bit of injustice a smart blow. The farmers who paid their men properly, and employed sufficient labour, had a better chance of pulling through a hard time. Those who labour-starved the land were simply, " labour wise and land foolish," and they began to find it out too late. Those farmers who had cultivated their land well, had enriched it and not spared labour, could afford to retrench in a very bad season without sinking. Their invested capital showed up its worth in the day of scarcity.

But whatever was said it always resolved itself in the last resource to this—better security, more freedom. The farmer's hands were tied by fear of a twelve-months' notice, and the landlord's hands were too frequently tied by the law of entail. I said at this period: "The land has been kept for a number of years under such a series of restrictions, and of so binding a character, that now we have the agriculturalists in such a position as cannot be found in any nation under the sun, I believe, with something like twenty-five per cent. of the occupiers of the land turning bankrupt, or on the brink of bankruptcy."

Land, land: that was what we were all thinking about and talking about, and the idea of an Allotment Act was in the air. Jesse Collings was taking the matter up after his fashion in the House—he was Member for Ipswich—and at a big meeting I was at in December 1881 we had a petition on hand in which it said: "Your petitioners view with grave concern the uncultivated condition of much of the land of England, and the consequent distress amongst the unemployed labourers, and respectfully but most earnestly pray your honourable House to pass the motion of Mr. Jesse Collings in favour of peasant proprietorships, which they believe would practically remedy the existing evils."

When before the Commisioners, I said: "If you want the labourer to rise, if you want him to get above being a pauper, if you want to make him self-reliant—we have been too dependent a class—if a man can make a good profit out of his quarter of an acre (and I know some men will make it more than others), let him do so. If that man could take an acre or a couple, and by that means save himself from pauperism, let him. I think it is highly desirable that the labourer should not be limited to a quarter of an acre, but that you should let him have some scope for his ability. A labourer should have a good quarter of an acre attached to his cottage; and if he can cultivate it and get enough out of it to take another half-acre it would be a wise step for any landed proprietor to let thrifty and persevering men have it. Those, of course, who do not properly cultivate their plot should not be allowed to keep it on.

"And I think the same rent should be charged to the labourer as is charged to the farmer. The rule, however, is to charge the labourer excessively; to make him pay twenty-five, thirty, and even forty per cent. more for his land than the farmer does. I have gone exhaustively into the question. A farmer will pay at the rate of thirty shillings an acre for land which the labourer has to pay for at the rate of five pounds per acre. This is land let to the labourer in addition and apart from his cottage garden-land, on which the men grow vegetables for their families.

"Take my own village, or Hampton Lucy, or take a number of villages in the west of England I have gone through; there is the field of allotments, and they have been paying from five shillings to eight shillings, and eight shillings and sixpence to ten shillings for twenty perches. Now five shillings for twenty perches equals two pounds per acre, and yet a farmer on the other side of the hedge will get his for twenty-five shillings. If the landlord can afford to let allotment-land at twenty-five shillings per acre to the farmer, he can surely let the labourer have it at, say, thirty shillings.

"Bad seasons affect the little plots of land just as much as the larger. I know that, owing to the bad seasons, labourers have had to pay for the vegetables they were unable to raise on their plots. I think 1879 was, taking it all round, about the worst season we ever had in my experience. I know that in my own garden, which I cultivate well, the produce was not worth so much in 1879 by about £3 10$s.$ or £4 as it is worth to-day. It is a fact that labourers suffer just as much as the farmers, and more, because of their very limited resources, in bad seasons. It is another example of what I have always taught, that when you come down to facts the interests of labourer and farmer are identical.

"Then, again, a labourer should have good security for his plot. He puts good labour into it, and clears it, and improves its value. I know how my father suffered—he had his allotment shifted four times in the course of his life. The labourers were put into a field in very bad condition, such that no farmer particularly cared to cultivate it; they held it for three or four years, and got it thoroughly clean and capable of bearing anything, and then they were shifted on to another.

"I consider that granting land is the only practicable way by which labourers can extricate themselves from pauperism and serfdom. I say, let a thrifty labourer be a small farmer if he can save enough; sufficient land should be open to him at a reasonable rate. I think, as things are, that it would be a great blessing if some of the farmers could be upset, as they have more land than they can cultivate, and here are labourers crying out for it.

"Let the labourer raise himself by the land. I teach the farm labourers never to be satisfied while there is a chance of advancing in life. To teach a man to be content to stick in the mud, is to teach a man to curse himself. I think we should increase within his mind a just discontent for every year of his life, to make himself a better man, and go one better every year he lives."

"Yes," I used to say to the men, too, "stand on the land and rise on the land." Now legislation was taking up the matter, and in 1882 the Allotments Act was passed.

CHAPTER XV.

I ENTER PARLIAMENT.

ALL during 1882 I spoke a great deal on the land question and on the franchise. Of course the Allotments Extension Act was very much discussed. Howard Evans was the real author of the Act, though he said the question was first stirred up by Mr. Theodore Dodd, the son of an Oxfordshire clergyman. Mr. Dodd wrote some articles on the subject, and he declared that the Act of William IV. applied to all local charity lands. Of course, there had been a lot of talk in different parts about these lands; and Howard Evans, when travelling about the country for the Union, saw that something had to be done. Many of our district secretaries got hold of the county charity reports and began to agitate. When the trustees were applied to about the lands they generally made both their ears conveniently deaf. Then the Charity Commissioners were applied to and they would have nothing to say to Evans, and showed him the door. Evans got a Bill drawn up and Sir Charles

I Enter Parliament

Dilke promised to lay it before the House; he did so, but it ended in being dropped. Then, after the election of 1880, Jesse Collings took up the matter. We all knew the labourers were divorced from the land, and that this was neither good for them nor for the country.

As soon as Parliament opened in 1882 Jesse Collings pressed on the "Charity Lands Bill"—a boon to the rural labourers it was meant to be. The Act was originally intended to give the labourers a cheap and easy remedy in the nearest county court. The moment, however, we attempted to apply it, the Charity Commissioners made all the difficulties they possibly could. They were not friendly to the Act, though they were obliged to administer it. As Evans said: "The tricks resorted to by some of the trustees are simply infamous. In some cases they have let the land on a long lease so as to evade the Act; in others they have, contrary to law, charged exorbitant rents; in others they have, contrary to law, refused to let except to farm labourers, and sometimes only to farm labourers who are householders; in others they have ignored the Act altogether; in others they have illegally demanded half a year's rent in advance." There were so many complaints, that Jesse Collings asked for help to start an Allotments Extension Association. I must say that Evans worked like a slave over this Act, and he wrote on it in our paper, and gave extracts from the Charity Digest.

I did my part by speaking on the subject. I told the men that they must see to it, and have the pluck to move themselves, for they had to force the hand of the Charity Commissioners. In many and many a village the charity land had been diverted from the purpose intended and enclosed in the farms, and when a poor man wanted a piece of land he had perhaps to pay the parson at the rate of £3 or £4 an acre for it.

I had to stir them up about the Union, too. Reports got about that the Union was dead, or next door to it. In an article I contributed to the *English Labourers' Chronicle* at the end of 1882, I said: "What are the labourers' hopes for the coming Christmas? They have let the Union go down, and instead of getting thirteen or fourteen shillings a week, they are receiving ten." I also said: "I ask, can any labourer who has read the *English Labourers' Chronicle* sit down to his Christmas dinner on Monday, December 25th, 1882, and not say that the Union, assisted by such men as Mr. Jesse Collings and Mr. Howard Evans, has enlightened his mind?"

"In some parts of the eastern counties an attempt was made to keep harvest wages down," I told them, "notwithstanding there was more to cut and gather. The men being strong in Union in many parts gained a ten shillings advance on their wages of the previous year. But in some parts of Gloucestershire, Wilts, Hants, Berks, Somerset, yes, and even in some parts of Warwickshire, they have been obliged to take whatever wage the farmer chose to pay."

Of course the Union was strong in parts, and where it was so it was very strong. As usual, I came in for

I Enter Parliament

any amount of abuse because of my notions about the land question; but I pegged away all the same, and I said: "Let them write till their pens are worn to a stump, until their ink-bottles are dry, and until their fingers ache, and their arms also to the shoulder; but, so long as I see millions of my fellow-countrymen, who have to eat to-morrow the bread they earn to-day, and who have to struggle hard to keep the wolf from the door—so long as I see them suffering as they do; so long will I labour to remove the cause of that suffering, and the great evil which I believe the land laws inflict upon the country. The landlords say, 'Touch these laws, and our political power will wane and wither.' I say, if that be so, however great the calamity—and it would not be great—for the sake of a prosperous trade, for the sake of a secure agriculture, let their political power wane and wither; but perish the laws that have so long been a hindrance and a curse to the country."

At this time the question of the labourer's cottage accommodation was a great deal talked about. It was always cropping up, and little wonder. Scores of the cottages were nothing but garnished hovels at their best when I was a boy; they were much the same in my young manhood, still the same when I was working for the Union and many are not much better to-day. In the sixties the overcrowding entailed a condition of things among the agricultural labourers which made a man blush for his country. Again and again I spoke out on this subject. I cannot think what the country clergy were doing not to have called high Heaven to witness on the terrible things going on in the parishes. In some cases the accommodation in labourers' cottages was so limited, that whole families of seven, eight, and nine, of both sexes, lived and slept in one room, and the sanitary arrangements were appalling.

Well, in 1881, when I was before the Commission, I had my say on the matter of bad cottages, and also on the question of cottage right. I said: "I think if the farmer is going in for tenant right, which of course I hold with, that there should be legislation to grant the labourers' cottage right." I knew of farms myself where the cottages were let with the farms, and of course it bound the men hand and foot. I said: "I never would live in one of those cottages myself. When a cottage is let with a farm, a man is compelled to labour on that farm from January to December." I knew of a case in 1872, but seven miles from my own house, in which, when the junction railway passed through the district, the railway companies were offering three shillings and sixpence to three shillings and tenpence per diem, and young, strong men, who were at work on this land for eleven shillings, left it; but they were pretty quickly told that unless they came back for twelve shillings they should leave their cottages. I said then: "Why, this cottage question has been going on forty years, to my knowledge."

I always thought this a shameful injustice. I said to the Commissioners: "The principle of cottages on farms being at the farmer's mercy is not sound at bottom.

If I, as a labourer, rented a cottage from you, and paid my rent, I would not be bound by you or any man living to labour as he wished. Let the farmer go into the market for his labour, the same as any other employer of labour. If a labourer," I said, "has a proper notice to quit, well and good; but I call it a monstrous injustice that he should be driven out of his cottage on a week's notice." I said, "Both tenant farmers and labourers have a precarious holding; it should in both cases be made more stable."

I know, too, that in my own village I strongly opposed overcrowding and indiscriminate sleeping. I called the attention of the Nuisance Inspector to the matter, and he soon stopped it. He made the farmers, in some instances, build new cottages with proper sleeping accommodation. There ought always to be, in my opinion, two bedrooms at the least; three bedrooms should be the general rule, because, even if a man has to pay a little more rent, his sons can then stay at home longer, and so help to keep the house going. Besides, it would have another effect: if the sons were comfortably accommodated with their parents, they would not be in such a hurry to make hasty marriages while only lads, as is far too often the case.

I will quote here from an article on the Franchise, which I contributed to the *Nineteenth Century*; because it touches on the question from another side. I said: "We are asked sometimes why we urge our claims so strongly. Is there anything in a vote which will do you any good? Do you believe it to be the panacea for all the ills you have to bear? Well, let us see. Have we in our own rural villages the same sanitary arrangements as there are in our enfranchised towns? It is true there are in some parts nuisance inspectors, but there are many—very many—villages where there are no sanitary arrangements at all? I must not name villages; any one who travels must observe the bad sanitary condition of the rural districts. But whoever brought a Bill into Parliament to compel the great landowner to properly drain his cottage property?

"There are, it is true, many improvements needed in our towns, but they have the means in their hands to rectify them. If an enfranchised town is suffering from bad sanitary arrangements—it may be the local squire or lord may object to certain measures the town authorities have seen fit to adopt—where do they apply? Why, to Parliament, where they have their representatives. But how is the rural workman, without a vote, to make himself heard on a matter of this kind? He may call the district inspector in, but what follows as a rule? It may be he complains of some nuisance which may emanate from his rich neighbour's neglect; if so, if he cannot ply his trade to profit without begging the custom of his rich neighbour to keep his trade going, no matter how bad the nuisance, he must hold his tongue or be prepared for the consequences.

"And while such laws exist as the law of primogeniture and entail, it will be more or less the policy of the present owner to get as great a rent as he can, while doing as little in the shape of improvement as he can. Only the other week in Wilts I saw cottages unfit for human beings to live in; fast going to decay, and the sooner the better; but will the present owner build more? Question!

"During the last twenty years how many of our cottages have been pulled down, and more built to replace them? thus driving the farm labourers into the towns, and in tens of thousands of instances robbing the land of their useful labour. Had the labourer been enfranchised half a century ago, the land as well as the villages would not have presented such a serious picture of dilapidation. Of course there are exceptions to this rule.

"Then there is pure water. If the water of a town is bad, means are set on foot to improve it; a town water Bill is brought into the House. And yet in many of our villages the water is not fit for human beings to drink; but who is to call the attention of the legislature to that? Some one may raise the question; but not until the vote is extended to every householder in the counties, will that question receive its due consideration—not only good drainage and good water, but good and decent cottages. Why is there an Artizans' Dwelling Act for our large towns? Why are the inhabitants to say where the law should take effect and where it should not? Why not an Agricultural Labourers' Dwelling Act? He would have had his Act the same as the artizan, but he had no vote. When the same right to send men to Parliament as the artizan in town has is given to the labourer, he will no longer be content to live in a fever den. He will no longer be content to drink impure water."

I had made up my mind that, if the cottages remained in their bad condition, it would not be because I had failed to have my say on the subject.

For a good many reasons I was very glad when I saw the last of 1882. From 1878 up to that year I had a very rough time of it at the hands of certain persons who had been inside the Union, and who wanted to bring about my downfall. In fact, they followed me everywhere like a lot of sleuth-hounds.

In 1883 I was chosen President of the Birmingham Radical Union, and we kept agitating for the franchise harder and louder than ever. In 1884 we got it. Next to the famous year of the start of the Union, the year which saw the agricultural labourer enfranchised was the great year of my life. We had a vote at last; we were now politically alive and existent, and there were those amongst us who intended to use that existence to the utmost of our power in pressing forward our best interests. I told them at Kenilworth in 1885, where I attended a meeting in support of Mr. P. H. Cobb's candidature for the Rugby division, that from the time I was ten years of age I made up my mind that, if the day should come when I could make my voice heard, I would make it heard against the landocracy of this country. I had made it heard, and I had by no means done; for now I hoped soon to be in the House of Commons to give the landlords a word or two about the periodical increases of rent and a few

I Enter Parliament

other things. In the autumn of 1885 I remember speaking at a great demonstration of miners at Burslem. Thomas Burt, M.P., president of the Miners' Union, was there, and he and I sat on the platform together. Burt is a very fine man, a solid, straightforward party politician; and being a working-man and a representative of the miners, he was particularly interesting to me. I was great friends with him, and I am proud to say so. That Burslem meeting was a downright good one, and they gave me a very hearty welcome.

In the November of 1885 came the general election and with it my chance of entering Parliament. I was told that the working-men of North-West Norfolk had been holding meetings at their branches and had determined to have me as their candidate. They asked me to contest the seat, and promised, if I would stand, that my expenses should be paid. They sent for me to go down to the Blackfriars Hall at Lynn when the candidates were selected. There were two Liberal candidates for the vacancy; Sir Bampton Gurdon, whom the well-to-do and upper classes wanted to return, and myself, whom the labourers wanted to represent them. I went down, and when the poll was taken I polled exactly double the number of votes Sir Bampton did. I therefore stood in the Liberal and labouring class interest. My opponent was Lord Henry Bentinck. In my address to the electors, I said I would support the extension of Free Trade to all articles of food; a measure for conferring local government by boards upon county districts; the complete reform of the land laws; compensation for improvements in the soil; total abolition of the law of distress; power to government or local boards to acquire land at reasonable purchase value, and to relet the same in allotments; disestablishment of the Church; free, secular elementary education; Sunday closing of public houses, except to bona-fide travellers; abolition of perpetual pensions; substitution of arbitration for war; and equal laws for all parts of the United Kingdom.

Lord Henry Bentinck was a young man and of course trained in a very different school; with the best will in the world he could not possibly enter into our feelings and understand our particular needs. The two millions of new voters wanted some one of their own class to speak for them. I was ready. The voting took place at Lynn on Tuesday, December 8th, 1885, and the votes were cast up on the Wednesday, when it was found that I was returned by a majority of 640. I polled 4461 votes, and Lord Henry Bentinck 3821. There was a great scene when the poll was declared. I remember how put about the Tories were, for a Liberal had not captured the seat for sixty or seventy years. They sent a troop of men down to one of my meetings to cripple me. They gave them five shillings and a gallon of beer each; but it so happened that a new line was being cut to South Lynn, and all the navvies knew me—the majority of them had come off the land on to the line. One day the ganger went to Lynn to draw the money to pay the men, and on his way he called in at a public house, and overheard

I Enter Parliament

the men who had been sent down by the Tories discussing the best way to pay me out. That night he told the navvies what he had heard, and they all attended my meeting armed with sticks. When the Tory crowd commenced to set about me, the navvies went for them and thrashed them most unmercifully, and the Tory roughs, with the navvies' mark on them, were regularly cowed and slunk off out of the way. I remember I rode through Lynn to the Town Hall in a donkey cart; and after the poll had been declared, when I rose to thank the electors for the honour they had conferred upon me, I said that while my opponents with carriages, horses, servants, and all their aristocratic paraphernalia, had failed to accomplish their object, Joseph and his brethren had accomplished *their* object with a donkey cart. The humble donkey had drawn me on to triumph and a majority of 640.

The day I entered Parliament as Joseph Arch, M.P. for North-West Norfolk, was a proud one, but pride was subdued by responsibility. Joseph Chamberlain and Jesse Collings were my sponsors. Chamberlain was smiling all over his face, I remember; if I was smiling, it was an inside smile at the thought that my entry marked the triumph of our enfranchisement. I took my place in the Council Chamber of the nation as the representative of the labourer and of the Prince of Wales—the Sandringham estates are in the North-West division—and I said to myself, "Joseph Arch, M.P., you see to it that neither the Prince nor the labourer has cause to be ashamed of you." I did not put on a black coat—I aped nobody—I wore my rough tweed jacket and billycock hat; the same I generally wore at my country meetings. As I was, so I wished to be. A few weeks after I entered Parliament Mrs. Peel, the wife of the Speaker, sent me an invitation to take tea with her. I went, and found her very nice and interesting, and the Speaker very friendly. He gave the first Levée in morning dress, and I also went to that. I met with a great deal of friendliness from different people with whom I was at this time brought into contact. When I went down to Leamington in January to attend the annual soirée in connection with the Liberal Working Men's Club, I told them that, though a club which was being formed in London had written to ask me to become one of its vice-presidents, I did not intend to waste my time in London clubs. My place was within the walls of the House of Commons when important business was before it. There I should sit and listen, and there I should speak when the proper time came. I said, too: "The return of the twelve working-men's candidates is only the beginning of brighter and better days for the working classes, and you may rest assured that when the carpenter, the glass-blower, the man from the forge, and the agricultural labourer put their shoulders together within the walls of St. Stephen's, they will scatter so much Radicalism that a great number of gentlemen will catch the dreadful disease." I said, too, that I meant to wear my ordinary dress in the House, not to make myself conspicuous, but because I was determined to do like the Shunamitish woman of whom I read in the good old book, and who had great opportunities of enriching herself—I would live and die with my brethren.

I rose to make my maiden speech on January 26th, 1886, in which I opposed Mr. Chaplin's Allotment Bill. In this speech I said: "When I read the speech of Her Most Gracious Majesty the Queen, which expressed sympathy with the distress that was prevalent, not only in trade but in agriculture, I took it certainly to mean this—'You are in a terribly poverty-stricken condition. Your lot in life is hard. You are without employment, and without money, and consequently must be without food. I know your lot is hard, but I have no remedy.' It seems to me something like this—that, supposing as an individual I were suffering intense bodily pain, and I sent for a medical adviser; he looks at me, he sees me writhing in agony, and he says, 'I have not a single ingredient in my surgery that I could apply to assuage your pain.' Would it not be natural enough to me to seek the advice of some more skilled physician? If Her Majesty's Government have no remedy for this distress, then, I think, the country will very soon look out for another physician, who has a practical remedy already to hand." I went on to say: "Honourable gentlemen have said that about a quarter of an acre is sufficient for a working-man in a village. There may be some working-men, such as shepherds and carters, who perhaps would be contented with a rood of ground; but I venture to say that a very large number of the labourers in Norfolk—and I am speaking now from my own experience in that county—would only be too glad if they could rent an acre or two at a fair market price. On the other hand, I do not find any human or Divine law which would confine me, as a skilled labourer, to one rood of God's earth. If I have energy, tact, and skill, by which I could cultivate my acre or two, and buy my cow into the bargain, I do not see any just reason why my energies should be crippled and my forces held back, and why I should be content as an agricultural labourer with a rood of ground and my nose to the grindstone all the days of my life." I said: "I cannot understand for the life of me why, if an English workman can, by thrift and industry and care, manage to secure to himself and his family a cow, he should not have the opportunity for doing so. The Amendment of the honourable member for Ipswich (Jesse Collings) means that. We do not ask for borrowed funds, or for the land to be given us, and we have no desire to steal it. What the Amendment asks, and what I ask honourable gentlemen on both sides of the House, is whether the time has not come when these thousands of industrious and willing workers should no longer be shut out from the soil, and should have an opportunity of obtaining a fair foothold, and producing food for themselves and their families?

"Why are these men out of work? Is it because the land is so well cultivated that no more of their labour is required? I travel this country from one end to the other, and I have an idea I know when land is cultivated and when it is not, as well as any gentleman in this House. I say, fearless of contradiction, that there are tens of thousands of acres of land waiting for the hand of the workman; and what this House ought to consider and aim at, is to use every legitimate means to bring the land that cries for labour to the labourer as soon as possible. I am addressing in this House large landed proprietors, and will any honourable gentleman attempt for one moment to deny that the best cultivated estate is the best for the landlord?

"When I look at this question, I go almost out of the region of party politics. It is not a landlord's, a tenant farmer's, or a labourer's question; it is the question of the people, and they will very soon make it their question. We are not Socialists—not in the accepted meaning of the word; but to a certain extent we are Socialists, because we are social beings. We like social comforts and social society, but we have a great aversion to social society paid for out of the poor rates. An honourable gentleman said last night that it was beyond the power of the honourable member for North-West Norfolk to raise wages. I thought it was equally impossible for landlords in this country to force up rent. We have always been told that the price of labour would be regulated by what it is worth in the market. That is just what land has got to be. My idea of justice in land is this—that if I have to sell, as a tenant farmer, my produce extremely cheap, then I say the rent of my land should be extremely cheap.

"But the time has come for, and this Parliament has been elected very largely to carry out, some just and wise measure, not only for the improvement of the tenant farmers—and Heaven knows they want something, many of them—but for the benefit of the labourers, and for the benefit of the country. When I look around on this side of the House I see several honourable gentlemen—a fair number of Liberal members—who have been returned by the votes, very largely, of the agricultural labourers. They know that during the contests in various divisions the labourers expressed a very great desire for land to cultivate for themselves. They naturally concurred with that idea; but I have never heard any Liberal candidate promise the labourers 'three acres and a cow.' For myself, I never made such a vain promise."

The fact was, I considered "three acres and a cow" all moonshine. The Allotments Act was a miserable failure until the labourers got the vote, but since then thousands of acres have been put into their hands. In my opinion allotments ought to be compulsory. I fought Mr. Chaplin three times across the floor of the House over that Bill.

I supported Gladstone's Home Rule Bill. It was thrown out on the Second Reading, and so we were brought face to face with another election. As every politician knows, the Liberal party split over it, and

I Enter Parliament

the Gladstonian Liberals stood on one side and the Liberal Unionists under Hartington, Goschen, and Chamberlain stood on the other, rejecting what they called the new policy. I went with Gladstone, for I believed in doing justice to Ireland; but I was never—not for a single instance—a Separationist. Freedom and justice in Union was my motto. The feeling was very bitter at this election, and there was fatal division in our ranks. The polling for our division took place on July 9th, 1886, and Lord Henry Bentinck was returned by a majority of twenty votes. Of course, apart from other things, I had to fight against heavy odds. To begin with, I could not leave my place in Parliament, and I had no machinery in the shape of carriages, the Primrose League, and great territorial influence, to put in motion, even if I had wished it. Then the "three acres and a cow" fallacy did me a good deal of damage, for too many of the labourers expected to have them at once.

Gladstone took a very warm interest in my election, and sent me a telegram on the day preceding the poll. I remember, as I was driving along past a hayfield, the men recognised me and the driver pulled up. I shouted to them, "Been to the poll, lads?"

"Yes, walked there and back this morning," they shouted back.

I jumped down, pushed through the hedge, and gave round copies of Gladstone's telegram. They read them, and then they stuck them on their forks and waved them, giving me a hearty cheer.

As I passed by another place I got into a crowd of Bentinckites, and had to encounter a regular volley of abuse and groans, with only a cheer or two. As I crossed the railway at Massingham the porters shouted that they were all for me. I made a speech on the green to over five hundred men and women, and I made another at Rudham. When I left I was escorted by about three hundred men and boys, singing an election song and beating a drum.

When the poll was declared there was a tremendous yell of joy from the Bentinckites. I made a short speech, and I said: " Though I am defeated, I am not disgraced. I hope Lord Henry will advocate in Parliament those measures which I myself would have supported had I been returned. In the meantime be not dismayed, for before long I shall come back and claim the confidence of my fellow-labourers." Though I often wished that my work was done, and I could go back to my cottage home in Barford to labour in peace, I felt I could not leave my work half done; that as soon as ever I had the chance I must again raise my voice in the people's cause in the Council Chamber of the nation.

I did not waste time crying over spilt milk, for directly after my defeat I started off on an electioneering tour through Norfolk. I also visited Lancashire early in 1887, on an educational, political tour, and began with an address at Caton on the land question. We had a splendid meeting, and among other things I pitched into Chaplin's Allotments Bill. I said that, " As an agricultural labourer I looked upon it as a perfect insult to me, and what was an insult to me was an insult to my class. I did not intend the labourers and the working men of England to be bamboozled with such a miserable Bill. If a working man in any village required half an acre of land—and he was not to have any more—he was to be compelled to get four ratepayers to sign a requisition to take to the county magistrates 'in petty or general sessions assembled.' 'Why,' I said, 'who would be the four ratepayers to sign the requisition?' I asked a noble member of the House of Commons whether four ordinary farmers would be induced to sign, or four tradesmen, say the blacksmith, the butcher, the grocer, and the baker in a village? They would not sign it, for the simple reason that, as soon as they set themselves up to do anything for the social elevation of the agricultural labour, they would be boycotted.

"I told Mr. Chaplin, coming out of the House of Commons, that I would make his Bill stink in the nostrils of the nation before I had done with it. Suppose there were four persons, however, who had the courage to sign a requisition for another person to rent half an acre of land. They get up the requisition and make it duly suppliant in tone, and they take it to the county magistrates 'in petty or general sessions assembled.' But the third clause in the Bill distinctly stated that these magistrates should have the power, if they thought fit, to refuse the application if they did not consider it satisfactory—that is, you know, giving it 'their most serious consideration.' Well, I insisted on a division upon the second reading of the Bill, and I beat Mr. Henry Chaplin and his Conservative friends by a majority of fifteen, and so far his Bill lay dead.

"Look at it in another light. Why should any working man be treated any less courteously and considerately, because he is poor, than a gentleman? If I was a gentleman and wanted a farm or a large house, do you think I would stoop to go and ask four ratepayers, say in Caton, to sign a requisition for me to take to the magistrates and ask their permission whether I was to have this farm or house, or not? Certainly not. But the case is no different from that of a working man who wants to rent a piece of land. My claim is a common-sense one, and it is this, that if there are sixty or seventy men in a village who want to rent land let them go direct to the landlord and have done with it, and leave the magistrates to officiate as the rabbit-killers. Don't you think I did right in helping to defeat that Bill? I think I did."

I spoke out about State-aided emigration. I said: "We have a great deal said now by some of our landed proprietors about adopting a scheme of State-aided emigration. They want Government to 'copper down' about a million of money to send the surplus labour out of our country to other countries and the colonies. They tell us it is not 'emigration' but 'colonisation.' I was asked to sit upon a Board of Directors for promoting this scheme, and I said, 'If you are going to emigrate Bishops and Deans I would be on your Board of Directors to-morrow.' The men who go in for

State-aided emigration are those who have made such a wonderful clamour about the Irish Question. They want to put their hands into the pocket of the State to emigrate—whom? If you are going to emigrate the drunken loafers out of your towns—the cadger, the idle fellow, who won't work at all—I say that the colonies don't want that class of man. If you are going to emigrate the most intelligent and the best workmen, the men with the most skill and the strongest muscles and the highest courage, then I ask, Can we as a country afford to lose them? I say, Certainly not. I cannot understand State-aided emigration unless it is to emigrate those who 'toil not, neither do they spin.'

"There is another phase of the question that I would like to draw attention to. A good many agriculturists have grumbled to me about the low price of produce, and they said, 'Gladstone's a lot to do with it, and you have helped'; and I have said, 'Thank God, the people's bread is a bit cheaper then.' But I said also, 'You have made this rod for your own back. Go back to the year 1874, when about four thousand men in the Eastern Counties and others in Dorset and in Wilts were locked out, for the abominable crime of daring to unite together to better their social position. These men were wandering about your villages willing to work, and you refused them. Then your colonial emigration agents came over, and they took thousands of the most plucky and most intelligent of your workmen away. You would not let them till the land here for you, and now they are cultivating land of their own with perfect freedom in the colonies; and these men, whom you drove from their homes in England, are now your competitors there, and fifteen thousand miles away are sending to England in countless shiploads the corn which you cannot produce.'"

I said too: "We are told through the papers that every year we have to send about a hundred and twenty millions of money to foreign countries for eggs, butter, cheese, meat, bread, and so forth, for food for the people of this country. Yet, notwithstanding this enormous outlay, you have hundreds of thousands of men, women, and children in this country who are not more than half fed. Compare those facts with this—we have thousands of acres of land in this country that are not tilled, and that would repay tilling if the 'Dead Hand' were taken off, and if the cultivator had fair play; and would it not be wise in us therefore, instead of sending away a hundred and twenty millions of our hard-earned money for food, if we raised, as we could raise, more than one-half of that amount at home, if the land was only tilled? It has been going on for years within my recollection, that the smart lads of our country villages find out that there are better markets for their labour than to work upon the land, and they rush off, as they have done by thousands, into your large centres of industry.

"And now that trade is a bit depressed you are told that you are over-populated. It may be said that you are over-populated and that trade is depressed, considering the demand for the articles you produce in trade; but how on earth can British agriculture be truly said to be in a depressed condition when there is a demand every year for a hundred million pounds' worth more of agricultural produce than we can supply? Talk of supply and demand! As far as this is concerned the farmers of this country have got the game in their own hands, if they will cease to be Tories and take a right view of their own interests and those of the nation! It is a serious mistake for farmers to send landlords to Parliament to look after farmers' interests. You may just as well expect the cat to guard the cream."

I also said: "It is said a man has a right to do what he likes with his own. That is not true. You cannot put a nuisance under your neighbour's window or where you choose; you cannot put a pigstye where you choose; you must do nothing which is an injury to your neighbour. Take the same idea and carry it into our landed system. Take my own little property of half-a-quarter of an acre, the productive power of which was valued by a competent gardener at £6 a year. If there were a hundred men in my village who owned the same quantity of land and cultivated it, they and the neighbourhood would be the richer by £600 annually. But if I and my neighbours happened to have a pocketful of money, and because of that neglected to till our land, there would be, in the first instance, a loss to the community of £600 annually; but that would not be all.

"These men would go into the neighbouring market with their money to buy what they wanted, and would buy up the produce which should be available to those who had no gardens—the poor artizans of the town. I say this, that if we dared to rob the public in such a way, and competed with the man who has no garden and but little money in his pocket, then the Government ought to step in and say to me and my neighbour, 'If you won't cultivate this land, here is the full market price for it—you must either cultivate it or sell it, one way or the other, because you have no right to waste the public food.' This may be rather Radical doctrine, but I maintain that it is pure Conservatism. I mean to say that I am a far better Conservative than Lord Salisbury, and for this reason—I wish to create the greatest possible wealth out of the land. It is a Conservative measure to place a lot of industrious working men upon the land, and produce from the land all the wealth it is calculated to produce, for the inhabitants of our towns and for the prosperity of the whole country."

I wound up my speech by saying: "The few thoughts I throw out to-night are for your interests and the interests of the whole country. Society is like a great building. You cannot remove the foundation stone of a building without moving all that is above it, even to the top. Just so with society. Let the lower classes of society rise and become thrifty, and provident, and happy, with plenty to eat and plenty to do, with good wages fairly earned, and then every other class of society will be raised, will be strong and happy in proportion. I want you working men to set your heart upon these things; and when the next election comes let no bribe, no intimidation, no temptation lead you from the path of duty; and if you do that duty honourably and well, though you may not realise all that you hope for yourselves, this at least you will do—you will leave to posterity after you, to your children and your children's children, a brighter and a better heritage than it has been your lot to receive."

When I was speaking at Badsey, in South Worcestershire, I told them that I had worked for fifteen candidates and written for twenty-nine, and how it had hit me hard when these men I had helped voted against Gladstone and Home Rule. I had rather an exciting meeting at Broadway, I remember, in the August of 1887. It was held in a field, and shortly after I began to speak a balloon in the shape of an animal, which had been set up in a field some distance off, floated over the meeting, and several of my opponents—I had a good many there—raised a cry of "Oh, look, here comes the cow!"

I said, "I know very well what you mean. I am not surprised that the calves first spied out the cow!"

In the February of 1888 I spoke at Southam, in my county, to a splendid meeting. I dealt with the Irish question and the detestable coercive policy of the Government. I was as hot as fire about it. I had been most careful to sit through the debates on it in the House, and I said to the meeting, "I sat close to the feet of Mr. Gladstone when he delivered his three hours and twenty-five minutes' address upon the Home Rule question, and if I live I shall sit there again."

I also said: "It is one of the happiest things for England, Scotland, Ireland, and Wales, that Mr. Gladstone introduced his Home Rule Bill. Why are the Irish people so law-abiding, in spite of the greatest possible persecution? How is it we do not hear of explosions of dynamite and shooting of landlords? It is because of the Home Rule Bill; and when I sat at the feet of our great political Gamaliel, and listened to his words, the thought flashed across my mind, 'Ah, Mr. Gladstone, you are raising a star of hope in the horizon of Ireland, and whether this Bill is passed or not, this star will shine on and on till poor Ireland is free.'"

I spoke also on the Fair Trade question. I said: "I want you to examine logically this Fair Trade dodge. I don't think they will try it on in my division again. They got it pretty well when they tried it on there in 1885. But in Warwickshire I find there is a number of gentlemen who are trying this dodge upon you. How will it act? Suppose one of you men with your family consume twelve quartern loaves weekly. If Fair Trade raised the price twopence a loaf, your bread bill for the week would be increased two shillings a week. But then the farmer will say, 'I could afford to pay you two shillings a week more money.' Well, if I were at work for a farmer, and he said that to me, I should say, 'Is that all, sir? Can't you give me more than that?' Bear in mind that if Fair Trade makes your bread cost you two shillings more, you ought not to rest satisfied unless your wages are raised at least four shillings a week. I will tell you why. The shoemaker will charge you more for your shoes; the tailor will charge you more for your clothes; and the butcher will charge you more for your meat; and you will never get bilious through eating beefsteaks. You won't see a leg of mutton on your table very often. Beware of this. I want you to see that it is very easy to draw you into the net, but it will be difficult to get you out when you are in. I don't want you to get into the snare.

"I was recently addressing a large meeting in a manufacturing district, and I said to the manufacturers: 'Suppose the food of your operatives is raised thirty per cent., they will immediately come down upon you for an increase of wages thirty per cent. Suppose for instance they do this, and the present Government put a tax on imports of ten per cent., the foreigner will then put a tax upon your exported goods of say twenty per cent.; and knowing you cannot do without his bread-stuffs, he will say, "Very well, if you don't like that we will manufacture our own goods." You will lose his trade with you, and still be obliged to buy his goods. If you want to ruin your manufactures put on the taxes at once.'"

The points which covered the Fair Trade Controversy were—any tax put upon goods imported into this country would have to be paid by the English consumer and not by the foreigner; protection could not be limited to any one single article. If corn were protected, the manufacturers would ask for their goods to be protected also. And also the cry for protection was simply a landlords' cry, started and kept up for the purpose of maintaining rents at their present high position, and enabling them to ride about in their carriages. This was the way a speaker at the meeting put it.

For some time past I had been in bad health and suffering a great deal at times, so it was often as much as I could do to get through my meetings and keep the political ball rolling. But now, as ever, I kept pegging away and toiled on. Enemies were still on my track, and I had to face another accusation about our Union funds. Major Rasch was reported in the *Daily News* as having put a question to the First Lord of the Treasury respecting the Agricultural Labourers' Union, couched in these words:

"Whether the Government would take steps to prevent misappropriation in connection with this body?"

Well, as you may guess, I was up in arms on the spot. We had a correspondence on the subject, in which Major Rasch did not come out well. Another thing; the very allegation made by him was the subject of a judicial inquiry in the Court of Chancery in November

I Enter Parliament

1887, when Mr. Justice Stirling, after reading the affidavits of all the parties to the suit, decided in my favour. He declared the charges were false, and made without the slightest foundation.

Sir Selwyn Ibbotson wanted me to send all the books and vouchers, and everything in connection with the financial arrangements of the Union, to a firm of chartered accountants in London. I replied that I had nothing at all to do with the books or the accounts of the Union, this department being in the hands of the committee and secretary. But, even if I had, I should certainly decline his request on these grounds: (1) That from the commencement of the Union we had submitted the accounts every six months to two chartered accountants in Birmingham, which they had audited and found correct, and it would have been an insult to those gentlemen if we had placed the accounts in the hands of London accountants to audit again. (2) That, provided I should feel myself at liberty to send the accounts of the Labourers' Union to the accountants he suggested, would he kindly send me the balance sheet of his estate, so that I could see that he was sound and solvent? That was my answer, and I did not hear anything further from Sir Selwyn Ibbotson.

As for me personally, I never received any money on behalf of the Union; I was only a hired servant year by year. At the Annual Congress the labourers elected their president, and they elected me. They paid me so much a week and my travelling expenses,

I travelled for them for about twenty-four years on those conditions. I received no contributions, and the only moneys I paid away in any shape or form were my own travelling expenses, which they refunded to me in due course. During the whole time I was connected with the Union I had nothing at all to do with the financial accounts. The Union paid my Parliamentary expenses. My salary was so much, and my expenses were so much, which amounted in all, taking one week with another, to between £4 and £5 a week.

When I went to the House of Commons they allowed me my expenses in addition to my salary. My election expenses came to about £800; they were found for me by subscriptions from wealthy men. From 1876 to 1879 my salary was £3 a week, and from 1879 to the time the Union collapsed it was £2 10s. The cause of the reduction was this: when the wages of the labourers began to be reduced they cried out about the salaries of the officials, and said that these also ought to be reduced. The majority of the officials did not like this, and did their best to keep their salaries up—it was natural enough—but I was willing to take ten shillings a week less, and told them so. The labourers accepted my offer, and the other officials had to come down also. After the year 1884 the Union began to go down, largely owing to the fact that an important part of the work was done (though by no means all); the men had the vote; it was as if they had a wide door set open before them, and they thought that they could get all they wanted by means of their representatives in Parliament. They did not understand how slow a thing reform is, and there were too many of them who thought they had only to ask and they would receive—three acres and a cow, for instance. I myself felt at this period that the main thing to be done next was to get a hearing in the House of Commons. We had our vote, and we were not to let it rust. Well, I was not rusting out through these years, and I never worked harder in all my life at speechmaking than I did in 1887 and 1888. I did not spare my lungs, nor my throat, nor my legs, nor my head; and my heart was as warm for the cause as it had ever been.

CHAPTER XVI.

AT THE END OF THE DAY.

AFTER County Councils were created by the Local Government Act of 1888 I stood for County Councillor for the Wellesbourne division; and though squarsons and squires, landlords and moneybags, were leagued together against me, I was returned by a majority of thirty-four. My opponent was Mr. Cove Jones, a magistrate, who of course had great influence behind him. He had carriages at his service, I had "Shanks's mare"; he had the Primrose League to work for him, I had a few trusty friends to speak for me. I did not canvass; I merely addressed three meetings from the distance of the platform. After the victory I received many kind letters which were as balm to me, for I had to submit to a regular torrent of scurrilous abuse from enemies and false friends. It was a bitter experience. Many of them were so prejudiced against me, and looked at all my doings with such jaundiced eyes, that I gave up trying to right myself with them. I was not going to play the part of the miller in the fable and I consoled myself by saying, "Never mind; fierce is the light that beats upon a prominent man, and many are the clods of mud pitched at him. Go ahead as before, and let snarling dogs snarl and bark till they bark their bark away; they'll only hurt themselves most in the end."

I sat in the County Council till the end of 1892, and attended regularly. I was appointed on various committees and was able to do good work, more particularly on the Highways, Roads, and Bridges Committee. I liked the work and regretted having to give it up; but needs must when illness drives, and work elsewhere called me away.

Not long after this I unveiled a bust of Mr. Gladstone at the Bingley Liberal Club, and in my speech on that occasion I said: "I can say that, as a working man, I think no man has stronger claims upon my sympathy, support, and affection than Mr. Gladstone. When the election of 1880 came we had him placed at the helm of affairs. Although I was twitted by weak-kneed Liberals and Tories that he would never concede the franchise, my faith in his honesty, in his sense of justice to the people, and in his love for the people, was not in the slightest degree shaken by these jeers. I was perfectly certain that he would enfranchise my class. In taking off this covering to unveil to you the bust of this great statesman I can say, fearless of contradiction, that he lives in the affections of thousands of men, aye, tens of thousands, who dwell in our rural villages in humble cottages, and who, I believe, whenever a wise Providence shall call him aside from this scene of action, will mourn his loss with a great and profound depth of feeling. I do not believe that Mr. Gladstone or any other living being is free from mistakes; but of this I am certain, that whenever he has made a mistake and has found it out, he has been honourable, he has been manly enough to acknowledge it, and has done his best to rectify it."

I had the honour, by the bye, of paying Mr. Gladstone a visit at Hawarden Castle in 1884, and I was received by the Rev. Stephen Gladstone, Vicar of Hawarden. It was a red-letter day in my life, for I hold my political chief in the highest honour. He is a very great man indeed, and when I was brought into close personal contact with him I realised it more than ever. He is one of the mighty men of the earth.

We held our eighteenth annual council this year, and we had to present a very unfavourable report. The fact was, the Sick Benefit Society was pulling the Union to the ground. I had always been against it. A lot of the workmen who were getting advanced in years—men of sixty years of age and thereabouts—began to feel that they would like to start such a society in connection with the Union. I objected to it at once, and the harpies who were around me tried to divorce the men from me, by telling them that I wanted them all to go into the workhouse. My reason for objecting was that I did not want the men to embark upon an undertaking which I foresaw they could not possibly keep up, and they found out in the end that I was right. I only wish I had been wrong. I paid into the society all the time it was in existence, but I had nothing from it. They tried to make a whip out of that affair wherewith to flog me, but it was no good.

The society was started in 1877. At that time district benefit societies were springing up in different directions, so ours was started, and men of sixty were eligible for membership on payment of an entrance fee of one shilling and sixpence. In addition to that, members of district sick benefit societies, irrespective of age and standards of health, were taken over in a lump, provided they had funds amounting to £1 per member. Then the standard of entrance fees was fixed at one shilling and sixpence, a sum preposterously low; in fact, men who would have had to pay £1, and even more than that, for admission into a Court of Foresters or an Odd Fellows' Lodge, were admitted into our society for one shilling and sixpence each. The admission of men over and above that age, where other societies have found it safe, and indeed necessary, to draw the line, resulted in the enrolment of members who were almost constantly on the funds. So it came about that for almost every ten shillings paid in, twenty shillings had to be paid out. Then the neglect of enforcing a proper entrance fee, the amount of which should have been regulated by the age of the applicant, deprived the fund of considerable sums. The basis of the fund was false hopes, and so it was bound to collapse; but, unfortunately, it helped greatly to kill the Union too.

I told them at the annual meeting that the Sick Benefit Society had neither been the handiwork of myself nor the present committee. It was what the members themselves had made it. Two years before we had been obliged to impose a levy of one shilling and sixpence per member. At that time, other societies, owing to the great amount of sickness, had also been obliged to impose levies varying from one shilling to one shilling and sixpence a week.

In 1888 the council and the executive committee sat till nearly midnight to see what alterations were advisable, with the view of saving the society from a collapse. The reforms then adopted were directed to be embodied in a circular, and submitted to the members for their approval. Neither the council nor the committee could do more. What was the result? The members refused to sanction what had been done, and there was consequently no alteration. I told them that I had gone carefully into the measures of reform then proposed, and had the men accepted them, the funds in hand would have been from £1,000 to £1,600 more than they were. That reform need not have lasted more than two years, or three at the outside; after which, they could, if they had thought proper, have reverted to the previous system of grants.

That refusal—and that refusal alone—had forced the council of the Union, to report a very large outlay in connection with the sick funds, considerably more than in any former year.

I said that the council would have to face the question like men, and if they did so they would see what had been the cause of the increase in expenditure. They all knew that when the funds were locked up in Chancery that the parties who locked them up professed to be extreme friends of the Union. Well, this was what the papers said: " The gentleman who did that was the only guardian of the labourers, and the president and the executive council were a lot of extravagant spendthrifts, who were running away with the Sick Benefit money, and wasting it in all that was bad." They now all knew that instead of that having consolidated the Union, the idea got abroad that the Sick Benefit funds were being improperly spent, and, as a consequence, a very large number of young men, who would have been paying members to this hour, became alarmed and left the fund. The consequence then was that we were left with the aged members on our hands; and as the sickness among them was necessarily greater than among the younger men, the demands upon the Union funds had largely increased, while the contributions had decreased. So that instead of benefiting the old men, the locking up of the funds had done them irreparable mischief. I told them I had paid into the fund nearly £40, and never drawn a farthing.

Another thing which had militated against us was this. In some villages a notice had been received by the men of a reduction in their wages. The men at once recognised the value of their Union. They appealed for help; I responded and went to their aid. Sometimes a new branch of forty or fifty members was raised and the reduction notified did not take place. But perhaps in a month or so the branch was again broken up, and when the reason was asked, the answer was given, "Oh, we have read such and such things in the papers about the Union funds, and we don't know what to think." All these reports did us a great deal of damage when we could ill afford to stand it.

Then there was the Widows' Relief Society, which was started in 1881 at two places; but it soon fell through. My name was printed on the papers and pamphlets of the society; but that was done without my consent, and I strongly objected to it. I opposed this society, simply because I did not see how it could be properly worked. All this worried me greatly and helped to keep me in bad health. We were being found fault with in certain papers, first for this and then for that. Why had the Union touched politics? Why had there been such a Sick Benefit Society? And so it went on; and of course all this affected our numbers most seriously. I wrote on the subject, to try and stem the tide, and showed how wages invariably fell back to the old rate, or nearly so, whenever the branch in that particular neighbourhood broke up. I begged the labourers to combine once more, and win the ground they had once so nobly fought for and had so foolishly lost by their own indifference.

From 1875 up to 1885 the Union had comparative peace, and moved steadily and calmly on; but after the 1885 General Election the Union was all wrong. It was venomously assailed by men who up till then had declared they were its very best friends. The truth was, some of these vipers were furious because they could not get the labourers to send them to Parliament, and they tried with all their wicked spite to howl and hoot the Union down. They wished to crush it out of existence. They tried to smash me up over and over again. They kept repeating that I misappropriated the funds, and of course some thought it might be true. I told the men once that my private diaries from 1872 onward could be inspected by a practical accountant any day, and that I had brought into the funds of the Union by my own individual efforts £14,000; a sum four times greater than any that had been paid out for services rendered.

I would not have gone into this miserable question here, but for this—it shows what I had to go through; that being president of a Union was not all sunshine and honey; there was plenty of gall and wormwood forced to my lips by those who were no better than Judases. I am not the first, nor shall I be the last, while human nature is what it is, to bear the brunt of such cowardly and persistent attacks on name and fame; but I can honestly say that what distressed me most was the injury they did to the Union.

In 1890 the Union, largely owing to the indefatigable efforts of Mr. Walker—he pushed it hard and fast, and never spared himself—began to look up once more. The morphia of lying and misrepresentation of myself and others who were working hard in the cause laid the majority in many villages in Norfolk and elsewhere fast asleep. For four years delegates and officers had been like so many John the Baptists crying in the wilderness without avail; but in 1890 the men began to wake up once more. The fall in wages touched them up and made them jump into Union. I spoke a good deal on Union just at this period, but the strain and anxiety were beginning to tell on me. I held up as long as I could and got along through 1891; but in the spring of 1892 I had a very serious illness, which it seemed to me I should never be able to shake off. I was regularly done up, worn out, and pulled down. The thing that cheered me was to hear of our progress.

By the time the General Election was on I was up and about again, and felt strong enough to warrant me in coming forward once more as a candidate for my former division. In this election the Liberals captured four seats in our part, my own and three others. I felt so confident that I should be returned that, when the business of the last executive committee was concluded, I said, "Gentlemen, that's the whole of the business, and when I meet you again at our next committee meeting I shall be Member of Parliament."

Well, I was returned by a majority of 1089. The Tories were completely staggered by it. In 1885 several of the local gentry lent me horses and carriages to take voters to the poll, though

I used a "dickey cart" myself; but in 1892 they would not lend me a wheel. They all turned against me because I voted for Home Rule. On polling day the men came in and polled for me well, and the old women lent their donkey carts to bring them in. When the High Sheriff saw the figures, he was so much annoyed that he refused to declare the poll, and the under sheriff had to do it. I then went up to the High Sheriff, held out my hand and thanked him for the very able way in which he had conducted the count. He shook hands with me, then deliberately pulled his handkerchief out of his pocket and wiped his hand. After that I just went up, shook hands with him again, and told him I was perfectly satisfied with the state of the poll, if he was!

Before the figures were declared there were ten carriages and pairs from Welbeck Abbey drawn up by the Assembly Rooms, awaiting the result of the poll; five minutes after it was declared, lo! they were all gone. The High Sheriff, I remember, was white with rage. When I left the Town Hall there was a tremendous crowd outside. Policemen were there in force to see that I was not crushed to death. I noticed five big, burly fishermen walking behind me, and when I got to the first donkey cart they laid hold of me and lifted me in and started hurrahing, and the crowd took it up; and then the donkey was started off and I was carted round the place, the people cheering all the time. It was a splendid ovation—right down splendid.

After that I went to the Liberal Club and addressed a meeting from the balcony; there were between seven and eight thousand people there. I noticed several prominent Conservatives in the crowd, and after thanking my supporters and agent, I addressed myself to them. I told them I hoped the election which had just taken place would teach them a lesson which they would never forget. In 1885, when I had the patronage of several of the local gentry and the loan of their horses and carriages, I won by 640; in 1886, when my opponents had all the forces of Welbeck Abbey and all the forces of every baronet and squire in the division to help them, they managed to beat me by 20 votes. "And now," I said, "I have stood the test again without the support of any of those gentlemen who have turned out to be Tories, and what has happened? Why, Joseph and his brethren have licked you in a donkey cart—a glorious licking this time it is too!" Well, after this the Conservatives cleared out of that meeting as soon as they could. The enthusiasm was tremendous, and the people shouted and hurrahed and sang songs:

> Shout a loud hurrah! boys,
> Raise your voices high,
> Arch is going to Parliament
> With a grand majority.
>   Shout hurrah! boys.

They sang this and "For he's a jolly good fellow," etc. How they did shout, bless their hearts! There was riding and running all the country-side round.

One man I heard of mounted his grey pony directly he got the news and rode from house to house spreading the glad tidings: he was a shoemaker, and he had his sleeves turned up and his apron on—he could not spare time to titivate. Oh, there was a regular to-do! My welcome back to Barford I shall never forget. My wife and I travelled down from London, and at Warwick we had a fine reception. A procession was formed at the bottom of Broad Street, and the Warwick Town Band struck up a lively tune when our carriage stopped. I got out and into another, and the men pushed and pulled it along. There was a large flag behind it, and also banners with inscriptions on them. I made a speech, and we had speeches and great cheering, and then off we drove to Barford and up to the old cottage. There we had more speeches and cheering and handshaking—it was a reception to uplift a man.

I forgot all my rough times then, all my struggles; I only remembered I was Joseph Arch, M.P. once more, the chosen representative of the agricultural labourers, and that by a glorious majority. It was a thumping victory for us and no mistake, and the labourers had done a splendid stroke towards breaking the back of the clerical and the territorial influences in the rural districts. They had got to see that what I had been telling them for years was the truth, that the ballot-box is the only weapon they possess, and by properly using it they can outwit the squire, the parson, and the land agent, with more effect than by holding arguments.

A pressman came to interview me just after the election and I told him what I thought, and what I meant my future policy to be. I said: "I tell you frankly, neither the Tory Allotments Act (1887) nor the Small Holdings Acts are of much, if any, good to the labourers. Our men realise that, and it is why they wish the Liberals to deal with their wants. After the Irish question is got out of the way we must have Parish Councils. By conferring upon these councils the control of the charities, and the administration of the Poor Law, many of the abuses at present existing will be disposed of. These councils, too, must take over the matters of rating and education in the villages. Then, above all, they must have the power to compulsorily acquire as much land for the labourer as he wants at the same rent as land is letting in the district. The labourers must, moreover, have conceded to them the right to sell their improvements if they choose." I was strong on the point that the meetings must be held in the evenings, so that the men could attend, otherwise parson and squire would manipulate them. There was another thing I said: "Hodge never forgets his friends and never forgives his enemies. He has been waiting like a tiger in his lair for the past six years, and now that he has sprung upon the Tories he pretty well frightens them out of their Conservative wits."

While I was up in London attending Parliament the Union was being actively worked in Norfolk and Essex. More than twelve thousand had joined during

1890-91, and some hundred and eighty-nine branches had been put in working order; but I saw that the work of the Union was practically done for the time being. It was a sort of final flicker up before the candle went out, and my Parliamentary duties left me no choice but to look on. I was now moving in the political sphere on my fellow-labourers' behalf. In February 1893 an article of mine appeared in the *New Review*. It was entitled " Lords and Labourers," and I wrote it in two goes of six hours each. Lord Winchilsea had broached the idea of forming the National Agricultural Union, which was to be a combination of landlords, farmers, and labourers. I opposed this because I thought the wolf and the lamb could not make common cause together, and I therefore warned the labourers not to have anything to do with it. In my opinion it was simply a Tory dodge to get the control of affairs into their own hands.

In this article I said : " The ranks of selfishness and class privilege are broken and routed, but the enemy has not yet given up the contest in despair. He is wise enough to abandon his old attitude compounded of tyranny and neglect, and now he comes fawning and smooth-tongued, saying, ' We are your friends ; we wish you well ; our interests are one ; let us make common cause ; join us in defence of our common livelihood.' This is the attitude which the landlords, and, following their example, the tenant farmers are taking up to-day. While I have breath I will raise my voice to prevent my brethren the labourers from falling into this skilfully baited trap. The labourers' interest is that of the farmers! He should join with them in defence of a common livelihood! Yes, when the mouse can lick the cream from the cat's whiskers!" I went on to say: "The British farmer is still the same selfish, stubborn animal that he ever was, and God help the labourer who has to trust himself to his tender mercies. We are told agriculture is so depressed that there is no longer a living to be made out of the land, and unless the labourers join with landlords and farmers to obtain legislative reforms there will soon be neither work nor wages left for them. I agree with the French minister who said he would be prepared to abolish capital punishment if the assassins would lead the way. When I can see a sign that landlord and farmer are prepared to consider the claims of labour, when I can assure myself that these new-fangled schemes and unions are something more than a plot to make the labourer pull the chestnuts out of the fire for the benefit of these autocrats, then I may be prepared to give the scheme a favourable consideration.

"At present I must confess that to my mind the evidence tends the other way. On one hand I read the words of my Lord Ravensworth, who says that for the salvation of agriculture it is necessary that all three classes interested in it should band together, and that as a preliminary step to this holy alliance the labourers must consent to a reduction in their wages all round. On the other hand, I see our old friend, Mr. James Lowther, openly advocating a duty on corn! A holy alliance truly! Increased rent, more money to waste in London frivolities for the landlord, more hunters for the farmer, and more silk gowns for his wife; and for the labourer, less wages and a dear loaf—the rich to be filled with good things, and the hungry to be sent empty away! My best thanks to these gentlemen who have so discreetly let the cat out of the bag.

"Lord Winchilsea, the proud parent of the embryo union, is more astute. *He* does not commit himself to heroic reforms—his words are softer than butter. The reforms, to obtain which it is necessary to establish this proposed gigantic organisation, and to induce the ermine robe (with many a dainty shudder, without doubt) to embrace the fustian smock, are harmless, not to say trivial: the decrease of the burden of taxation on land, a revision of railway rates, and a better system for the collection and distribution of agricultural produce—which last grand reform, as I shall shortly show, it only requires a little energy and enterprise on the part of the farmers themselves to secure. A fortnight ago these three reforms comprised the whole of his lordship's programme.

"But it seems he has discovered that the tea he is providing for the labourers is not sufficiently sweetened; therefore he has, within the past week, dropped another lump of sugar into it. The latest addition to the programme of the Agricultural Union is a sliding scale of wages for labourers dependent on the price of corn. When corn rises five shillings a quarter the wages of the labourers are to rise concomitantly threepence a day. Bravo, my lord! When once the door is open to concession—even a crack—pressure from without may very soon fling it wide. I do not despair of seeing our sultans of the soil, in their eager angling for votes, swallowing wholesale the programme of the Agricultural Labourers' Union. But I should very much like to have the details of the scheme from Lord Winchilsea. What about the grazing and dairy districts? Are the men who are employed there to tend cattle—are the shepherds and the horse-keepers to share in the benefits of this sliding scale? If not, there will be pretty general discontent among them supposing the price of stock or dairy produce rises while that of corn sinks. If they are to share in it, the proposal at once stands out in its true light as a bribe to catch votes in favour of a measure intended to raise the price of corn—that is, stripping off the frippery of language and looking at the naked fact, in favour of Protection. For not one of the remedies proposed, except Protection, makes for the raising of the price of agricultural produce. Revision of railway rates, reduction of the burden of taxation on land, better methods of collection and distribution, all purport to benefit the agriculturist, by cheapening the cost of production, not by increasing the price of produce.

"A precious benefit for the labourer this last truly! Raise the price of his bread a penny a loaf, and give him an additional eighteenpence a week! And suppose, instead of rising, the price of corn falls while our noble lords are carrying out their Protection agitation? Are the wages of the labourers to *fall* threepence a day for every five shillings' fall in the price of wheat? Presumably so; otherwise the proposal would amount to stereotyping the rate of wages at present obtaining in the country.

"This, then, is the halter which the noble Earl of Winchilsea and his henchmen are hoping to put round the necks of the labourers as they go to the polls. 'Vote for the candidates of our union,' they say, 'for those only who will promote measures tending to raise the price of corn; if you do not—if you reject our programme and vote for the "cheap loaf"—you will cut your own throats, for you will bring about a fall in your own wages.' It behoves all true friends of the labourer to speak up. The proposal is so spurious and so fair-sounding that I cannot conceal from myself that there is danger that the flies may seek the honey-pots.

"It is no wonder landlords are anxious for the return of Protection. In the course of a close observation of agricultural matters, extending over a long series of years, I have found it an invariable rule that whenever the price of corn rises rents rise also; but I have not observed any proportionate increase in the labourers' wages. Under Protection the landlord would improve his position, the farmer would, at the least, maintain his, while the labourer, who is least able to bear loss, must inevitably suffer. Under these circumstances, can I, as one of his own flesh and blood, allow him to be cozened into a partnership which means ruin to him without raising my voice to warn, and, if possible, to save him?"

I said too, that "We who had worked and toiled to raise the condition of the British labourer would not cease from our endeavours to tear off the smiling mask of plenty with which the authors of this Union's being have covered the grinning death's head beneath, until we can say, 'Surely in vain is the net spread in the sight of any bird.'

"The labourer," I said, "is the child of the soil—the others are parasites who have affixed themselves to it; and before agriculture can become prosperous again they must go." I went on to say that the "squire must have his London house; he must entertain 'the county' in a sumptuous and ostentatious manner; he must find money for his sons to spend three or four years of idleness and extravagance at Oxford or Cambridge, or a longer period in a cavalry regiment; he must give marriage portions to his daughters. To do all this the money must be wrung from the land; to give it the land is starved for want of cultivation, and the labourer, who is the least able to protect himself, is kept in penury.

"The tenant farmer," I went on to say, "is no less to blame than his landlord. I have no hesitation in saying that no man can farm at a profit unless he and his family are willing one and all to give close attention and hard work to their business. But the modern farmer must hunt and shoot, he must go to evening parties, play cards, and smoke and drink with his friends, while his wife dresses in silk, reads novels, and plays the piano. Hence only the merest outlines of his business are attended to, and those 'inconsidered trifles' which turn a loss into a profit are utterly neglected.

"Let the farmers," I said, "once become manufacturers as well as mere producers of raw material, and Lord Winchilsea's desire for a better system of collection and distribution of produce will speedily become an accomplished fact without his lordship's interference."

I also said: "High rents, charges on the land—*i.e.*, mortgages, jointures, tithes, etc., and a desire for luxuries on the part of landlord and farmer, with its consequent inattention to business on the part of the latter—I believe lie at the root of the present serious condition of agriculture." I said: "The vampire land-starving farmer is in, and has been allowed to lay field to field, to take three or four farms perhaps, each one of which ought to afford a good living. Those farms are the second curse of agriculture which must be done away with. The system had a political origin. The Whig or Tory owner of a dozen farms found some of his dozen tenants opposed to him in politics. Therefore his policy was to 'boil down' the constituency by reducing the tenants to the lowest possible number."

"If landlords were wise," I went on, "they would get rid of the land-starving farmer, and return to the old system of farms from fifty to one hundred and fifty acres. We are not without object lessons as to the great results to be obtained from small holdings of land. In the village of Barford I have been able to obtain for the men a number of small holdings of land, from one to three acres in size, with astonishingly good results. In by-gone days the County Court officer was a familiar figure in Barford; he has not been in the place for several years. There is not a careful man in the place who has not got one pig or more in his stye, and a more manly, independent set of fellows could not be found in the land. They are under obligations to nobody, and they fear nobody. One man, who is not, as a labourer, much more than half a man, told me that even in this last year of scarcity he obtained sufficient wheat off half an acre to supply his family with bread till the winter was over. Where is the tenant of four to six hundred acres who could say that his land produces in like proportion? Even at the present low price of corn there is a handsome profit to be obtained when this quantity is grown."

I wound up by saying: "We must make the profits of his own skill and energy secure to every man; we must get rid, by free sale, or otherwise, of burdened estates; and we must have a class of farmers to work the land who are industrious and attentive to their business, who will work, themselves and their families, instead of playing at being ladies and gentlemen.

"Nemesis is at the door of those who in their selfish ease and soft living never regarded the cry of the poor.

Ruin is upon them, and they will fall unmissed and unregretted, to give place to a newer, brighter state of things. I do not in the least regret the blight which has come upon the present agricultural system of England. Sharp diseases require sharp remedies, and if only the present depression can make a root-and-branch affair of the fungus-growths of feudalism and class privilege which have for centuries choked the tillers of the soil, I for one shall count it gain. But I will never, if I can help it, permit the labourers to be drawn into a trap, however daintily baited, which has for its object the bolstering up of a pernicious system. It was a saying when I was young, that if you saw the fox's brush sticking out of the earth you might be sure the fox was at home. The brush of my Lord Ravensworth and that of Mr. Lowther are plain for all to see, and I think I can see the tip of that of my Lord Winchilsea."

As you may guess, I was full up to the brim and overflowing with my subject when I wrote out this article for the *New Review*. I was not going to have the men bamboozled without trying to stop the lordly game. No, it was too much of a good thing, and I could not sit quiet under such a proposal. Not only my tongue should speak, but my pen should be a point to show the labourers what a Jack-o'-lantern was being dangled before their eyes by the smooth-tongued gentlemen who advocated this protectionist union. It tickled me a good deal to watch the tactics of Lord Winchilsea and Mr. Henry Chaplin and others of the same kidney. Why, after all their talk about the evils of agitation and unionism, they were nothing but aristocratic agitators and Unionists themselves. It suited their convenience now to adopt the methods they had tried to cry down. They laid themselves out with honeyed smiles and buttered words to entrap Hodge; and why? Because Hodge had a vote. Well, Hodge has the ballot-box, too, and he has learned how to use it as a free man should.

I have, as I said before, but little faith in Special Committees and Royal Commissions, but there was one to inquire into the condition of the poor which I hoped might achieve something. I sat on it, and the Prince of Wales was also a member of this Commission. I should like here to bear testimony to the invariable kindness and courtesy which I have received from His Royal Highness. Among other things the Prince of Wales sent me two tickets for the opening of the Imperial Institute; he sent me his good wishes with them, and that pleased me most of all. I am his member, you see in a manner of speaking; and I will say this—should I be spared to see him King of England, he will not have a more loyal subject in all his vast dominions, in all his great empire, than Joseph Arch of Barford, the agricultural labourer who has had the honour of representing his division in Parliament. I was representing it in 1893; and at the last election, when so many big guns went by the board, I was chosen to represent it again—once more I was the Prince of Wales's own M.P. So I am Joseph Arch, M.P. for the North-Western Division of Norfolk still.

The introduction of the Parish Councils Bill was

another day of triumph for me. I said to some one with whom I was discussing the matter, "The Bill is a great stride in the right direction. It is going to revolutionise our villages; it will give England back her vanished peasantry, and add immensely to the prosperity of the country. These are surely great things to set against the loss of their influence by the squire and the parson, who have squandered away their chances of binding the labourer to their interests by assisting the farmer to grind him into the dust."

And now as to the Union—the starting and the leading of which I look upon as my real life-work, the great thing I was specially set apart to accomplish by the help of that All-seeing, All-knowing Providence which overrules the destinies of men and all things—*its* work was, for the time being, accomplished, and so it died a natural death. For about the last four years it has been practically non-existent. The men had got the vote, they were getting on the land, their path was being smoothed for them, and so they thought they no longer needed their Union. Well, time will show.

As I sit here in my little cottage at Barford and review the past, it seems at one minute a long look back; at another it seems but yesterday that my grandmother sat in the chair I am sitting in now —a chair which is over a hundred years old—and I stood by her, a little chap of six. And there is the old eight-day clock which my father bought in Leamington more than fifty years ago. He, I have heard him tell, carried home the case over his shoulder, and my mother trudged at his side with the works in her market basket. I can see my good mother cutting the barley bread for us, with tears in her eyes because there is so little of it for the children who are so hungry. I can see my father step in at the door, come home from his work for a bite and sup of whatever is going. I can see myself tramping off in my little smock-frock, clapper in hand, to scare away the birds; then jumping the clods at sixpence a day; and so on, right away on to the great year of 1872, when I held that first meeting under the Wellesbourne chestnut-tree on the February evening which saw the birth of the Agricultural Labourers' Union.

I know that it was the hand of the Lord of Hosts which led me that day; that the Almighty Maker of heaven and earth raised me up to do this particular thing; that in the counsel of His wisdom He singled me out, and set me on my feet in His sight, and breathed of the breath of His Spirit into me, and sent me forth as a messenger of the Lord God of Battles. So I girded up my loins and went forth. It was from the Lord God of Battles I came, that there might one day be peace in the land. Only through warfare could we attain to freedom and peace and prosperity; only through the storm and stress of battle could we reach the haven where we would be. I was but a humble instrument in the Lord's hands, and now my work is over, my warfare is accomplished.

But there is a great work still to be done in the

century that is close upon us, and I call upon the young men among us to rise up in their strength and do it. Let them set their hands to the plough and never falter, never look back. Let them face the day that is dawning, and let them go forward with stout hearts. There is none so lowly, none so humble, none so poor, but he has his work to do; and it is a bit of work set for him, and no one else can do it but he himself—to each man his appointed work.

To the future of the agricultural labourer I look forward with confidence. I know—none better—that all is not glittering gold in his lot; but the bettering of that lot, the brightening of that lot rests with himself. When I began he had nothing. Now he has the political telephone of the vote, his Board Schools, his County Councils, his Parish Councils. I say, then, here are the means of betterment and progress lying ready to his hand, if he will but use them with discretion and manly, independent judgment. I am all for self-help. Let the labourer think and reason, let him use books and every chance of improvement that comes in his way; but let him never be ashamed of his work, of his calling in life. If he honours his own manhood, if he honours his labour, if he honours all other men and all other honest workers, he will be honoured in his turn, and his labour also. Do not let him ape any man; let him be himself, and let him aim at being himself at his best. That is what we have all got to aim at—to be ourselves at our best.

"The land for the people" is the goal the labourers

are working for. What I want to see is, when a labourer has no work to do for others he has something to do for himself. He can attend to his allotment and grow fruit, vegetables, and keep a pig for himself and his family, so that when the winter comes round he will have, like the busy ant, a good store laid up to keep them all going till the spring comes round.

Get on the land, I say, but by your own help—I do not believe in State-aid and land nationalisation. Get on a bit of land at a fair average rent, and then do the best with it—that is what the labourer should do. As a last extremity I would employ compulsion, but only so. Self-help and liberty, order and progress—these are what I advocate. I think that in the course of time new ideas will spring up—they are bound to do so—and when the labourers' present legitimate grievances are satisfied they will settle down to steady progress. Present-day Socialism will die a natural death sooner or later. To my mind the Socialism of the future will consist in the improvement and upward tendency of the strength—physical, moral, and mental—of the rural and urban population of England.

A great, a very great responsibility rests with the press of the country. I say to that press collectively: "Do not abuse your power, do not shirk your responsibility; but use your power, face your responsibility, and be a beacon of light and leading to the agricultural labourers. Teach them to be steady, industrious, sober, and independent; teach them to take advantage of every turn of the tide, and to be for ever striving to get nearer the goal of improvement, the goal of perfection. Point the way to them, and keep pointing."

Will there ever be another Agricultural Labourers' Union? If it should be found necessary to form another, the new one will, I believe, differ in many important respects from the old; for the times are changing. But now as ever union means strength, and disunion means weakness. Combine, co-operate in manly independence, that is the main thing; help yourselves and help others, that is the point; the machinery will then take care of itself. There is a union coming, a mighty union, but I shall not live to see it in its glory. I see the beginning of it though. And here to my mind is one sign of it—that the noble lady whose name adorns the title-page of this book should have displayed such generous and un-prejudiced impartiality as to edit the Life of Joseph Arch.*

Yes, it is a sign of the grand union that is coming, when prince and peer and peasant shall combine and co-operate for the good of one and all. It is a union that will be as big as all England; it will be as big as the empire; and some day it is going to be as big as the whole world. The world in union! That is what is coming, that is what all must work for. I shall not live to see it, but as sure as the sun shines in

* I want this to stand; I don't want it edited out.—J.A.

the heavens the great and glorious day when the world will be in union will dawn at last. In that sure and certain faith I lay down my pen and bid my readers farewell. A last word I would say to all; it is this—Courage, and work for union! the union of the world.

INDEX.

Abbot's Salford, 305.
Afghanistan, 314.
Agricultural commission, 127.
—— depression, 323-345.
—— Holdings Act, 337.
—— Labourers' Dwellings Act, 353.
—— Labourers' Union, formation, 73, 93-116; rules, 87; songs, 97; trustees, 108; congress, 109; constitution, 111-113; emigration, 188.
Agriculture, Chamber of, 108, 130.
—— Warwick County Chamber of, 104-106.
Alcester, 315.
Allan Line, 179.
Allington, G., 112.
Allotments Act, 345, 359, 362, 364, 390.
—— Extension Association, 347.
Ancestors of J. Arch, 3-5.
Arch, J., foreword, 1; birth, 3; childhood, 3-22; ancestors, 3-5; parents, 5-9, 14, 15; religion, 21, 47, 48; boyhood to manhood, 23-41; death of mother, 38; marriage, 46; death of father, 57; politics, 49, 58; visits Canada, 174-198; enters Parliament, 346; charges against, 235, 374, 375, 385.
Arnold, A., 110, 113.
—— J., 108.
Artizans' Dwellings Act, 353.
Ascot women, 139.
Ashantee, 315.
Ashley, T., 4.
Attenborough, Rev. F. S., 142, 199, 276.
Australia, 254.

Badsey, 371.
Ball, 123, 125, 199.
Ballot, 146, 326.
Banbury, 118.
Barford, 3, 73, 79, 389, 398.
Beach, Sir M. Hicks-, 145.
Beaconsfield, Lord, 223, 311.
Bedfordshire, 114.
Bennett, Sir J., 123.
Bentinck, Lord H., 355, 363.
Berkshire, 138, 348.
Besant, Mrs., 123.
Biddle, J., 112.
Bingley Liberal Club, 379.

Birmingham Radical Union, 354.
Blackwell, H., 112.
Blandford, 99.
Board of Trade, 315.
Boston, 196.
Bowpark, 192.
Bracebridge, 190, 191.
Bradlaugh, C., 123.
Brassey, Lord, 255.
Brazilian emigrants, 202.
Bright, J., 312.
Broadway, 371.
Brogden & Sons, 122.
Brooklyn, 195.
Buckinghamshire, 99, 109, 114.
Burgis, C. R., 199.
Burslem, 355.
Burt, T., 355.
Butcher, 118.

CAIRD, —, 337.
Cambridgeshire, 108.
Campbell, J., 109, 199.
Canada, 174-198, 183, 188, 254.
Carters, 31, 32.
Castle Bytham Farm, 277, 278.
Cat-o'-nine tails, 324-326.
Caton, 364, 366.
Chamberlain, J., 125, 357, 363.
Chaplin, H., 359, 362, 364-366, 399.
Charity, 8, 15, 18, 53.
—— Commissioners, 346-347.
—— Lands, 279.
—— Bill, 347.
Charlecote, 73.
Church and sexes, 17.
Church schools, 25.
Clayden, A., 179, 183, 199.
Clothing, 31.
Coat of arms, 45.
Cobb, P. H., 354.
Cobden, R., 312.

Collier, R. W., 199.
Collings, Jesse, 91, 108, 110, 113, 118, 342, 347, 357, 360.
Collins, Jeanie, 197.
Combination, 64.
Communion, 19, 20.
Coombe Bisset, 328.
Coombs, —, 301.
Corn Laws, 6, 10-12.
Cottages, 4, 44, 57, 125, 126.
County Council, 378.
Coventry, 153.
Cox, J. C., 135, 235.
Criminal Law Amendment Act, 142.
Cromer, 165.
Cross, Sir R. A., 257.
Cubbington, 79.
Cuckfield, 256.
Curates, 227, 228.

Daily News, 83, 199, 324, 374.
Davenport, Bromley, 103.
Davies, C., 207.
Dawson, S., 257.
Denbigh, Earl of, 104.
Denham, 99.
Denison, Col., 183, 187.
Devonshire, 85.
De Witt Talmage, —, 195.
Dilke, Sir C., 123, 347.
Dixon, G. 109, 263.
Dodd, T., 346.
Dorsetshire, 70, 99, 114, 191, 303, 340.
Dufferin, Lord, 182.

EASTON, —, 264.
Edwards-Wood, —, 199.
Elementary Education Act, 146, 246.
Ellicott, Dr., 121.
Emigration, 96, 122, 132, 178, 181, 194, 199-220, 254, 255, 313.

Index

English Labourers' Chronicle, 275, 276, 329, 348.
Essex, 79, 390.
Evans, H., 346, 348.

FAIR Trade, 372-374.
Faneuil Hall, 197.
Farmers, 30, 31, 76, 84, 102, 229-232, 301.
Farringdon, 135.
Fawcett, Professor, 110.
Fenny Compton, 79.
Fenwick, 188.
Fine Old English Labourer, 98.
Fitzmaurice, Lord E., 110.
Food, 10, 12, 13.
Forbes, A., 83, 89, 94.
Foreword, 1, 2.
Forster, W. E., 271.
Franchise, 252-273, 330, 331, 351.
Fraser, Dr., 127, 222, 224-226.
Freehold property, 43.
Free Trade, 355.

GAME Laws, 118, 145-173.
Giffen, —, 339.
Girdlestone, Canon, 85, 110.
Gladstone, Rev. S., 380.
—— W. E., 323, 327, 335, 362, 363, 371, 372, 379, 380.
Gloucester, Bishop of, 121.
Gloucestershire, 100, 114, 121, 348.
Gooch, —, 210.
Goschen, G. J., 363.
Granville, Earl of, 327.
Ground Game Act, 171.

HAIGH, G. T., 199.
Hambridge, —, 139.
Hamilton, 189.
Hammet, —, 70.
Hampshire, 348.

Hampton Lucy, 73, 343.
Harbury, 84, 97.
—— Vicar of, 102.
Harris, J., 112, 261.
Hartington, Lord, 263, 327, 363.
Hawarden Castle, 380.
Haynes, 108, 112, 113, 199.
Herbert, Hon. A., 91, 94, 110, 118.
—— Hon. S., 323.
—— Lord, 323.
Herefordshire, 79, 110, 114, 281.
Herring, B., 112.
Heyford, 228.
Hills, Luke, 256.
Holloway, —, 141.
Home Rule, 174, 362, 371, 372, 387.
Household Franchise Counties Bill, 263.
Hughes, T., 123.
Hunt, G. W., 145.
Huntingdonshire, 108, 114.
Huntsville, 190, 191.
Huron Indians, 182.

IBBOTSON, Sir S., 375.
Ipswich, 342, 360.
Ireland, Home Rule, 174, 362, 371, 372, 387.

JENKINS, E., 94, 107, 113, 136.
Jones, Cove, 378.
Jordan, G., 112.

KENILWORTH, 354.
Kent, 275.

LABOURERS and land, 300, 322.
—— and Lords, 391.
Labourers' Union Chronicle, 235, 275.
—— wages, 100, 110, 125, 133, 156, 300, 384, 386, 393.

Lancashire, 110, 255, 364.
Land and labourers, 300, 322.
—— Question, 271.
Langford, Dr. A. J., 91, 109, 110.
Leamington, 86, 89, 104, 112, 199, 294, 333, 358, 401.
Lefevre, Shaw, 279.
Legislators, 111.
Leicestershire, 79, 223, 250.
Leigh, Lord, 85, 152.
—— Hon. and Rev. J. W., 109, 118.
Leighton, Sir B., 91, 109, 118.
Leintwardine, 110.
Lennoxville, 186.
Lesage, —, 181, 182.
Lewis, John, 86, 94.
Liberal Working Men's Club, 358.
Lincolnshire, 108, 125, 275.
Littleworth, 134.
Liverpool, 179.
Local Government Act, 378.
Locksley, 73.
London, Canada, 193.
London Trades Council, 85.
Longfellow, —, 197.
Long Sutton Marsh, 99.
Lords and labourers, 391.
Lowe, —, 187, 189, 194.
Lowther, J., 392, 399.
Lunnon, G., 112.
Lynn, 355, 356.

MACDONALD, Sir J. A., 187.
——, —, 284.
MacKellar, —, 202.
MacKenzie, —, 135.
Magistrates, —, 152, 153,
Manchester, 222, 224.
Manitoba, 187.
Manning, Archbishop, 123, 125.
Massingham, 364.
Mechi, —, 304.

Mill, J. S., 305.
Mitchell, G., 123, 126, 287.
Montreal, 186.
Moreton, 73.
Morley, Samuel, 122.
Mundella, A. J., 123.
Muskako district, 189.

NETTON, 328.
Newbury, 174.
Newcastle, 221.
Newport, 301.
New Review, 391, 399.
New York, 195, 197, 313.
—— Trades Unions, 196.
New Zealand, 96, 122, 254.
Niagara Falls, 188.
Nineteenth Century, 351.
Norfolk, 79, 99, 114, 303, 355, 357, 386, 390.
Norris, —, 323.
Northamptonshire, 79, 123.
Northcote, Sir S., 314.
North Eastern Railway, 96.
Norton, Chipping, 138, 140, 142, 143.
Nottinghamshire, 114, 250.

O'NEIL, Rev. A., 109.
Ottawa, 193.
Oxfordshire, 79, 226, 291, 321.

PAKINGTON, SIR J., 210.
Paris, Canada, 191.
Parish Councils, 390.
—— Bill, 400, 401.
—— relief, 35, 36, 101, 258.
Peel, Mrs., 358.
Pelham, 188, 189.
Pembroke, Earl of, 323.
Penrhyn, Lord, 254.
Phillips, Wendell, 197.
Pigott, Rev. C. F. C., 109.

Pill, E., 112.
Pillinghurst, 233.
Poaching, 13, 14, 153-155.
Politics, 58-60.
Poor Law Amendment Act, 124, 125.
Pope, —, 187, 194, 202.
Post Office Savings Bank, 5.
Pratt, H., 110, 113.
Press, 275, 276.
Prevention Act, 155.
Prickett, J., 112.
Primrose League, 363, 378.
Protection, 394, 395.

QUEBEC, 180.
Queensland, 254.

RADFORD, 79, 84.
Radnorshire, 114.
Rasch, Major, 374.
Ravensworth, Lord, 392, 399.
Religion, 15-17, 19-22, 47, 48, 265.
Richmond, Duke of, 332.
Rogers, T., 237, 242, 318.
Roscoe, —, 136.
Rudham, 364.
Rugby, 354.
Russell, E., 103, 105, 112, 114, 199.
Rylands, Miss, 96.

SALISBURY, Lord, 370.
Saw mills, 186.
Schoolmaster, 26.
Schools, 25, 26, 50-53.
Scott, —, 185, 186.
Scottstown, 185.
Shaftesbury, 99.
Shanklin, 301.
Sharnbrook, 257.
Sherbrooke, 183, 186.
Sheen, —, 136.
Shropshire, 114.

Sick Benefit Society, 34, 297, 380, 384.
Small Holdings Act, 390.
Snitterfield, 84.
Socialists, 361.
Solley, Rev. H., 118.
Somersetshire, 79, 348.
Southam, 95, 371.
Squire, 34.
St. Louis, 180.
Stafford, L., 180, 181.
Staffordshire, 110, 114, 301.
Stand like the Brave, 97.
Stanstead, 183, 185.
Stephen, Fitzjames, 136.
Sterling, Justice, 375.
Strange, T. H., 110.
Stratford-on-Avon, 3.
Suffolk, 114, 222.
Summer, —, 197.
Sussex, 124.
Sweeting, R. G., 199.

TAYLOR, H., 87, 199.
Tenants' Rights, 271.
—— Bill, 304.
Toronto, 187, 189, 191.
Trebeck, J. J., 109.
Trevelyan, —, 263, 331.
—— Sir C., 123.
Trocks, Captain J., 179.
Trustees of Union, 108, 113.

UNION, see *Agricultural Labourers' Union*.
United States, 174-198, 217.

VACCINATION, 54-7.
Vincent, J. E. M., 113, 199, 275.
Voting, 59, 326.

WAGES, 14, 100, 110, 125, 133, 156, 300, 340, 384, 386, 393.

Wales, 254.
Walker, —, 385.
Walton, 84.
Ward, G. H., 132.
—— W. G. 110, 199.
Warwick County Chamber of Agriculture, 104-106.
Warwickshire, 3, 108, 314, 340, 348, 389.
—— Labourers' Union, 108, 132.
Washago, 189.
Watkins, Sir E., 236.
Welbeck Abbey, 387, 388.
Wellesbourne, 68, 72, 73, 76, 84, 86, 103, 286, 378, 402.
Wells, 165.
Weston, 68.
West Suffolk, 264.
White Star Line, 179.
Widows' Relief Fund, 384.
Willey, 68,
Wilton, 323.
Wiltshire, 20, 114, 191, 348, 353.
Winchilsea, Lord, 393-395, 397, 399.
Woodstock, 272.
Worcestershire, 79, 100, 114, 281, 300, 340.
—— Chamber of Agriculture, 210.

YARMOUTH, LORD, 311.
Yorkshire, 110, 114.

ZULULAND, 314.

www.ingramcontent.com/pod-product-compliance
Lightning Source LLC
Chambersburg PA
CBHW062125160426
43191CB00013B/2198